The
Alphabet
of
Modern
Annoyances

Also by Neil Steinberg

COMPLETE AND UTTER FAILURE
IF AT ALL POSSIBLE, INVOLVE A COW

Doubleday

New York
London
Toronto
Sydney
Auckland

Neil Steinberg

The Alphabet of Modern Annoyances

PUBLISHED BY DOUBLEDAY
a division of Bantam Doubleday Dell Publishing Group, Inc.
1540 Broadway, New York, New York 10036

DOUBLEDAY and the portrayal of an anchor with a dolphin
are trademarks of Doubleday, a division of
Bantam Doubleday Dell Publishing Group, Inc.

Library of Congress Cataloging-in-Publication Data
Steinberg, Neil.
The alphabet of modern annoyances / Neil Steinberg. —1st ed.
        p.   cm.
1. American wit and humor.   I. Title.
PN6162.S77   1996
818′.5402—dc20   96-24612
                                                        CIP

ISBN 0-385-48171-3
Printed in the United States of America
December 1996

10 9 8 7 6 5 4 3 2 1

FIRST EDITION

For Edie

"If you wish to overcome the repulsion certain disgusting creatures inspire, study their loves, their intimacy, the hidden and unexpected sides of their characters."

—BARON GEORGES CUVIER

Contents

Introduction

Rob Sherman is a pest. He'd be the first to admit it. A professional atheist, Sherman has spent years pressuring suburbs around Chicago to purge their town hall lawns of nativity scenes and their crests of crosses and other religious trappings. He is as common a sight at city council meetings as folding chairs.

Needless to say, people hate him. Sherman is pushy and aggressive and gets communities worked up over issues they'd rather not think about. And he never goes away.

Even those who sympathize with Sherman sometimes find themselves blanching at his tactics. He is locally famous for having dragooned his young son, Ricky, into being a reluctant poster child for the atheist cause. The most notorious incident took place eight years ago, when a columnist visited Sherman's home and Ricky, then six, was trotted out for display.

"Do we celebrate Christmas?" asked Sherman.

"No," Ricky answered.

"Why not?" Sherman quizzed.

"I don't know," Ricky said.

"Because we're what?" Sherman persisted.

The son was puzzled. "Smart?" he ventured.

"Because we're what?" Sherman prodded. "It starts with an *A*."

The child thought for a moment. Then it came to him. "Assholes?" he said eagerly.

Like all living organisms, human beings want to operate at equilibrium—to be at peace with the world, the fat and dry newspaper ca-thunking against the porch steps just as the teakettle sings and the eggs sizzle. If bluebirds happen to be fluttering around the forsythia bushes, decorating their branches with ribbons, all the better.

Nature, however, hates balance and is constantly upsetting it with earthquakes, fires, plagues, thunderstorms, supernovas.

Equally disruptive is human society, which savors steadiness while at the same time destroying it. Ninety thousand years ago, when the first band of wandering hominoids united for the purpose of huddling together at night for warmth, their social order no doubt lasted only until they stumbled upon a second, larger troop, who promptly fell on them and killed them to take possession of their brightly colored sticks.

We have, fortunately, evolved a bit since then, especially in the United States. Despite the common perception that the country is a vast sink of violence and suffering, modern-day Americans of a certain economic level tend to be immune from crisis. We go about, working, consuming, re-creating, unconcerned that we will be crushed in a riot or eaten by a bear. When our worlds are intruded upon, the intrusion is usually not by meteorites or murderers, but by the Rob Shermans of the world—steely-eyed advocates and pesky phone solicitors and rude neighbors and careless shop clerks. The far smaller, far more numerous problems of life. Annoyances.

We like to pretend otherwise; it isn't very romantic to recognize that the central difficulty of your existence is a lousy boss or balky car or the need to lose fifteen pounds. Where's the drama in that? So we ignore our own annoyances, or try to, and instead scare ourselves by concentrating, via the news media, on great tragedies in distant parts of the world, monitoring closely, as if at any moment we'll need to brief the Security Council. As if keeping track were a form of compassion.

Our thoughts may be on the big picture, but our hearts aren't. The reality is, no matter how many graphic images of misery CNN collects from the famine in Ishmaelia and squirts into our living rooms, they don't disturb the average person, not really, not in the way that city workers cutting sheet metal in the alley at 7 A.M. do.

That's human nature. Or, as Thurber said: "The confused flow of . . . relationships with six or eight persons and two or three buildings is of greater importance than what goes on in the nation or in the universe." Large problems close to home—poverty and racism and pollution and the like—may frighten, but only in bursts. The big perils are just too big to fixate on.

So we are left fretting privately about tiny matters, too embarrassingly small to air much in public. Nobody dreads advertising the way they worry about, for instance, crime.

But while muggings and burglaries come to an individual rarely, if ever, advertising is a constant, daily if not hourly assault: an army of petty felons, hanging from rooftops, shuffling ever closer, hands outstretched, mumbling pleas, pressing their faces against the glass from within your television set, slipping their nimble fingers into your pockets.

While common annoyances have to strike just the right mixture of low-level distress and bland ubiquitousness, the truth is that anything can be annoying. I have a friend—a handsome, well-known Chicago writer—who is irked when beautiful women come up to him in public and compliment his work. I guess that gets dreary after a while, but I'm taking his word on it. Or maybe complaining is his way of bragging about it.

Annoyance is like taste—every person decides what is pleasant, what is obnoxious, what hangs somewhere in between. The things you hate the most are certain to be beloved by other people—which in turn makes your feelings of dislike even keener. Computers would be vexing enough if they were universally mistrusted, like furnaces or automobile salesmen. But they are boosted to the heights of major annoyance by cadres of zealous devotees who love computers and want nothing more out of life than to think and write and talk about computer technology until the rest of us go mad.

This popularity is what makes the common person hesitant to speak up. McDonald's spends nearly a billion dollars a year celebrating its complex McWorld—the food, the clown, the whole schmeer. Millions of people worship Elvis Presley as a near god. Praise of Disney characters pours out of children's mouths as soon as they can form words, if not before, their droolings and cluckings perhaps a form of preverbal praise of the Lion King.

But where is the anti-McDonald's? The counter-Elvis? The yang to Disney's yin? Where is the person willing to stand up and whack a few common annoyances on the side of the head and say, "*Stop* that! You're *bothering* us!"

Here I am. Identifying annoyances is a perilous course, to be sure, since, to many, calling something an annoyance is itself annoying. There is a human tendency to react strongly by turning against the complainer: "Oh yeah, you think Mickey Mouse is annoying? Well, *fuck you,* buddy! My wife *loves* Mickey Mouse. . . ."

Still, someone has to do it. We can't just surrender, can we? Can't just turn our faces to the wall and die. That's the coward's way.

So I offer up this modest barrage of return fire at the annoyances assaulting us daily. Not in the hope of turning back the tide of vexation—that would be too much for even the giddiest optimist to expect. Rather, I'd like to provide a bit of encouragement and comfort to the beleagured, scattered forces of the fed-up; on the run, yes, but trying to make a good show of it nevertheless.

—Neil Steinberg
June 10, 1996
Chicago

A Is for Advertising

Doubleday

I was pumping gas yesterday at the Shell station on Ontario Street when the gas pump started singing the praises of the quickie mart inside. If you need milk, it told me, you're in luck: milk is waiting for you. I looked dumbly at the pump, the way I would look at my toaster if it abruptly suggested that I please consider Wonder Bread next time the occasion calls for toast.

Then the flash of recognition: Boom. Welcome to the future. Someday I'll rush into an airport rest room to take a pee, and the moment I break the little electronic zone that tells the urinal to flush itself, the porcelain receptacle will deliver a quick spiel about low air fares, timed at exactly fourteen seconds, or whatever researchers determine is the average time it takes a man to do his business. The Hertz rental car story will be printed on hotel sheets. Smirnoff vodka will find a way to insert tiny slips of paper—the size of fortune cookie fortunes—under the skin of oranges, reminding us how nice a freshly squeezed screwdriver would taste right about now. And with so much advertising all around, Smirnoff will be right.

The talking pumps were a shock, but not a surprise, not the way things have been going. As an increasingly jaded and overwhelmed audience tunes out even the slickest, big-production TV commercials and singing, flashing, holographic magazine ads, advertisers must cook up new ways to cut through the clutter and raise a tingle in our blown-out senses. Corporations stick ads in the back of paperback books, before movies, on the side of yellow buses taking children to school and in the classrooms when they get there. They wiggle their names more and more prominently into the titles of events. We already have the dreaded Poulan/Weed Eater Independence Bowl, can the Philip Morris CBS Network be too far behind? Or Searle brand physicians? Or the Federal Express Presbyterian Church?

With police cars renting out themselves as rolling billboards, how long can David Foster Wallace's dystopian vision of corporate-sponsored years—the "Year of the Trial-Size Dove Bar" and the "Year of the Depends Adult Undergarment"—remain in the realm of fiction? They're already talking about selling the street names in Atlanta.

The only limit is the superheated, greed-stoked imaginations of advertisers, which is to say no limit at all. They'd tattoo brand logos on babies' butts at birth, underwriting the procedure, if a significant minority of people— the malcontents and complainers—wouldn't object. Outcry being the sole defense left nowadays, all barriers of taste and restraint having been washed away in the mercenary torrent.

What makes the sudden appearance of advertising in

new places so worrisome is one can't at first tell whether the development is intrusive in some fundamentally unacceptable way or just new. Look at ballparks and stadiums. RCA Field and United Center and USAir Arena seem gross and commercial—now. But what about Wrigley Field? That must have stung at some point in the hazy past. Perhaps fifty years from now writers will invoke the reassuring image of San Francisco's beloved 3Com Park when railing against the naming of Betcha Can't Eat Just One Field.

Perhaps I am being wistful, but in my heart I can't believe the chatty gas pumps will become accepted as part of ordinary reality. People do not like to be talked to by inanimate objects. They get yelled at enough as it is. Car manufacturers learned this when they introduced dashboards that spoke to drivers, who loathed disembodied voices nagging them to wear their seat belts.

Just because a development is horrid, however, doesn't mean it won't prevail. I remember when the only voice I heard at the gas pump was Jack's—Jack ran the Clark station in Berea, Ohio—saying hello to my mother and offering us kids in the back seat sticks of spearmint gum. If you had shown me then the dreary routine of pumping your own gas and shoving payment through a slot toward an indifferent and anonymous clerk protected by a slab of greasy bulletproof glass, I would have thought it an impossible image culled from some science fiction nightmare.

But it wasn't.

The service station decay is made grimmer by the realization that it is something we did to ourselves, a deterioration embraced by a craven public in order to save three cents a gallon. The average citizen does display a sickening willingness to jettison the quality of life if it will save a few dollars. A survey done in 1995 claimed that 35 percent of Americans would support putting advertisements on dollar bills if it would lower their taxes. The survey was done by Visa/PLUS International ATM network, obviously hot to put its logo on our bucks, and only too happy to take advantage of the perception that prostituting national symbols is an effective path to financial health.

But would the return to individuals balance the blow to the stature of the nation as a whole? If Visa paid a billion dollars for the privilege of slapping its logo on our dollars (replacing, say, the funky hovering-eye pyramid that nobody understands anyway) would the individual tax reduction of $4 per person really be worth the national humiliation? Think of how they'd laugh at us in France.

In a similar vein, there's always some bright boy suggesting that ads be put on stamps, or the sides of the space shuttle, or the presidential seal, as a way to grub up a few bucks for the impoverished body politic.

For the reader who wonders why this is bad, as long as it saves money, I'd like to introduce a concept known as the "slippery slope." The slippery slope says that, once you take a baby step in certain negative directions—that first step, perhaps itself benign—the tendency is to roll downhill faster than you expect or desire. Shooting up heroin once might not be so bad if it didn't lead directly into using it again and again.

PBS, which once carried grateful little nods of acknowledgment to its corporate funders, now runs full-body kowtowing commercials that fall only a little short of Cher sitting on a couch for half an hour, touting hair rinse.

Harper's magazine waited fourteen years before it allowed any advertising at all, and when it did, the magazine had a strict policy about liquor and such. Now it carries ads for lonely Thai women and posters of penises.

The tasteful VISA logo stuck on the back of dollar bills this year inevitably leads to the MTV logo carved into Mount Rushmore next year and the President receiving $100 million toward balancing the budget for downing a can of Coke at the Superbowl during half time the year after that.

By focusing on advertising's ubiquitousness, however, I don't mean to give a pass to the content of advertising, which is the underlying horror that makes its proliferation so offensive. Trees and flowers are everywhere, too, but nobody seems to mind them. If thoughtful, creative ads and commercials were the rule, and not the rare exception, they might not be so odious.

But ads are for morons. That might sound harsh, but who else could be swayed by them? By the lame I-can-*see*-myself imbecility of cleaning-product ads. The blatant drink-Miller-and-screw-a-pretty-girl subtext of beer commercials. Did anyone ever see a Chrysler racing down a country lane, spewing leaves behind it like a trail of applause, and then run out to get one? Did that idiot Brit actor, Jonathan somebody, really sell anyone a Lexus with all his talk of "luxury cahs"?

Car commercials are particularly noxious. A Chicago new car dealer seems to be offering to kill someone for you. "If you want the lowest prices, *or something else,*" he insinuates, emphasizing his cryptic offer, "come and see me, Erwin Weil. *I'll do it!* I'll do whatever it takes."

At least I thought he was talking about murder the

first fifty times I saw the ad. Now I think Weil is just offering himself, physically, to any customer savvy enough to catch his meaning.

We all have our own areas of advertising concern. Homegrown Puritans and frothing moral fanatics focus on nudity in advertising, unconsciously contributing to its impact. I give Calvin Klein credit for not rubbing his hands together and cackling with glee, at least not in public, after the religious right raised a howl against his billboards of sallow, emaciated teens sprawled against the fake wood paneling of some pederast's basement. The inevitable result of the protests was to slap the offending images onto every news show and in every magazine in America. Next time why not just cut Calvin Klein a check for $10 million to buy more ads? The result would be the same.

I think there should be more nudity in advertising. It might redeem the profession. Why limit naked teenage models to touting brassieres and perfume? Have them hawk mortgages and vacuum cleaners and cooking utensils, the way they do in Europe. If Ed McMahon in a tux can sell insurance, imagine how many more policies could be sold by Cindy Crawford in a bubble bath.

Sadly, that's not the direction we're going. With the demographic bulge heading into decrepitude, we're going to see fewer nymphets, not more. Already half the ads are suddenly canted toward old people—or should I say toward some fantasy image of old people, whether it is that couple in the vintage convertible, toasting each other orgasmically with Sustacal while roaring down a desert highway, or those insane Humana commercials in which the ancient geezers talk about how young and full of life they are. "When spring has turned to fall, comes the sudden realization, I'm really not old at all," Mimmie Horowitz, ninety-four, says, prompting me to shout at the screen: "You're ninety-four, for Christ's sake, Granny, you're *old!* Don't fool yourself!"

Commercials, one might argue, are God's way of punishing you for watching television. Print ads aren't quite as bad, just because your eye can dance over them, registering nothing. You just assume they are lies. If I saw a newspaper ad which read: "Marshall Field's Big Spring Clearance—100 Percent Off! Prices Slashed to Nothing! All Merchandise Free!" I don't think it would stir me. One assumes there is a catch, and why waste your time trekking downtown to find out what it is? ("Why sure, mister, everything's free . . . *if* you run the Gauntlet of Fire.")

The rare ad that does catch your attention just makes you feel like a fool. One Christmas, recently, Absolut vodka trumped themselves by running a musical magazine ad that lit up, little Christmas tree lights dancing while some carol played. My wife and I shut off all the lights in the kitchen and ogled it in the dark, with what struck me then as childish glee and now seems like infantile gullibility. To make matters worse, I subsequently bought a bottle of Absolut, and can't in good faith claim that it wasn't the fancy little ad that inspired me to do it.

Maybe I'm extra sensitive to advertising, having written the stuff myself, briefly, during low points in my career. No crime—there is a fine tradition of serious writers contributing to advertising's banal oeuvre. F. Scott Fitzgerald can be remembered not only for having penned *The Great Gatsby* but also as the author of the line "We keep you clean in Muscatine."

No wonder he was a drunk. I've written ads for Republic Steel, for Glidden Paint, for Epson computers, and I'll tell you, it's a dark night of the soul for a struggling young writer to realize he has just crafted the sentence: "Republic's new IMF fine-grade alloy increases speeds and feeds in line bar production."

Time has taken the sting out of those memories, thankfully, without an undue reliance on gin. It is rare that I wake up screaming, thinking about writing ads for a used car dealer who insisted his mother show up in a funny hat at the end and deliver the tag line.

But I do find myself talking back to the television, more and more. I try not to. It seems curmudgeonly, the step before you start shaking your fist at young hooligans in their hot rods. But the inanity and illogic of certain ads gets under my skin, especially after dozens of numbing repetitions.

I couldn't bear those Bud Lite commercials, for instance, in which the grizzled Johnny is always trying to cadge a Bud Lite from his unwilling friends and family, who reject his admonishments of love with a stern "You're not getting my Bud Lite." Why does everybody in the commercials have a beer but Johnny? He's obviously some sort of broken alcoholic, pathetically trying to beg a drink. What a strange spokesman to have for a brand of beer.

Soon, whenever I saw the ad—and it was playing every ten minutes there for a while—I would turn to my wife and start raving: "What's wrong with Johnny? Why won't they give him a beer? What has he *done?*"

It was another beer ad, however, that nearly drove me to a breakdown. About a dozen years ago, a brand of German beer called St. Pauli Girl began blanketing the air-waves with a commercial, the tag line of which was: "Because you never forget your first girl."

As it happened, I had just been dumped by my first girlfriend, after a heart-wrenching relationship that lasted six years, through all of college and most of high school. The St. Pauli Girl commercials came on constantly while I was sitting, damaged, in some bar, drinking anything but St. Pauli Girl. When the commercial delivered its invariable tag line—"Because you never forget your first girl," I would turn toward the offending television and snarl, "But you sure as hell try!"

B Is for Bureaucracy

The Chicago Park District had reason to celebrate. They took a dilapidated Olympic pool, dating back to the 1930s, and turned it into a showcase—a dazzling blue expanse, with eleven spouting fountains and a "zero-depth" shallow area giving young children a gently sloped entry into the pool, plus two 36-foot double-loop water slides, all of it blue and white and marvelous.

This of course called for a formal opening. The press was invited, as were a couple hundred inner-city kids, plucked from a park district summer camp. The kids filed in, already wearing their bathing suits and swim caps, grasping their towels, all arms and legs and energy. They took seats in the pool's bleachers. It was a hot, sunny, hot, mid-July, hot, cloudless, hot day. The kids eyed the pool with hunger in their eyes.

The children arrived about 10 A.M. and were told they could swim for an hour before the ceremony at noon. But

15

first there were festive balloons to be blown up, and the kids were put to work puffing into the white, blue and aqua balloons. The balloons then went into the pool, speckling the shimmering eight-lane, 50-meter expanse. Quite a pretty effect.

By the time the kids finished blowing up balloons, however, it was nearly noon. Almost time for the ceremony. They were told they could swim afterward. The festivities kicked off with an opening address, followed by an invocation blessing the pool, the singing of the national anthem, the introduction of the master of ceremonies and the many special guests, including the ward's alderman and the incoming and outgoing superintendents of the park district. All had things to say.

"I would clearly be remiss if I did not acknowledge and publicly thank an individual I worked with very, very closely over the years," said the outgoing superintendent, who proceeded to do so, in great detail, as balloons burst, from time to time, in the burning noontime sun.

"It's hot out here; I want to get in the pool," said Seneca Scott, eleven, up in the bleachers.

". . . I would be remiss if I didn't mention another person . . ." said the superintendent, who did so.

"We're supposed to go swimming today," said Sequita Stuart, ten.

After the speeches, entertainment. A water ballet. And a folk dance, by the Washington Park Steppers. And the formal handing over of a gold-painted life preserver from one park district official to another.

"I'm bored sitting right here," said Nakita Clayborne, nine.

Finally, the pool was inaugurated—by the park district

brass, who laughed and cannonballed off the slide. "It's great, great! Oh boy, I love it," enthused a park commissioner, emerging from the water, laughing and dripping wet.

By then it was nearly 1 P.M. and the two hundred kids were being ushered out of the bleachers, back onto the buses. Three hours had passed and it was time to return to camp for lunch. They never did get a chance to swim, not that day, anyway.

This, in a nutshell, is bureaucracy. The arrogance and obliviousness of those in office—in this case, the park district officials fixating on their beloved ceremony—lead directly to the agony of waiting and disappointment for those of us expecting to be properly served.

Defenders of bureaucracy—those savoring jobs in the endless warrens of federal, state, county and city governments, plus their counterparts in a thousand becalmed business offices—will defend themselves by pointing out that many fine, thinking, efficient individuals also work in bureaucratic settings and have accomplished many fine accomplishments, such as Hoover Dam, and it is wrong to tar them because of the fumblings of a minority.

I call this the Post Office Rebuttal. Whenever mail carriers are found setting fire to bundles of letters in barrels under lonely viaducts—as they so often are, in Chicago at least—or firing weapons at their cowering coworkers, some poor post office official is inevitably produced who clears his throat and, staring at a spot on the ground in front of the cameras, observes that billions of pieces of mail are not stashed into trunks or burned in barrels but actually find their way to their rightful destinations, eventually, just as the vast majority of postal employees never go on deadly sprees, and thus the post office should not be judged too harshly.

This is the equivalent of a mass murderer standing before the judge and explaining that there are many, many people whom he *didn't* kill, and the court should take that into account.

Since the post office holds a central position as the Beast of Bureaucracy, a post office episode best illustrates the great existential question of bureaucracy: is there something intrinsic to organizations which turns the people working in them into idiots? Some process whereby intelligent, well-meaning individuals—people with parents who loved them—are changed into rule-spouting, foot-dragging, form-shuffling incompetents?

Some sort of dumbification, perhaps.

Or are bureaucracies, as entities, blameless and neutral systems that would function like clockwork were they not staffed by flawed humanity, who are generally stupid to begin with and only deteriorate with time, bringing their own idiosyncratic stupidities to bear on whatever tasks they can't succeed in shirking?

A puzzle worthy of Descartes.

The answer appeared magically when I went to the post office the other day to buy stamps. Just the fact that I was there at all was a bad sign. My post office branch is always packed like the steerage section of an immigrant steamer, with twenty or thirty people waiting in line, all glaring holes through two or three indifferent clerks, who are going through their motions with agonizing slowness, as if underwater, weighing packages and affixing postage with the sort of measured, methodical intensity one normally associates with the defusing of a bomb.

I got in line, as always, behind the special case—a couple in their fifties, the man holding a rolled oriental carpet that must have been seven feet long.

I have a certain genius for this, not limited to post offices. In a bank, I'm behind the guy trading in his Krugerrands for dollars, exchanging the dollars for dinars and wiring them to Tunisia. In a supermarket, I'm behind the woman trying to pay for her unpriced, unlabeled canned goods with expired food stamps from another state.

Seven feet long, at least, the carpet was. Maybe eight. A prudent person would have wheeled around and left at that point, cutting his losses, waiting for another day to try to stock up on stamps. I've done that before. Or I could have attempted to use the lobby postage machines. But I'm loath to do that. Almost phobic about it. I picture myself feeding a $10 bill into a machine, then getting nothing. No stamps, no money back, nothing. Perhaps a brief electronic flash of the message "Sorry, pal" on the little blue screen. Filled with righteous indignation, I would then attempt to get my money refunded by the United States Postal Service, a quickly escalating quest, calcifying into a mania and then into a Kafkaesque nightmare that would take years out of my life. I would end up living in one of those survivalist compounds in Idaho. That's where those people come from. One day you are a meek writer feeding a $10 bill into a stamp machine. The next you are a glittery-eyed, skinheaded maniac, field-stripping your weapons, checking the cisterns of water stored under the floorboards and waiting for the postal police to come creeping up through the woods.

19

Mild curiosity over the rug-toting couple kept me in line, however, shuffling forward behind them as the non-carpet-bearing patrons ahead of us were, eventually, served. Sure enough, when the carpet couple got up to a window, the clerk told them they couldn't mail the rug. It was too tall. I was next in line, two feet away, and could hear everything. The man launched into a protracted defense—the rug had come to them through the mail; two had, as a matter of fact, that's why they were sending this rug back. It was the extra. Here was the mailing label the company had sent.

The clerk crossed her arms and held firm. The carpet was too tall. Their machinery wouldn't accept it. End of argument. It didn't matter if the post office brought it, the post office wasn't taking it back. Try downtown. Try somewhere else. Go away.

The couple weren't about to go away, however. They had suffered the embarrassment of schlepping this big rug through the city streets; they weren't leaving with it. The conversation went on for some time. The clerks at the other windows stopped working and watched.

Suddenly, *deus ex machina,* a second clerk stepped over. "Fold the carpet in half," she commanded. "What?" the man said. "Fold the carpet in half," she repeated. He did so, easily, and the savior clerk took a roll of strapping tape and bound the two ends together. *Voilà!* Not too long anymore. The refractory clerk accepted the bundle without a word and tossed it into the bin of packages. Business resumed. The great gears of postal efficiency began slowly turning again.

This is the entire spectrum of bureaucracy—from the refusal of the rigid, rules-are-rules martinet to the swift, effective intervention of the nimble-minded second clerk, who probably risked being fired by stepping out of her space and inserting herself into the other clerk's transaction.

All within the same organization. Which means, much as we'd like to blame the system, there is a frightening possibility that the real problem is the people.

I tried to draw the heroic second clerk into conversation to learn more about her—maybe she had just been hired the week before and hadn't had her humanity squeezed out yet. But she was demure, mumbling a few noncommittal phrases in response to my observation that she should be elected to high public office.

But barring some sort of scientific study ("Question 47: Please rank your level of efficiency before association with the government: a) inept; b) very inept; c) tremendously inept . . ."), we have to assume that the problem is a little of both—listless incompetents gravitating to official service like silt sinking to the bottom of a pond *and* dynamic, well-meaning and brisk individuals transformed into inert cogs and shirking functionaries by the perverse dynamic of organizational breakdown.

Maybe this is a good thing. "The evil would be greater, the more efficiently and scientifically the administrative machinery was constructed," John Stuart Mill wrote, noting that bumbling is sometimes all that keeps bureaucrats from giddily "rushing into some half-examined crudity which has struck the fancy of some leading member of the corps."

And there are things that bureaucracy is good for, after all. Self-preservation being number one. Despite years of zealous rhetoric about pruning back the official tree, all manner of superfluous agencies and antiquated bureaus continue to exist. The federal tea-tasting board has lasted from the nineteenth century to the present day, and while the government is making noises again about getting rid of it, they haven't done so yet. I wouldn't hold my breath.

At least the tea board exists benignly, a quiet tumor, as opposed to actively mucking things up. In 1981, when the federal government wanted to secretly move $20 billion in gold bullion from the U.S. Assay Office in Manhattan to its repository at West Point, the feds met with local officials beforehand, arranging to close bridges and divert traffic so the gold-laden trucks could speed to their destination. The only sticking point was the Port Authority, which at first insisted, $20 billion or no, that the trucks stop, one by one, and pay their tolls before taking the tunnel into New Jersey. I don't know how the federal government persuaded them to relent, but they would have been within their rights to send in the army. The provocation was there.

Whole books, such as Philip K. Howard's *The Death of Common Sense,* catalogue with horrified fascination the lurchings and clankings of bureaucracy, which seems in general to have only two speeds—agonizing slowness, the gear it uses when going about its rightful functions, such as patching roads or issuing refund checks, and blinding swiftness, which is reserved for folly.

Howard concludes that the solution to bureaucracy is to jettison all these rules and regulations and just let bureaucrats, individually, be responsible for running their organizations as they see fit.

There is some sense to this. As seen at the post office, improvisation at the grass roots of bureaucracy can assume the level of genius. My brother Sam, who runs a livery company, cherishes the charming story of going to the State of Illinois building in Chicago to register a new limousine license. The form he was required to fill out had a line on it for the signature of the man who sold him the license, something of a problem, since the man was in St. Louis. Sam complained that he couldn't possibly be expected to go back to St. Louis and get the guy to sign the form. The mails would take a week, at least, and until then the car couldn't be rented out (and, worse, he would have to return to the government office and wait in the line). The clerk at the Secretary of State's office had obviously dealt with this problem before.

"He's here—the guy who sold you the license; I saw him in the food court. Go get his signature," the clerk said.

My brother, stunned and dubious, trotted off for a look. He scanned the tables in the area where fast food is sold. Of course the guy wasn't there. Sam returned to the window. "He isn't there," my brother said, with that thick probity often afflicting ordinary citizens. The clerk seemed almost annoyed with him.

"No, no, you must not have looked hard enough. The guy's there. I saw him. Go back and look again."

Sam was halfway back to the food court when the head-slapping revelation came. The clerk was doing him a favor, telling him in every way short of semaphore flag to sign the form himself. A bit of bureaucratic idiocy passed down from on high was being circumvented in a neat way that only required my brother to forge somebody's signature, which he happily did.

The problem with depending on such ad hoc cleverness, however, as a matter of routine, is that, for every bureaucrat who makes a decision for the ease and benefit of a member of the general public, there is someone, if not a group of someones, making decisions for the ease and benefit of themselves. City workers park their trucks behind warehouses and catch lengthy naps. County officials thrust their arms, up to the elbow, into the till, along with all their ghost-payroll cousins. Federal officials commandeer military jets to deliver their poodles to the hairdresser. That these acts are felonies only encourages stealth on the part of the perpetrators and doesn't raise our confidence that, left to their own devices, governmental workers would forge efficiency utopia.

Government is not the only place where bureaucratic stupidities occur. Businesses have plenty. We used to see them all the time at the *Chicago Sun-Times,* the newspaper where I often work. The day would be going along fine when suddenly a new unenforceable edict shrieked in to land. Sometimes the new policy would be immediately discarded, in the name of expediency. Sometimes there would be a momentary, Potemkin-village sham of following it.

The situation was almost funny. The managers were constantly rushing away to weekend retreats at swank resorts, where they ran barefoot over hot coals, fell backward into each other's arms in trust drops, broke boards, whatever. (We reporters even got to break boards once, in a day-long, touchy-feely seminar we were all forced to attend. "Write the problem you'd most like to overcome on your board," the charlatan instructor said. I wrote "BAD MANAGEMENT" on mine in big green letters. The board broke nicely, but without immediate practical result.)

The managers would then return from the mountain-top, tanned, invigorated. People who had never spoken to you in your life suddenly materialized in front of your desk, asking about the kids you didn't have. Reporters were saddled with all manner of complex editorial systems and story schedules and electronic update boards and Byzantine command chains, some of which were implemented with great fanfare, vigorously maintained for a week or two, and then swept away in the mad scramble to publish a daily newspaper.

Thank God the new owners arrived, in the nick of time, to install bright and decisive editors blessed with astounding powers of organization and deep intellectual clarity, the sort of people who, almost immediately, gave me a column.

Which reminds me of one of bureaucracy's rare benefits. It has elevated fawning to an art form. Unappreciated, yes, but an art form all the same. Truckling and groveling are still held in ill repute by a tiny group of abstract dreamers who don't recognize their power and importance in the operation of any well-oiled system. But the rest of us know better.

C
Is
for
Computer

The first time I ever sent a letter by fax, I made a photocopy of it beforehand, so I could retain a record for my files.

Now, I'm sure I knew, intellectually, that the sheet being fed into the fax machine would not go squirting through the wires and disappear. But I wasn't acting on that knowledge; I was acting on habit, which told me that, when you send something, you no longer have it. I can still feel the shiver of surprise and embarrassment when the letter came sliding slowly out the other end of the fax machine and fell into the tray.

That moment defined me, technologically. Gradually, and without realizing it, I had become one of those aborigines who, finding themselves in a hotel room for the first time, sleep on the floor next to the bed and build a cook fire in the sink.

I glanced guiltily around the newsroom. There is a distinctive shame associated with bungling new technology, part of what makes its relentless change so perturbing. As soon as you master one device, zip, it's gone, and a battling new box of knobs and wires is set before you.

Computers, like many annoyances, are doubly perturbing. First there is the thing itself—expensive, prone to catastrophic collapse, available in a superabundance of forms, all of which are technically unfathomable to the average person.

Second, there is the enthusiasm of the people hyping the thing—the brainless fanaticism of the digital heads crying that this is the Revolution, that a new Cyber-Civilization is rearing up to replace the crumbling old order with its dead white philosophers and their silly paper books.

I'm not sure which is worse.

Had I recognized the deep symbolic value of the fax gaffe, as I stood at the machine, I might have glanced around the newsroom and noticed that part of my problem was within sight: the place was a graveyard of defunct technology. In the walls slumbered the outlets for the pneumatic tube system that once sped news copy to the composing room, the little entry hatches awaiting compact brass cylinders that were never going to arrive. On a few isolated tables sat manual typewriters, salvaged for decoration and nostalgia. By the filing cabinets, dusty and alone, a glue pot waited to be thrown away, dry and mooted into uselessness by electronic paste-up on brilliant, perfect-quality Radius terminals. A few stray photo reduction wheels and pica poles cast here and there, as unnecessary as sextants.

Yet, somehow, like the brittle yellow copies of the old, defunct *Chicago Daily News* or *Herald-American* shoved in the bottom of many desk drawers, these technological *memento mori* had just enough claim on the heart to avoid being thrown away.

Computer zealots are always striving for more memory, but others of us already have too much. Perhaps the curse of my generation—an uncomfortable and unlabeled band of mid-thirtyish people whom *Newsday*'s Wil Bunch described perfectly as "always too late, always missing something"—is to be never quite at home in the present. We don't spend enough time with a certain technology to develop an unbreakable bond with it, yet we are caught off guard by the new system that comes down the pike to replace it. We are dragging along at the tail of the Baby Boom, the hind end of this giant demographic bulge that beats a path for us whether we want to go there or not. At the same time, we are prodded forward by fear of being run over by the thundering herd of nostril-ringed slackers just behind us.

Or maybe it's just me.

Either way, before we slump our shoulders and shuffle off into the digital future, I think a few observations about the personal computer need to be uttered in our defense.

First, despite the manifest self-regard of the computer aristocracy, there isn't necessarily any intellectual difference between those who giddily run toward computers, their arms flung open like the kids in *The Sound of Music,* and those of us who linger behind, worrying. The cyberspace whiz kids of today are not more open-minded than their forebears, just earlier along the curve. Thirty years from now they'll be clinging to their ridiculous, outmoded Windows software and arcane digital systems, complaining that they can't make heads or tails of all this electron bubble diffusion nonsense. Will they remember how they sneered at dear old Dad? Mocked his bumbling attempts to run Lotus 1-2-3? Will they remember when they are struggling to get their front door voice security units to recognize their thin, reedy pleas and let them in out of the rain? ("Geez, Pop," their kids will grin, "no wonder it won't let you in, with you wheezing so asthmatically into the microphone like that. Say it slowly, in a deep, well-modulated voice: 'My . . . name . . . is . . . Winston . . . Smith. . . .' ")

Probably not.

Second, you can only be amazed so many times. After watching men walk on the moon, live, a person can be forgiven for being blasé about subsequent developments, even if this baffles those whose most dramatic life memory is rescuing the lady in Donkey Kong. Computers may be the ultimate thrill for people who encounter them immediately after pecking through their shells and emerging wet and blinking into the sunlight. But for others, who are older, emotionally if not chronologically, it may be too late. Computers just aren't that big a deal.

The junior Bill Gateses of the world will probably view this as a lot of crap. But I'm sincere. If, by my life's end, I can write by taping a pair of electrodes to my forehead and drafting my thoughts onto a screen projected inside my mind's eye, then downloading them telepathically to a molecule-infusion turbojet printer that produces a finished page the moment I squeeze my left earlobe and blink twice, it won't mean an awful lot if the sentence I write is: "Tiffany bit her knuckle and leaned hard against the heavily polished cherry dining-room table, her eyes wild with despair, thinking: 'Then he really does not love me.' "

Engineers might be striving toward shrinking an entire Cray supercomputer onto a mote of dust small enough to float in a shaft of sunlight on a sleepy summer day, but I'm still planning on buying, eventually, that IBM Selectric II I've always wanted.

The IBM Selectric II was the last advance in technology that made perfect sense to me, whose revelation did not carry a trace of fear or anxiety. Hit a key, and you heard a ca-thunking sound solid as a Cadillac door slamming, confident as the double click of a shell being jacked into a shotgun.

And that aluminum ball. A technological icon. A sphere, spangled with the letters of the alphabet, like a cosmos. Heart-stopping. You could change fonts, too.

But my love for the Selectric was thwarted by progress. When I got out of college, in the early 1980s, and began to set myself up as a writer, I knew I could no longer rationalize getting the IBM, and felt cheated. Oh, I could have grimaced and bought the Selectric, I suppose, but by then word processors had already ruined the dream, already pointed a rude finger toward the comparative disadvantages of the typewriter. Using a typewriter had become an affectation, like wearing a cape or taking snuff.

I also had the cautionary tale of my father, who in 1956 bought the most expensive monophonic stereo system ever sold—nearly—a fantastic array of Marantz tubes and Fisher tuning and a cast aluminum turntable whose platter probably weighed ten pounds, all of which doomed him to spending the next thirty years of his life listening to music in high-fidelity mono.

So I bought a Kaypro 2X, queasy at the cost—as much as three Selectrics, by the time you added the Juki daisy wheel printer and the tractor feed and the software and all the associated bells and whistles. The Macintosh I had dismissed as a toy—particularly with that mouse, which, as an old touch typist, I knew was a fatal error in design. Nobody would want something that requires you to take your hands off the keyboard. The keyboard of the Macintosh didn't have a solid feel, either. Typing on it was like drumming your fingers on a bunch of loose Chiclets poured into a plastic tray.

When buying the Kaypro, I didn't pay attention to factors such as memory or software. What sold me was that the Kaypro was made of steel. A gunmetal-gray body with a rock-solid keyboard that folded out to reveal a tiny green screen. It looked like something the army would design—a computer to go ashore at Normandy beach, lugged in a rubberized bag and set up in the shelter of a tank trap so that some sapper could use it to figure out artillery azimuths. I loved it.

The Kaypro was advertised as "portable," and, at twenty-four pounds, you could carry it by the handle for a few feet, in a fast trot, before your shoulder went into spasms. When, in later years, the screen sometimes froze up, I would address the problem by taking the flat of my hand and slamming the top of the machine as hard as I could. That usually worked.

After I finished my first published book, my wife started pressing me to replace the Kaypro. The company had quietly folded, evaporated in the tech wars like a soldier hit by a mortar shell. My machine had developed all sorts of weird symptoms—the screen speckled with a dozen or so exclamation points which, when you typed over them, would change the letter typed to the next letter in the alphabet, on the screen, while not affecting what would ultimately be printed out. I got to know where they were and adjusted to them.

I seriously considered simply keeping the Kaypro, suffering through greater inconveniences, more exclamation points, bigger expenditures of time and money trying to keep the thing running. It seemed good karma. I worried that giving up the Kaypro would be an act of treachery that would be reflected in my writing. And, at the core, I was afraid.

Afraid to plunge into the literature of computers, afraid to learn all that *stuff*. I didn't want to know about the specifics—the RAM, the bits, the whatever. Yes, that fascinates some people, but in truth they remind me of those guys in high school who loved cars and would sit around with *Hot Rod* magazine propped up behind their textbooks, itching to get home to adjust the carburetor on the wreck in the backyard. They seemed to be focusing on the wrong thing—it's where you go in the car, not why the spark plugs fire. But to each his own—I'm glad somebody knows about cars, and I'm glad that computers exist for the sole reason that they do indeed facilitate writing. At least you don't have to bother with those circular pink erasers with the stiff green brush on the end (although, now that I think of it, those erasers were quite pretty, and I should track a few down and scatter them around the office).

So I bought a new computer. Impulsively. The way I imagine amateur murderers close their eyes and strangle people. The way suicides stand on the bridge rail, hold their arms out for a moment, then pitch blindly forward into darkness. I never even tried the computer I bought— my brother liked his Dell, so I just picked the most expensive one I could afford out of the Dell catalogue. It had, I figured, five hundred times the capacity of my Kaypro, and cost about the same. It is the color of cold oatmeal and not an ounce of metal in the whole damn machine. But I adjusted.

I've never played a game on the Dell. I view playing computer games at home the same as drinking before 5 P.M.: fun, perhaps, but a dangerous road to go down. Writing is tough enough without having to compete against Myst, whatever that may be.

I did figure out how to use the fax modem. Making the modem work required about four hours on the toll-free helpline, at one point being instructed to actually type new lines of code into the master program. Being on those helplines is like being the passenger who has taken over the controls of a stricken airplane in a disaster movie, the sweaty Samaritan talked down by Charlton Heston in the tower. "Okay, Billy, you're doing fine. Now reach over to the FILE slug and bring it down. You should see an air-speed indicator. Click twice on it."

Once I got the modem up and working, I finally plugged in one of the discs that America Online was raining over my house like seed corn and connected myself to the Internet, albeit in its basic, constricted, America Online form.

Having shot many hours poking around the system, I

still can't figure out what the big benefit is supposed to be, the panoptic wonder that has caught human imagination like nothing else since the Peloponnesian Wars. While you can access certain articles in various publications, the practical services are almost nil. The *Chicago Tribune* does offer its computerized archive, but tags an incredible $1.25 a minute extra charge on it. For $75 an hour I could hire Robert Caro to go to the library and do my research for me, then bring back his results and present them, baked in a pie.

The rest of the features, particularly the chat lines, are merely a time-wasting sinkhole for shut-ins and perverts. Perhaps when I'm ninety years old and strapped to a chair and eating baby food I'll have time to devote to fractured conversations with twenty-two strangers, conversations focusing primarily on how old we are, what our sex is, and where we live. I know these details about myself already, and the fact that other people of varying ages and sexes live in cities around the country, cities that often differ in weather conditions, does not come as a startling revelation.

Claims that the Internet will unite the world in a bond of understanding will someday be seen as based on the same kind of whimsy that once prompted predictions that television would create an enlightened and encultured populace. Conversations with a constantly changing band of two dozen people, many of whom are horny teenagers, just can't develop into anything worth five cents a minute. As I tried to instigate some sort of actual communication of ideas among the various Wizard666s and HotChix and ShyGuys I found myself on line with, I couldn't help but wonder how the Socratic dialogues would have turned out had they taken place, not in low-tech Athens, but in Lobby 35 of America Online:

```
OnlineHost:
OnlineHost:        *** You are in "Lobby 35." ***
OnlineHost:
PoleMarChus:       Do you see how many we are?
Socrates469:       Of course I do.
PoleMarChus:       Well, you must either be stronger
                   than we are, or you must stay here.
PUSSLIQUOR:        WHO LIKES ICE CREAM?
Socrates469:       Is there not another alternative?
                   Namely, that we may persuade you
                   to let us go?
BuzzGrL:           party  hard!  hi  puss!  age/sex
                   check :)
PUSSLIQUOR:        I LIKE CHOCOLATE BEST!
PoleMarChus:       Could you persuade men who do
                   not listen?
Glaucon:           Not possibly.
PoleMarChus:       Well, you can take it that we are
                   certainly not going to listen.
BEAVIS298:         m/13. Any hot ladies here tonight?
Adeimantus:        Do you really not know that there
                   is to be a torch race on horseback
                   this evening in honor of the god-
                   dess?
Socrates469:       On horseback? That is a novelty.
Nambla6969:        Hola! Somebody talk to me.
```

Since people generally do not bother to form signifi-cant relationships with those around them—their coworkers, their neighbors, sometimes even their families—or express much interest in absorbing the mass of information already at their fingertips, in libraries or on their own shelves, it seems odd in the extreme to suggest that the world will be transformed when everybody has the chance to communicate in fractured sentences with faceless strangers, and download as yet untranscribed data from the great academic centers of the world.

Much of the appeal seems to me to be the same as that of the torchlight race on horseback: novelty. Being able to order a pizza via the computer might be convenient under certain limited circumstances. But is it revolutionary?

A computer is a tool. That this simple statement can be presented almost as an epiphany underscores the delusional quality of most discourse about computers. As tools, computers are no greater, or lesser, than the ends they are put to.

Or as Steven Levy points out in *Insanely Great,* a history of Macintosh, many people fall into the trap of "focusing on our tools instead of using them." He writes:

> I never spent a whole morning installing a new ribbon. Nor did I subscribe to *RemingtonWorld* and *IBM Selectric User.* I did not attend the Smith-Corona Expo twice a year. I did not scan the stores for the proper cables to affix to my typewriter, or purchase books that instructed me how to get more use from my Liquid Paper.

Sure, when you made a mistake on a typewriter you had to go through the little Wite-Out ritual, or zip the paper out of the platen and insert a fresh sheet. But at least you were always *doing* something. You never just stared at the thing, waiting for it to decide it was ready. People forget that, for all their lightning quickness, computers can also be slow, in the death-of-a-thousand-cuts sense, with a loss of five seconds here, half a minute there, two hours somewhere else.

Nor did the typewriter ever take a few days' work and toss it in the trash for no apparent reason. Nor did a typist ever unknowingly reach into the machine and unconsciously snap the type bars off, which is basically what I did when, in trying to free up memory in my Dell, I deleted the DOS files, figuring they were an antiquated system that I never used. A mistake, as I quickly learned.

But this is all work routine and procedure, and not the main issue. My central concern is that, rather than increasing literacy and communication and knowledge, computers will degrade them. Readers may come to expect tinny songs and animation with their prose; written communication will be delivered in a series of bloops and bleeps, slogans, abbreviations and smiley faces. The idea of reality, of history, will be lost to digitalization and special effects and computer animation.

More than ten years after society paused to pat itself on the back that George Orwell's grim totalitarian vision of *1984* did not come true on schedule, I find myself still thinking of that awful scene where Winston Smith is strapped to a table in the Ministry of Love, straining to look at a photograph—evidence damning leaders of the Party—held tantalizingly out of his vision by his tormentor, O'Brien:

. . . All he wanted was to hold the photograph in his fingers again, or at least to see it.

"It exists!" he cried.

"No," said O'Brien.

He stepped across the room. There was a memory hole in the opposite wall. O'Brien lifted the grating. Unseen, the frail slip of paper was whirling away on the current of warm air; it was vanishing in a flash of flame. O'Brien turned away from the wall.

"Ashes," he said. "Not even identifiable ashes. Dust. It does not exist. It never existed."

You put enough of your world on computers, you can do the same thing. Just because we missed Orwell's deadline doesn't mean we're out of the woods yet.

D Is for Disney

I've always disliked Disney—Mickey, Minnie, Snow White, Uncle Walt, Cantinflas, Fantasyland, Imagineering, Dumbo, Flubber, Herbie—all of it, for as long as I can remember. Ditto for the new stuff—Aladdin, Lion King, Pocahontas and the rest. Disneyland seems like hell to me, the Hieronymus Bosch *Garden of Earthly Delights* version, with weird creatures and tortured denizens scrabbling over each other trying to find a way out. Disney World, a bigger hell, with the limbo of Epcot tacked onto it. I never went as a child; never wanted to go. As an adult I visited the parks out of a mean, cold, anthropological curiosity.

This dislike was not articulate. I could not lean back, flop my leg over the arm of a chair, turn a palm up and hold forth on the various offenses against art and taste committed by the Disney Corporation in its films, TV shows and theme parks. Rather, the dislike was a mute shiver. My skin crawled, though I didn't really know why.

In truth, I did not *want* to know why. I did not want to stare the thing in the face.

Forced to put the feeling into words, as now, I would start by finding fault in the simplification of classics—turning *Alice in Wonderland* into a bad cartoon, *Tom Sawyer* into a dumb kids' movie, Quasimodo into a teddy bear. Rendering Abraham Lincoln into a jerky robot. Disney shares the shame of bowdlerizers and condensers everywhere—heck, Disney even homogenized its own star, reducing the manic, rubber-limbed 1920s Mickey Mouse, hopped up and jittering with his barnyard pals, into a diluted, beady-eyed, buttoned-down, soulless creature. A Smurf in a straw hat.

Dislike of this process is certainly reason aplenty to loathe Disney. No doubt it was foremost in mind of the Virginians who fought desperately to keep Disney from plowing under an actual Civil War battlefield and transforming it into a grotesque historyland. A special sort of perversity is required to want to destroy an actual historical site in order to construct a fake one. Disney swore up and down that it would give the Civil War the respectful treatment the subject deserves. The Virginians knew better. They knew Disney's project was akin to Bozo the Clown volunteering to officiate at your wedding—he might *promise* to do a good job, he might even *want* to do a good job, might *try* to give the event the dignity it deserves. But Bozo would be unable to, constitutionally, just because of who he is. You wouldn't even see the seltzer bottle until the stream of soda hit you in the eye, during the exchange of vows.

Still, the minimalization of both personality and history—which so bugs academic critics of Disney—can't be the entire problem, at least not for me. I have nostalgic affection for those "Classics Illustrated" comic books, and they certainly are as great an impoverishment as anything Disney ever did. Everyone needs a little simplification sometimes, if only to introduce subjects that might never be encountered otherwise. I didn't know the details of the Easter story until I saw *Jesus Christ Superstar* and, like most, I first heard opera in a Bugs Bunny cartoon.

Perhaps, then, it is the homogenized smarm. All that cuteness, all those cloyingly wholesome values, all those hydrocephalic characters trying to hug you. Disney is the filter designed to take our most basic cultural heritage—the fairy tales and fables and nursery rhymes, with their dark undercurrents of sex and plague and horror—and strain out the disturbing aspects that make them interesting in the first place, producing a consistent gruel bland enough for any palate.

The Disney characters do all have a certain sameness, a predigested, flat quality shared by the cartoons the United States Government occasionally produces—Mr. Zip and such—as if they had been vetted by one committee too many. Quick, name a characteristic of Mickey Mouse. Besides "ears." You can't, can you? He has been scrubbed clean of qualities. They all have. That's what Disney does.

But is that really the core problem? We live in a world of bland smarm. Disney is no worse than—I don't know, *Hello Kitty,* or *Polly Pocket* or *My Little Pony,* or any of the other warm fuzzies designed to pick the pockets of the young. Well, maybe a little worse, due to the stupendous size of the corporation and its global domination, making Disney's brand of idiotic characters a little less avoidable.

Think how bad Barney is; now imagine him, not in the backwater of public broadcasting, but on CBS, anchoring the CBS Evening News. That's Disney.

Could Disney be bothersome, not for any particular intrinsic flaw, but just because it's so huge and successful? There's so much of it, with the films and TV shows and theme parks and toys and books and comics. It never goes away, and eventually becomes grating. That would explain why, even though certain elements of Disney might be well crafted, the whole, taken together, is invariably annoying.

What trace of the charm that Disney creations presumably must have had at some point can survive after they are layered over society like a dew? After popping up on McDonald's cups and postage stamps and baby bunting and carved into the cornices of buildings? Anything would become annoying given a far more subtle treatment. Think of the most desirable house guest you can imagine—Elle MacPherson, say, phones you up, out of the blue, and asks if she can camp out at your place for a few days in between modeling assignments. "Great, Elle," you say reflexively, even if you're married, "come on over." You find yourself dancing to the store, stocking up on champagne and melba toast. And maybe it would be great—for a while, perhaps a long while. But eventually you'd find yourself irked that she is hanging her lingerie over the shower rod and using your razor to shave her legs and parking on the phone for hours at a time talking to her friends in Boongarooda and Paris. "Elle, for God's sake, put some clothes on and help me with the dishes," you soon find yourself barking.

Now imagine the house guest, instead of Elle Mac-Pherson, is Newt Gingrich. That's Disney.

Just the spectacular success of Disney, in itself, inspires disgust, a cousin to the envy that makes the United States loathed by every tin-can dump of a country on the planet, automatically, simply for having risen above them all.

Look at how the appeal of Warner Brothers characters—Bugs Bunny and his pals—has been devalued now that every mall in America has a giant store selling a million varieties of T-shirts and coffee mugs and bronze statuettes bearing their likenesses. There is some sort of basic contradiction in having your zany and lovable characters whelped from the maw of some multibillion-dollar megalith.

Or am I being naive? We're already well on our way to being able to trace every successful creative effort in society back to the same five or six giant entertainment conglomerates. Soon you'll strike up a conversation with Mr. Bongo, the decrepit old clown on the street corner, the one standing on a milk crate and cradling a motley performing bunny, and it will turn out that Mr. Bongo is represented by the William Morris Agency, which collects 15 percent of the change tossed into the hat, and the bunny is owned by Bechtel.

So what is it? Looking for illumination, I dug into the literature of Disney criticism. Over the years, every left-leaning ideologue, radical feminist and Derrida deconstructionist who owned a typewriter at some point went after Disney, beginning with 1930s Communists, who had no problem with Joe Stalin but found Mickey Mouse a threat.

"The Mickey Mouse demonstrates that the creature continues to exist even when it has shed all similarity with humans," wrote Walter Benjamin, arguing that Mickey was the vanguard of dehumanizing technology.

Disney criticizers pull off the neat trick of being more repellent than the thing they are criticizing. Reading the *South Atlantic Quarterly*'s hysterical dissection of Disney made me want to make a beeline for the Magic Kingdom to spend the day riding the Pirates of the Caribbean with a big happy grin plastered all over my face. Academics seem so outraged, so smugly superior. What did they expect? As they poured invective onto Disney—particularly the theme parks—I couldn't help but imagine a theme park that would meet the approval of sociology professors and aging lefties. The brightly colored Twirling Teacups Filled with Steaming Feminist Rage. The Hall of Wobblies, with an animatronic Eugene Debs lurching to his feet to denounce General Motors. The Water Ride of Anarchist-Syndicalism. Eleanor Smeal Land.

What drives academics nuts about Disney is the rigid control it has over everything. When Euro-Disney opened up outside of Paris, remember, it wasn't the aesthetic barrenness of fake medieval streets slapped together just a few Métro stops down from real ones that so enraged French intellectuals. It was the idea of some American company coming in and demanding that Frenchmen wear underwear to work.

The theme parks are indeed a strange inversion of the idea of festivity. Think of settings associated throughout human history with mass entertainment—fairs, carnivals, holidays; the emphasis was always on letting loose, the shedding of normal strictures, the donning of goat horns, the King of Fools crowned, the holy pieties mocked in plain daylight.

Disney's various lands and worlds are exactly the opposite—*more* constrained than real life, a maze of walkways and roped-off areas and crowd management systems. The implication is that our society has decayed so much that people will fly to Florida and pay $33 to walk down a main street that isn't cluttered with crack vials and dozing junkies.

Maybe it has. But the end result is something that is almost worse, the deadness of a wax figure, which doesn't suffer from the ravages of age but still isn't anywhere near alive. Disneyland is the same as if the city of New Orleans emptied out the French Quarter and hired actors to stage a pseudo Mardi Gras, which was then watched by tourists slowly rolling by inside sealed buses. Safer, yes, but also utterly false and more than a little frightening.

As if sensing this predilection for control, despots tend to find Disney irresistibly attractive. Krushchev, remember, when he visited America in 1959, wanted to go straight to Disneyland. He was frustrated that our government wouldn't let him, out of fear of demonstrations, and bitched about it, both in public at the time and later in his memoirs.

His desire was an amazing breach of dogma, when you think about it. The equivalent of Nixon visiting China and asking if he can drive a tractor on a collective farm, or play Li Po in the Red opera *Taking Tiger Mountain by Strategy.*

Hitler, too. For all the Nazi rant against Disney (Mickey Mouse struck them as both black and Jewish), Hitler privately liked Mickey. Goebbels wrote in his diary that he gave the Führer eighteen Mickey Mouse films for Christmas. "He is very pleased and quite happy over this treasure which will hopefully bring him much joy and recreation," the Minister of Propaganda wrote. All the Fascists seemed to carry a secret torch for Mickey. When

45

the Italians banned Western comics as reactionary in the 1930s, they made a lone exception for Disney. And Emperor Hirohito shocked the imperial court for a spell in the 1930s by wearing a Mickey Mouse watch.

Could that be it? The problem with Disney is it suffers from guilt by association. Not with Fascist dictators—not anymore, at least—but as something symbolic of the proletariat. Maybe hating Disney is a form of elitism. Middle America loves Disney, after all, and so loving Disney is seen as deep-kissing middle America, something we card-carrying squishy intellectuals find revulsive.

Maybe that's why, at heart, I find the whole thing so mystifying. Going to Disney World strikes me as akin to pretending to take a beach vacation by sitting in your living room in a deck chair, set up in front of a heat lamp and a fan, wearing sunglasses and sticking your feet in a pail of water. But other people don't see it that way; other people love Disney World. I somehow can't convince myself that, to most, Cinderella's Castle isn't a faux Burgundian pile of concrete and chicken wire that ought to be dynamited into eternity. It's romantic. Five hundred couples got married at Disney World last year. " 'Some weddings cost $100,000,' " I read aloud to my wife, my voice dripping condescension, " 'and come complete with the bride arriving in Cinderella's glass carriage drawn by six white horses.' " I paused, waiting for her bitter chuckle of acknowledgment. Silence. I looked up, thinking perhaps she had left the room, overcome by contempt. No, she was misty-eyed, gazing off into the distance, dreaming of her arrival in the glass carriage. "Oh, how wonderful," she murmured. I couldn't have been more surprised if I had read her a passage about Salman Rushdie and she responded by jamming a steak knife into the countertop and shouting, "He will be shattered by Islam's mighty fist!"

In the final analysis, I think I dislike Disney for the same reason some people hate going to hospitals or graveyards—I know that my doom is Disney World. Disney is part of the package that includes Indian Guides and PTA and Sesame Street and long, long hours at excruciatingly bad elementary school performances. The canyon floor toward which I am hurtling at terminal velocity.

Our boy Ross is just a baby, but I am considering trying to insulate him from Disney, just to forestall that awful moment when I find myself sweating in the Florida sun, feeling his little hand tear itself away from mine as he races into the embrace of a giant Goofy, its arms spread, down on one knee, beckoning. Burying his dear face into the bright polyester fabric dampened by the drool of sixty other children, his precious little body pawed over by the twenty-three-year-old deviant lurking within the costume. Horror.

That has to be the final ignominy of Disney. Children love it. When we reach tenure and settle down, late in life, because our self-expectations were so high, and finally do have kids, our precious Taylors and Maximillians and Beatrices, what are their first words? Mama? Dada? Bauhaus? No, *Lion King*. And *Jasmine*. Uttered the moment their upper palates fuse and repeated until either they reach adolescence or we throttle them one afternoon and go bury the body in the Forest Preserve. ("Little Max? He's been vacationing in Burkina Faso with his real parents. Sure you can have his *Aladdin* video. I don't expect him back any time soon.")

Perhaps resignation in the face of Disney's overwhelming power is the only rational approach. I could play Mozart for our baby twenty-four hours a day and he would never throw a tantrum demanding his favorite opera be played again. *("Madic Fwoot! Madic Fwoot!")* But even if I scrupulously shield him from all things Disney—as I plan to—it will still get in his blood, like a virus. He'll catch it from other kids, or from the air, and one day I'll drag myself home from work and find the walls of his room mottled with Mickeys and Goofys and Aladdins. It's the way of the world, and woe to those who struggle against it.

E Is for Elvis

 There was a guy in my freshman dorm named Andy Krivine, a slight, red-headed fellow who really liked the English rock group The Jam. Really liked them. So much so that, when he tried to express this gigantic like, sense had difficulty coming out, as if the monumentality of his regard had caught in his throat. "The Jam are so great, so . . . ah . . . *fucking great,*" he would say, almost strangling. "Gaaa, The Jam, I can't believe it." He would foam and pinch at himself and collapse to the floor, his legs kicking in the air, while raving about The Jam.

That was almost twenty years ago. The Jam are long gone, and since Andy is probably a partner in a huge law firm by now, perhaps specializing in litigating libel cases, I should probably add that some of this could be a mere trick of memory, particularly the foaming and kicking part. But he did really like The Jam an awful lot.

I was reminded of Andy's raging zeal while examining

how a significant minority react to Elvis Presley. While most of us view Elvis in his proper context—as a great singer whose sexy style helped create rock and roll—there are people who believe the ascent of Elvis was no less than a rend in the fabric of history. An explosion on a par with the Renaissance. A blast that shifted the earth off its axis in 1956 and still continues to echo today, as a source of study, wonderment, veneration and quite possibly something beyond the scope of human comprehension.

"Elvis was too big, too complex—too much—for any of us to quite take in, to see all at once, to understand," marvels Greil Marcus, the most vocal of the many writers whose careers have been spent, in part, parsing Elvis into tinier and tinier pieces, then rooting around in the mush.

Since his death in 1977, Elvis has crept into the marrow of the culture to an incredible, not to mention annoying, degree. "Elvis is everywhere," Mojo Nixon sang in 1987, and the situation has gotten a lot worse since then. A person minding his own business can hardly get through the day without having Elvis flung into his face in a variety of perturbing ways.

The small library of Elvis books—at least 400 titles—expands year by year, from scholarly tomes such as Peter Guralnick's *Last Train to Memphis* to utter schlock such as Gail Brewer-Giorgio's *Is Elvis Alive?* TV specials celebrate and ponder. Magazines lavish attention. The press cannot report on Elvis and his phenomenon enough—when Graceland announced that the tacky Memphis mansion's kitchen would now be included on the tour, the development was solemnly reported in newspapers nationwide, as if it were real news. The once respectable *New York Times* devoted a Sunday magazine cover to seriously analyzing whether Elvis mania represented a new "redemptive faith." When the University of Mississippi held an academic conference devoted to Elvis, more reporters than participants showed up.

Elvis's face adorns products from thimbles to statues, churned out by opportunists from basement entrepreneurs to the U.S. Government. At Graceland, the $17 tours begin every three minutes, eight hours a day, seven days a week, Christmas and New Year's excluded. Each year, around the anniversary of his August 16 death, there is "Elvis Week," a Festiva del Muerto for followers to wallow in his memory, well attended by another strange spin-off, Elvis impersonators, who themselves have had an impact on culture—the echo of an echo.

Ironically, the facet of Elvis least likely to be encountered nowadays is his voice singing a song on the radio. He is so frequently incorporated into other things—a clip in a rock documentary, a snippet of song in a movie, a face in an ad—the music that is supposedly the most important part gets overwhelmed.

Taken together, the books and the TV specials and films and CDs and references in songs and stand-up comedy routines and countless advertisements of ripoff products have pretty much tainted the thought of Elvis Presley for those of us who are not fanatics. Bach would be an annoying buzz if accompanied by the endless drone of praise and analysis and exploitation and ballyhoo lavished on Elvis and boosted by an array of fans as aggressive as Elvis fans.

Many deserve blame for this, but first I want to excuse the tiny sphere of sincerity—the Beulahs and Adelaines who saw the King at the Cow Palace in 1956 and, forty years later, after four kids and two divorces, realize that, by God, the concert was the only genuine moment in their entire lives, the one time they felt real and alive, and it must be honored by the purchase of a collector's plate from the Franklin Mint.

That's okay—weepy regret may be weak, but it's every person's God-given right, and whether you manifest it by closing your office door and drinking big tumblers of single malt, or by rubbing your sobbing face against the iron gate of Graceland, is only a matter of personal style.

Sad that this well of honest emotion should have been so quickly tainted by poisonous exploitation that began with Elvis himself. (I somehow can't refer to him as Presley. It may be proper style, but it sounds prissy, the way the *New York Times* once called the singer Meat Loaf, on second reference, "Mr. Loaf.")

What began on a primitive scale, with the fabled black velvet paintings and other back-room kitsch, has grown into a full-blown industry, particularly after Elvis Presley Enterprises worked out the legal kinks in the 1980s and began licensing his image to appear on every object that can carry it.

Elvis Mountain casts such a long and wide shadow of money that even the most unexpected organizations have a hard time resisting the urge to slip into its shade. *Life* magazine never put Elvis on its cover during the years when both of them were alive, but in early 1995 the animate corpse of *Life* produced an entire issue devoted to Elvis, an amazingly frank document, perhaps unintentionally so, on the occasion of what would have been his sixtieth birthday. After admitting that the magazine had reviled Elvis when he was in his prime, calling him a

"21-year-old hillbilly who howls, mumbles, coos and cries," executive editor Jay Lovinger explained that their epiphany came after Elvis finally did appear, post-mortem, on a cover in 1988. The issue "went on to become one of the best-selling issues in the history of the magazine," wrote Lovinger. "Mmmm..." thought Time/Life. The gears of journalistic excellence began to turn.

"A light dawned: maybe Elvis was nothing to be afraid of. Maybe Elvis was just a human being who brought a lot of pleasure to a lot of people," Lovinger wrote, restraining himself, somehow, from adding, "Maybe Elvis is a way for us to slap together some archival photos and sentimental drool in 14-point type, call the thing a 'Collector's Edition' and sell 300,000 copies at $3.95 a pop." The magazine felt comfortable enough about its ploy to tweak readers at one point, mocking a $65 photo tribute on sale at Graceland. "C'mon, you know LIFE is bound to offer something far better for only $3.95," the magazine ribbed. "By the way, did you remember to buy a copy for a friend?"

Life no doubt felt it held the moral high ground since the magazine hadn't plastered Elvis on its cover for, oh, sixteen months, since August 1993, when it hawked "Exclusive Lost Snapshots From His Army Years—Elvis Young and Innocent."

Even less sincere was the U.S. Postal Service's decision to honor Elvis in 1992 by sticking him on a stamp, a bald attempt to jack up revenues by tapping into the gigantic market for Elvisania, whipped into a froth by a sham contest to decide which Elvis image should be used: the trim young Elvis or the bloated Vegas Elvis. It worked, too—124 million Elvis stamps were sold, making it the most popular issue of all time.

Climbing on the bandwagon, both presidential candidates Bill Clinton and George Bush weighed in with their opinions on thin versus fat Elvis. Bush mentioned Elvis twice during his speech accepting the Republican presidential nomination in 1992. Elvis impersonators performed at Clinton's inaugural celebration, a low point in national prestige unmatched since the British burned the White House in 1814.

Naked commercial exploitation is usually near the bottom of the sewer of cultural life, but in Elvis's case it is only the foyer leading down to lower regions, such as the realm of those who find the whole thing wryly amusing and ironic, the twenty-eight-year-old assistant gofers who think that sticking a Salvation Army painting of Elvis in the living room somehow plants them on the cutting edge of hipness.

Worse yet—on the bottom rung of the Dantean levels of Elvis Hell—are not those who are ironic but those who take their Elvis seriously. I picked up the book *Dead Elvis* by the aforementioned Greil Marcus, thinking the former *Rolling Stone* critic had put together an examination of the latest phase of Elvis's career in keeping with the book's subtitle: "A chronicle of a cultural obsession."

Wrongo. Marcus does mention the various surprising ways in which Elvis crops up in the culture in a "seemingly permanent ubiquity," but he finds this state of affairs a good thing, succumbing to the obsession, inflating Elvis's deep impact on society into an epochal, universe-cracking cataclysm. No exaggeration is beyond him.

"Elvis was the first public figure since Jesus that couldn't be ignored by any segment of his civilization, yet that foretold and embodied a new mode of being that would eventually dismantle the very society that was so fascinated by his presence," he writes, vaulting Elvis over Newton, Einstein, and a few other notables who did their own society dismantling between the man from Galilee and the boy from Tupelo.

Not only does Marcus credit Elvis with any changes made in culture since the 1950s, but he adds the completely unsupported, almost insane claim that Elvis intended all of it to happen.

"If he redefined what it means to be American, it was because he meant to," writes Marcus. "He wanted change. He wanted to confuse, to disrupt, to tear it up."

Bullshit. What Elvis *meant* to do, as David Halberstam notes in his fine history, *The Fifties,* was to make the movies which his devotees later were to dismiss as a schlocky aberration. "What he really wanted from the start was to go to Hollywood and be a movie star," Halberstam writes. "It was almost as if the music that shook the world was incidental."

As for Elvis ushering in any "new mode of being," more sentient critics recognized that, rather than being the beginning of anything, Elvis was actually the end of an epoch, the last popular singer to grab mass adulation, the ultimate expression and final gasp of pop cohesiveness in American life, closer in spirit to Frank Sinatra and Al Jolson than to anyone who followed him. Two weeks after Elvis's death, rock critic Lester Bangs, in his sharp critique "Where Were You When Elvis Died?" writes of walking down the street in Chelsea, relaying the sad news to indifferent Hispanics and sneering shop clerks. "Not everyone liked Elvis," noted Bangs, musing that passersby might have been more affected if he told them Donna Summers had died. "Not everyone liked rock and roll."

Bangs saw the passing of Elvis, that "big strapping baby bringing home the bucks," as symbolic of atomization, which has indeed been the mark of the past twenty years of American culture.

"I can guarantee you one thing," he wrote. "We will never again agree on anything as we agreed on Elvis. So I won't bother saying good-bye to his corpse. I will say good-bye to you."

The problem with viewing Elvis as an end, and not a beginning, is that it doesn't pump up the ego of his critics, who, by elevating him, become gatekeepers of something Huge and Ongoing and Significant. Marcus compares Elvis—in addition to Jesus—to Lincoln, to Melville, to Franklin Roosevelt. His 1968 comeback TV special (possibly "a central moment in the history of American culture," Marcus pants, as if nothing else was going on in the 1960s) is likened to Lincoln's second inaugural, to certain lyrical sections of *Moby Dick*. Marcus tears into Elvis's detractors with a comical fury—Albert Goldman's book is more than a sloppy jeremiad, he says, it is "cultural genocide" committed against Elvis fans, who constitute "a people," no less. Golly.

The phenomenon of peeing Elvis to delineate your intellectual territory was astutely parodied a decade ago by Don DeLillo, who has a character in his classic 1985 novel *White Noise*—a prospective professor of Elvis studies—admire the handiwork of the more established professor of Hitler studies:

"You've established a wonderful thing here with Hitler. You created it, you nurtured it, you made it your own. . . . It has an identity, a sense of achievement. You've evolved an entire system around this figure, a structure with countless substructures and interrelated fields of study, a history within history. I marvel at the effort. It was masterful, shrewd and stunningly preemptive. It's what I want to do with Elvis."

In an odd inversion, the actual academics that DeLillo mocks are more grounded in reality than popular writers like Marcus. Take Susan M. Doll, whose unpublished doctoral thesis "Elvis Presley: All Shook Up; The Effect of Ideology and Subculture on Star Image" runs 560 pages and at least makes the cogent argument that Elvis's menace came as much from his Southern roots as from his swiveling hips, though it does so in chunks of verbiage like:

"That's All Right"/"Blue Moon of Kentucky" represents the first text of Elvis Presley, or the first bit of material that was coded with information by or about Presley, which was then made available to an audience to be enjoyed, experienced, or, from my point of view, read.

Rendered into vernacular, the above reads: "Elvis's first 45 rpm record was 'That's All Right, Mama.' The B side was 'Blue Moon of Kentucky.' " I couldn't resist tracking down Doll to find out how a person who writes a doctoral dissertation about Elvis Presley views the endeavor after the passage of a few years. Answer: tired of being mocked about it, particularly by disingenuous journalists pretending to share her perspective.

There *is* something that invites ridicule in the tone of academic prose lavished on Elvis. Midway through Doll's two-volume thesis I found myself chafing to try out her style on other cultural icons: "In encompassing states both real and magical, friend and star, person and dinosaur, Barney mirrors the dichotomous nature of the parent/child relationship. By freely moving between play/state and authority/leadership state, Barney presents an image of freedom to children, who are otherwise circumscribed by societal norms, giving added weight to his love message, and not incidentally presenting himself as an alternative and therefore a threat to parents, leading to the common perception of Barney as devil figure. . . ."

You keep this up long enough, they give you a doctorate.

The idea of Elvis has been so overworked, so ground to a nubbin, so worn down to nothing like a toddler's adored blankie, that, more than any other entry, I had qualms about even including him in this book. I was faced with a thorny logical puzzle: how can one write about the irritation caused by the endless analysis and celebration of Elvis Presley without in the process adding to the problem? Is any argument, no matter how apt, worth reading *Elvis and Me* by Priscilla Beaulieu Presley? Maybe the high road is to just walk away. E could be "e-mail."

Difficult questions. But what made my decision for me was a single, ineluctable fact. A fact which, compared to the constant blare of Elvis deification, is only occasionally whispered: Elvis is stupid. The whole thing is stupid.

Here's a guy—nice, by all accounts, at first, ignorant but well mannered—who crawls out of a *Tobacco Road* upbringing to find fame and fortune, which almost instantaneously transform him into a drug monster, living out the last two decades of his life in a stupor of Percodan and celebrity. He never writes a song. He never makes a good movie. He never attempts to wrest his life from the fawning handlers and leeches who cover him like a coral reef. The blank slate of his mind is, at the end, scribbled over with mysticism and guns and karate and self-regard. Then he dies, comically, on the toilet, and enters this creepy zone of Gothic myth and nightmare imagery.

Yes, Elvis is arch and tragic and American. Big themes—race, music, money, sex, drugs, movies, death—run through his story. And yes, he was important—just as Kennedy was important and Plato was important and the little gob of goo at the back of our brains telling us to breathe is important.

But does being important mean there has to be so much of him? Can't Elvis at some point *recede?* Metternich was important, too, but you don't see *him* gazing down from every coffee shop wall. Couldn't the general public allow Elvis's rotted corpse to return to the grave, to its proper place among other dead cultural figures? Or is our egocentrism so intense that anyone who affected us greatly has to be set on a pedestal and adored continually until we ourselves pass into the Great Beyond?

Everybody associated with Elvis has written a book—his ex-wife, his bodyguards, his former lovers, his fans. Thirty bucks will buy you *The Ultimate Elvis—Elvis Presley Day by Day,* a mind-numbing compilation of irrelevant facts, arranged chronologically. On September 19, 1967,

59

we are told, "Elvis fired his gardener, Troy Ivy." (Ivy's book, *The Day Elvis Fired Me,* is no doubt forthcoming.)

After 335 pages of this, with another 200 pages yet to go, including lists of Elvis's phone numbers, pets ("Fluff, a cat,") and favorite foods—the sort of stuff you would expect to read in *Tiger Beat* in 1959, not in a hardback book in 1995—author Patricia Jobe Pierce steps forward and delivers this bold trumpet blast of idiocy, made more acute by its bad writing, its stunning naïveté and complete irrelevance to the actual historical personage of Elvis Presley, plus its pitiable grab at political correctness:

> Elvis may be physically dead, but he's alive in people's memories and in every act that goes against a one-sided government, a narrow-sighted parent, a hypocritical minister, an uninformed teacher, a slandering member of the press, a person who feels alone, or anyone who shows prejudice against any person or race. Elvis is there when a person of poverty or color decides to make a difference and move on. Elvis is there whenever a teenager feels down and out because his appreciation of them and his message to them lifts their spirits and gives them a reason for being alive. Elvis is there whenever an individual or group challenges the first amendment. Elvis is there whenever the next innovative musician, composer, dancer, poet, or writer decides it's all right to be different and stands for beliefs that may go against the norm.

There's really nothing more to say after that, except it might have been better if Elvis had never happened along.

If we were all still sitting in our seats, hands folded primly in our laps, listening to the Mantovani Orchestra play "The Beautiful Blue Danube." If this is where the trip has left us—Patricia Jobe Pierce revealing the registration numbers of Elvis's airplanes—what was the point of rock and roll? If the music was so liberating, then why isn't anybody liberated?

Spike Lee, himself a minor annoyance, expressed it best when he said, "I wish he'd never died myself, so I wouldn't have to hear about him every single day." But I think the last word, as a sort of sorbet after a meal of excess, should go to the late, lamented Lester Bangs, who two weeks after Elvis died contemplated his legacy, then wrote: "We might all do better to think about waving good-bye with one upraised finger." Amen.

F Is for Fat

"Are you going to eat that chocolate?"

The question might not translate well onto the printed page. It might be mistaken for the words of somebody who wants a chocolate, of a person who is being polite before taking the last one.

But there were two truffles on the white paper doily on the plate by our bedside. It was midnight. We had just spent a lovely day at a resort in Wisconsin, hiking through the woods in the afternoon, attending a performance of Shakespeare's *Twelfth Night* in the evening. Later, we sat on a veranda with two friends, enjoying a post-performance cocktail. I was relaxed, happy, not on my guard.

Now we were back in the room. I was still hungry—am, in fact, almost always hungry, at least in my mind. I knew those chocolates would be there. I had been thinking about them in the hall.

"Are you going to eat that chocolate?"

My wife said it. Not really a question at all, of course, but a statement. A criticism, an expression of surprise, a polite way of saying: "I cannot believe you are eating that chocolate now after a day of vigorous gluttony, you oily pig you."

The chocolate was already in my mouth when she said it. I chewed and swallowed, though I might as well have spat it out. The pleasure was gone. Edie never did eat her chocolate. She threw it away, I suppose, so I wouldn't get at it.

My wife has always been lean. When she was thirty she could still wear jeans she had worn at eighteen. While women long to be a size 8, she bought a size 4, sometimes even a size 2.

Yet she eats whatever she wants, whenever she wants, without thought to consequence. Food just doesn't have the central place in her world that it does in mine. I remember once, when she was in law school, I fixed her a cup of tea and set it out for her with a brownie. She took a bite out of that brownie and let it sit there for, oh, I don't know, three hours. I kept passing her, looking at the brownie with the bite taken out of it, astounded. I couldn't have been more amazed if she had used her mystic feminine powers to levitate the brownie and was reading case studies while it hovered several inches above the table.

The brownie became part of my private mythology, one of the tales I tell to illustrate the marvelous, otherworldly quality of my wife. Cassandra could see the future, and Edie can ignore a brownie for hours.

I could never neglect a brownie like that. I might be

able to eat it slowly, rationing myself, taking a bite every five minutes, or whatever. But it would take will, planning; it wouldn't be an accident.

Some people are no doubt fat because of glandular disorders or the wrath of an angry God. I am not one of those people. I am fat because I eat a lot.

Since fat people are held in such low regard, I should say immediately that I am not *that* fat. Not fat in the Chinese Buddha, Daniel Pinkwater, spilling-out-of-the-airplane-seat sense. Not the size-48, Jeez-look-at-that-thing-coming-down-the-block sense. I don't have the neighborhood kids skipping behind me in the street, singing derisive songs and banging tin cans together.

Not yet, anyway.

I've always wondered how people let themselves get that way—if a man is 400 pounds, what was he thinking when he hit 350?

I can say this because I made a goal-line stand when I reached 200—a fine weight if I was 6′2″ and not 5′8¾″. As it is, I cut a figure that was once called husky. Round, pearlike, plump or, in my wife's love-clouded eyes, bearish.

Two hundred is enough for me to think of myself as fat, particularly because I was thin, for about five years, in my middle twenties. After I realized that women were not attracted to fat guys and shot down to 148 pounds. I looked gaunt just long enough to snag my poor wife, who thought I was this svelte little guy. Now she is stuck, forced to forever wage a low-level campaign to nudge me back toward thin. Too many failures have gone by for a direct approach, so now the battle is fought on the periphery, a guerrilla war of veiled statements and subtle sarcasm. "Are you going to eat that chocolate?"

Of course I am. Just as I am going to eat that club sandwich, and those fries, and these cookies, and this double-stuffed baked potato along with the thick steak. And why not? Aren't you? Can I have yours, then?

Eating is what life is about. My life, anyway. Sure, I would prefer to experience my deepest and most profoundly alive moments while swooning over a book of philosophy or free-climbing K2.

But I ain't that way, and my guess is that neither are you. We live in a society preprogrammed to make you fat. Forty thousand years of the body hoarding every gram of fat, every calorie of gristle gnawed raw off a wildebeest shank bone, set us up for the fall. And now suddenly, poor us, we find ourselves in late twentieth-century America, awash in the greatest concentration and variety of food ever assembled in one place. No wonder we go crazy. No wonder we get fat. No wonder that one third of the U.S. population is overweight, up from one fourth just a few years ago and racing toward a half and then two thirds.

I suppose it's better than starving to death.

The surprise is that anyone manages to be thin. Surprise and, if I may say, pain. Bothersome as fat people can be, with their greedy-puppy plowing back of food, elbows raised defensively, and their sad obliviousness to their own condition, thin people are worse. If they are naturally thin, you want to strangle them, since they don't know how lucky they are. My friend Larry must have tapeworms or something. He literally eats all day long, digging his hand up to the wrist into the big bowls of M & Ms scattered around his house, lifting out softball-sized handfuls and, tilting his head back, cascading the candy in. Thin as a rail. And I know he doesn't appreciate it, because otherwise he would go to Mecca every year, or light a candle, or something.

Even worse are people who work at it. They seem shriveled, anhedonistic. I was at a party once where the hostess was, like my wife, another wisp of a woman. She prepared some intensely fattening dessert—Bananas Foster, I believe it was: thick slices of ripe bananas awash in sugar and cinnamon and butter and liqueur. I was halfway through mine before I noticed that she wasn't eating any. I challenged her, nicely. She fluttered a little smile and demurred. Oh, she couldn't eat that, she said. But it was fine for us, she didn't say, fine for her piggish guests, who would ruin themselves and enjoy doing it. I wanted to take my dessert and grind her face in it—why serve dessert, if you are going to step back and decline the poison yourself?

That moment of shame, your cheeks packed gerbil-full with Bananas Foster while confronting the slim resolve of your betters, is the heart of the fat experience. The yin of the primal pleasure of satiation, the lips closing down on the tip of a thick triangle of stuffed Chicago pizza, balanced against the yang of catching sight of yourself in the mirror, of being photographed in profile, of packing your corporeal being into tight pants and binding jackets.

Being fat would be wonderful, if not for the social stigma. Well, that and debilitating medical conditions. And premature death.

"Nothing tastes as good as being thin feels," the old saying goes, and, having been both thin and fat, I can vouch for that. Sometimes I battle ten or fifteen pounds off my frame, and can even enjoy the process, a little. I *like* carrots. I love those new soyburgers, those chocolate-flavored rice cakes. They too are food after all.

But the fact is, if there was a God, we fat people wouldn't have to think about this. We'd slip our trim forms into our fashionable outfits and then go out for a steak. There would be no piper to pay.

Alas, fat is here and always will be. And, despite the desires of the resignedly fat, it will always be unacceptable. When the day comes that five sixths of the nation is 20 percent overweight, fat will still be looked down on. How could it not? Ignoring the obvious medical concerns, there is the sheer discomfort of it. Those fat-acceptance activists in their muumuus, whining because some airline charged them for the second seat they need to accommodate their bulk, can talk all they like about inner beauty, about false and arbitrary aesthetic standards. They can hurl barbs at poor Kate Moss. They can never argue they're comfortable, however. They can never say that carrying around an extra hundred pounds *feels good.*

The irony is that, as more and more people become fat, fatness will be seen as less and less desirable. To aesthetic and medical complaints are added spiritual ones, unfair as that may be. The modern world both encourages fat and then condemns it. Hillel Schwartz's riveting history of dieting, *Never Satisfied,* finds the entire streamlined sweep of fast-paced progress as being, at its core, anti-fat.

"Fatness was awkward, imbalanced, inefficient, un-economical," he writes of the growing unacceptability of fat at the dawn of the twentieth century. "Fat men and women were increasingly self-conscious, and society was more embarrassed for them. Cartoons showed them to be at odds with the scale of modern life: a fat man dwarfs a hotel bed or a Pullman sleeper, a fat woman plugs up the aisle of a streetcar or the compartment of an elevator."

To find comfort, we fat must cast our gaze back to the nineteenth century, to Diamond Jim Brady sitting down, uncriticized, to his endless banquets of oysters and champagne. To a time when the image of feminine beauty was zaftig Lillian Russell and her jewel-studded gold bicycle.

Did I say "uncriticized"? Heck, "lauded" is more the word.

On August 14, 1879, the Fat Men's Association of New York City held its annual outing, a boat ride and clambake at Gregory's Point. By the account in the next day's *New York Times,* under the simple headline "Fat Men and Clams," the gathering was a festive affair and drew great notice. People on shore cheered as the fat men floated by. "A large proportion of the population of Connecticut waited on the pier to see the New Yorkers land," the story noted. A brass band played. The *Times* estimated that nearly a thousand fellow revelers took the trip with the twenty fat members of the club. "The few fat men, surrounded by the many lean men, had a delightful sail up the Sound . . . as fat men were never known to be in a hurry, they enjoyed the ride, drank all the beer on board, and were supremely happy."

Ahhh . . . that's better. What a lovely image. I can squint my eyes and see it. The sunny day. The lapping water. The proud, happy fat men.

Let's leave it there. Isn't that what fatness is all

about—being happy, the happiness that comes from keeping your maw well stoked with the kind of food it likes best? An infant contentment, rudely interrupted by all the societal scolding and shame. Okay, being fat is a death sentence. What isn't?

G Is for Gimmick

Now I found myself in sullen middle
    age
Gazing sadly at the world material,
Noticing that when form and
    substance engage

The free prize overshadows the cereal.
I called out to the heavens for guidance.
The heavens sent a message ethereal

In the form of a figure in checked pants
Appearing in a flash of acrid green smoke,
Dapper from his yellow shoes to hat from
    France.

He twirled his umbrella, winked, then spoke:
"Ev'ree durn fool knows ya need a gimmick.
Plain substince loozs out t'emptee baroque."

I stared at this strange-speaking lunatic
For a moment, then said, "Who the hell are
you?" A rude enjambment, yes, not politic.

But what I really said, in vernacular.
Though I regretted saying it immediately,
Seeing how shocked he was by my vinegar.

The man composed himself rather readily,
Squared his shoulders and extended his hand,
Saying, "Kall me Petroleum V. Nasby."

Now it was my turn to fail to understand:
An obscure humorist, a century dead,
Speaking dialect, alive, walking the land.

He spoke again: "Twill all mek sense,
    copperhead."
Then reached out, taking hold of my elbow,
And heavenward, high into the sky, we sped.

I was not frightened to see the earth below
Glowing blue and radiant, white at each pole,
The better to show up against black cosmo.

Next we entered what seemed a hot glory-hole,
So fiery, I thought we fell into the sun
But then we were back on land, a curving knoll,

In a crowd, he and I, almost overrun
By masses of pushing, paint-streaked persons,
Each trying not to let himself be outdone.

"Fust," he said, "uv wut wel be niyne lessuns . . ."
"Stop that!" I said. "Ghost or poetic device,
Talk normal, or I'll be reduced to a dunce."

He smiled. "My rude friend, I'll be precise.
Look at self-expression, if you have the heart.
Any frill, any technique, all to entice.

"The boldest young climbers dare to call it art
To reside in a cardboard box for a year
Or select their colors by throwing a dart.

"It sets you apart from a talented peer
To brandish your paintbrush in your butt.
Gathering more attention pays for the beer.

"This one limits himself to painting his mutt
Just in blue, to catch the eye of the *Journal.*
A thing like that will always cut through the
      glut."

We went by someone gilding a urinal.
Ceramic dog turds, Jeff'ry Koontz, sculpted mud.
"But, master," I said, "is this not eternal?

"Wasn't Impressionism first thought a dud?
Did not the critics see excess sensation
When Eakins gave a woman muscles and blood?"

He winked, but gave no amplification.
Simply took off, striding, down the steepish hill
I followed him, closely, with trepidation.

To a foul lake where sunken souls did distill
Upside down, while toothsome piranhas gnawed.
I stared at the water and felt a sudden thrill

Of recognition. "Master!" I said, awed.
"That one. With the beard. And the most
    piranhas.
Haul him up here. I know that person, by God!"

Nasby reached with the hook of his umbrella
And caught the bearded unfortunate man's feet,
Pulling him out, this poor, sopping-wet fellah.

Oh, to see him in this place was bittersweet!
"Nick," I said, "Nicholson Baker, tell me, please,
What lapses led to this unexpected defeat?"

He shook off water, shivered, gave a sneeze.
Then turned his blind eyes in our direction.
"Friends," he said. "Technique is often a disease.

"Like syphilis, pleasant in the infection,
But horribly lethal if left unchecked.
I began with an eye nearing perfection

"For nuance, and detail, and human defect
But I strayed into mannered fantasy sex
And found my ample talent nearly wrecked.

"Style is consistency while life is complex
Thus art and commerce clash, and I, like a cad,
Traded my vision for royalty checks.

"So I joined the manner'd, the banner'd bad,
Grasping for any stock character or tool,
Their tawny geniuses solving crimes unclad."

Nothing more did he say of this fate so cruel.
We three stood silent, then Nasby, with a groan,
Cast the unfortunate back into the pool.

"Let us go now," Nasby said in a monotone,
His eyes still fixed on the churning waters,
And I knew that while my fate is still unknown

Nasby was viewing his permanent quarters,
Reprieved, but not pardoned, for my sake
Soon to return to these suffering jotters.

I touched his arm. "Come, away from this lake.
We will both find ourselves returning someday."
He complied, his face reflecting heartache.

Oh, that I had the stamina to relay
Or you the attention span to follow me
Through the subsequent six levels of dismay

But our age is accustomed to brevity
And here I will condense the tale a little
So as not to lose those raised on MTV.

Down, ever down, Nasby and I did skittle
Past politicians, performing complex tricks
To attack while remaining noncommittal.

Next a nursery school of academics
Dressed in the costume of whatever new pose
Passes for theory, or aids in polemics,

Halting a moment to pity ad honchos
Using their own products; then to fashion's pride
Shivering in their gauze coats and lace ponchos.

At times we laughed, other times we cried.
I could barely look at the great iron grill
Where doctors pushing dubious cures fried.

At level eight the sky was black, the wind shrill.
Here news editors, each chained to a trend,
Ground every idea through the big mill.

Those who cut copy so to never offend
Now cursed in torment, begged me for peace,
But I was too shaken by their grim portend.

When we saw the river I wanted to cease,
So fearsome were the waters, so rank the smell.
I implored Nasby to grant me release.

"Do not keep me here in this terrible hell."
But he said I had not yet seen quite enough.
Across the river we strode, to a dim dell.

At last, the bottom, a ring scrabbly and rough.
We came upon souls, each with helmet-clad head,
Staggering in a version of blindman's buff.

They lurched and bumped, grasping fingers spread
In air, or else pushing at buttons and keys,
Their faces hidden, each to each, cable-wed.

Some roll on their backsides, some sway on their
     knees
In silence, but for odd whirring and clicking.
I turned to Nasby and said, "Tell me, please.

"Who are these people? What things are they
     flicking?"
He said, "Ask them yourself, do not take my
     word.
They dwell in a strange world of their own
     picking."

He culled someone at random from the herd
And worked at releasing his helmet strap,
Lifting it off to reveal a head ungird.

A pale, beady-eyed, quite frightened chap.
Staring at us as if he had never seen
People before, or else had some handicap.

"Who are you?" I asked. "What is this
     machine?"
He just stared, seeming not to understand.
"Why are you living like this? What does it
     mean?"

A long delay, almost more than I could stand.
I was about to suggest that we be gone
When, slowly, he raised his quivering hand.

"You . . . seem so . . . real," said this near
   automaton,
Grasping hold of my cloak, feeling the fabric.
"A stunning effect," he went on, weak and wan.

"The graphics, extraordinarily slick."
He held out his button box and twiddled.
"It must eat memory, it's not very quick.

"Pipeline burst cache," he said as he fiddled.
"Sixteen megabyte multi-session dual RAM.
You must be a glitch—the system is riddled."

I grabbed him by the nose, twisting. "I am,"
I said, "no glitch, but a person annoyed.
On a trip to discover trick and flimflam.

"So rouse yourself from your electronic void.
Provide answers to our most important quiz
And Nasby and I will be overjoyed."

Some color crept into his face. "My name is
Stuart Brand. I wound up here, as millions did,
Searching for any grail, any answer, viz.:

"Geodesic dome, tire sandal, pyramid,
Home canning, *The Whole Earth Catalog,* rolfing,
Holistic healing, home birth, Trans-Species Id.

"But no fad grabbed and held us like this thing:
God in a box and Information Engine,
The Gimmick Ultimo, the Contraption King.

77

"Theology and workshop and discipline
Always moving forward, always followed,
And ideas! Fast, numerous, crystalline

"A select group—self-selected, know the
    code
The rest are unconnected, while we chosen
Wait breathlessly for the new age to explode.

"Still waiting, living on cyber-food, frozen,
Running, virtually, across bit-green grass,
Welcoming all who, like us, are fresh-squozen."

He grabbed the helmet, fell back on his ass
And was soon happily working his device.
I looked to Nasby; he just said, "Alas."

Suddenly everything scattered like mice—
The helmeted ones, the place, also Nasby
With no more than "Alas," a statement
    concise

Though not as clear or instructive as could be.
"Wait, what did that mean?" I yelled, to the air.
"Tell me! Come back!" But no answer met my
    plea.

Now it struck me as absolutely not fair
To lead me through this nightmarish under-
    world
Then leave me with "Alas," back in my
    armchair.

I had seen the gimmickeers all swirled
But not been shown the line where content did
   stop
And extraneous trickery unfurled.

What of naming characters Bloat and
   Slothrop?
Anxious artifice or admirable art?
Which are the bubbles? Which is the soda
   pop?

Or does "Alas" mean that you can never
   start
To answer the question for any but you?
A trick to one is gold to her counterpart.

Sure, gimmicks are annoying, but it is also true,
Without Bat Day, few would see a bad team, a
struggling loser grabs something to break
   through.

Thus I wrote this chapter in terza rima
Not due to poetry being my forte
But since it seemed an impressive schema.

Arcane triple meter of poet Dante
Used in the *Inferno,* and little more
A rigid style suited to some old auntie.

To me it was a challenge, a noble chore,
Not just the rhyme, but eleven syllables
In every line, not a syllable more.

You can count them if you are prone to quibbles.
It made writing the chapter take forever,
Grinding out triplets, in drabs and dribbles.

Yet it struck me as so goddamned clever,
A gimmick within a chapter on the same,
Mighty impressive, digressive, whatever.

Another footfall on the road to acclaim,
Which is a slick and slippery thoroughfare.
Why not a facile trick to help hype your name?

Just be sure to pick that trick with utmost care.
For each one boosted, there are many it bars
From reaching the special vantage point where

A lucky person can catch sight of the stars.

H Is for Hip

Fifty years from now, when I would be a very old man, will the First Lady sport a small chrome ball dangling from her nose?

If the answer is "Yes," then I must pray that I am dead by then. I don't know if I could stand it—I had a hard enough time with Bill Clinton, yucking it up with Arsenio Hall and clomping through McDonald's in his horrible plastic running shorts.

I suppose the problem is mine—clinging to the outdated notion that high government leaders ought to maintain a certain level of decorum. If the Chief Executive wants to get a big tattoo of Grace Slick straddling a Harley on his back, or publicly praises his new cock ring, so what, as long as he balances the budget?

And what is decorum, anyway? The most outrageous excesses of one generation have a way of becoming the ho-hum normality of the next. As you age, you are left with the unpalatable choice of either abandoning the standards of your youth or seeing them in constant violation everywhere you look. No wonder old people retreat from life— it's the most attractive option.

There is probably little point in remarking on hipness, never mind fighting against it. Heck, the word itself shows I'm not with it—the term at the time I'm writing this, if my sixteen-year-old niece Julia is any guide, is "fresh," though by the time this is published it might be anything. She predicts "the bomb" will be the next preferred term for something attractively new, but then she might be just pulling the leg of her old, befuddled uncle. "I told him kids were calling cool things 'the bomb,' " she'll whisper to her giggling friends, "and he believed it!"

I know that the most dating, time-specific thing a writer can do is carp about the current fashion. Nothing I say about nose jewelry will matter in the long run. If the fad goes away, then my opinion on the topic will be meaningless, akin to some obscure mid-1970s satirist bitching that leisure suits are ugly.

And if the fad becomes a universally accepted practice, which is where it seems to be heading, then I'll look even worse. The fusspot who found pierced eyebrows disgusting, failing to realize they would be embraced by a populace rushing toward faux tribalism and safe perversion and the mildly occult.

But still—*nose baubles?* Somebody's got to man the ramparts. In the past several years I have watched, with growing alarm, as nose jewelry and facial piercing moved from a signal oddity among genuine sexual deviates to a mainstream fashion accessory aspired to by fresh young people, such as niece Julia, who would bolt off to get one this minute if her mother didn't brace herself in the doorway, forbidding it.

No amount of familiarity can accustom me to the trend. My neighborhood—admittedly a section of Chicago known for youthful pansexuality—is awash with facial jewelry. Yet no matter how many times I see the fashion, my brain is hardwired to always go through the same three-stage process of cognition: (a) "Hey, that girl has a piece of snot hanging out of her nose"; (b) "No, wait, it's metallic"; (c) "Oh, it must be a nose bauble."

The most annoying thing about people who embrace radical fashions, whether nose trinkets or spiked hair or tattoos, is not the outré quality of the fashion itself but the fact that, without their knowing it, they are still bowing to conformity. But instead of it being the JCPenney catalogue conformity of the mainstream, their fashion choice is an equally slavish grab at what the smaller, hip circle has deemed represents rebellion. My niece Julia didn't just decide out of the blue that she wants a nose bauble, among the galaxy of potential adornments she could use to terrorize her mother. She thinks she is rebelling, when in fact no teen would ever dream of adopting a truly odd fashion—pince-nez, or powdered wigs, or lip plates, or whatever—that would take actual individuality to attempt.

Radical fashions are even worse, intellectually, than regular ones, since both are sheeplike behavior, but at least in the JCPenney outfit you can still hold a real job.

Another mystery about radical fashions is that wearers seem to bitterly resent being noticed. What do they expect? When I pass a knot of teens loitering at the corner of Belmont and Clark, they invariably return my curious gaze with a hostile glare. It's hard not to chuckle, "Hey, kids, if you don't wanna be stared at, here's a thought: don't dye your hair green."

Since I am a card-carrying nonjoiner, I have always viewed most fashions with hostility. The fact is that I don't understand them. They zoom at me out of nowhere, and either disappear or become the rage. I can never predict which it will be. I can never react in time, and since I'm fat, nothing would fit me even if I did. I have not been fashionably decked out since I wore a diaper and plastic pants along with everyone else in my cohort.

Take three-button suits. They are back. Definitely. They returned in 1989, on fashion models, after having disappeared in the mid-1960s. I saw them and smiled. "Right," I thought. "Next they'll be bringing back Nehru jackets. No one will buy these things." The musical *How to Succeed in Business (Without Really Trying)* came to mind. ("How to commute/in a three-button suit/with that weary/executive smile . . .")

I was mildly surprised to see pedestrians in Chicago wearing three-button suits. Then people I knew at work wore them. Then my seventy-year-old father-in-law bought one.

To make matters worse, *How to Succeed in Business* came back too, returning to Broadway after thirty years. As if mocking me.

Still, I couldn't wear one. My torso isn't long enough, or something. I don't buy suits often enough to risk tacking after a fad. On the other hand, I worry that I'll cling to two-button suits and end up looking like those grandmothers you see still showing off their 1967 Carnaby Street caps and plastic op-art raincoats, the last clothing purchased before the frost set in.

The few times I have tried to embrace fashion have not worked out. When I was just out of college, and realized that women are attracted to dangerous men, I bought a black leather motorcycle jacket, the kind with the zippers and buckles all over. I wore it for a while, until I realized it made me look, not like a seductive rebel, but like a puffy Jewish guy on his way to a 1950s dance. I can still remember a girl whom I desperately wanted to impress, seeing me in the jacket and laughing so hard that she doubled over, struggling to catch her breath. "Neil!" she finally gasped out. "That *jacket* . . ."

After the motorcycle jacket fiasco, I have been reluctant to indulge my fashion tastes. I can assume that, if something appeals to me, I should resist it, the way I resisted those one-piece underwear ensembles most stores have been hawking, realizing they would make me look impoverished and slovenly rather than rustic and appealing, more like Rod Steiger in *Oklahoma!* than a character from Robert James Waller.

For instance. The fashion accessory I would really like right now is a fez. This is not a comic pose. Every time I am in New York City I stop by Nat Sherman's on Forty-Second Street to finger the imported British smoking fez, made of red velour with a long black tassel dangling down the side.

I know why I like it—besides its odd beauty. The fez suggests a life—of independence, of devil-may-care revelry (who could wear a fez and care about other people's opinions?). A sort of giddy, corpulent, Robert Benchley late bachelorhood. I see myself, in the fez and the matching smoking jacket, red with black satin lapels, sitting cross-legged on a coosh, smoking a water pipe, chatting happily with my crowds of visitors, offering them trays of marzipan and martinis. (In my fez fantasy, I am always entertaining at home. I somehow just can't picture myself going out in a fez, no matter how self-assured I might become. I once wore a bow tie to a dinner party and could not have felt more uncomfortable and odd had I worn a cotillion gown.)

But the time is not yet right for a fez. Society generally frowns on hats for men, one of the sorriest fashion trends over the past thirty-five years. Hats were a wonderfully expressive fashion accessory. When Thurber wrote of Columbus politicians as being the sort of men who "fanned their soup with their hats" you knew exactly what he meant.

If wearing a fedora is seen as a little strange, wearing a fez would be a perversion—I might as well wear a bonnet. And in addition to larger conditions being wrong, my own life is not conducive to a fez either. Everything is not in order. The support systems are not there. Buying a fez would be like buying a pair of riding boots—the rest of my world would belie it. "Clothes alone will never make you fashionable," fashion critic Kennedy Fraser writes. "Friends, thoughts, face and life must match." Mine don't. First, I am not a bachelor. I have a wife, and I don't think my wife would ever permit a fez. She would see it and let out a scream that would shake the radiator away from the wall.

So I am biding my time, waiting for the right moment. Perhaps my wife's anti-fezism will soften. Perhaps the strong subcurrents of society opposing fezzes will dissolve, making my adopting the fashion easier. A few chance occurrences—Jean Paul Gaultier drives past a Shrine circus; Tommy Hilfiger, flipping through channels, alights on *The Road to Morocco*. And suddenly fezzes are hot. I will be ready to seize my rightful place in the avant garde, as an innovator, someone who leapt to embrace a true and attractive fashion long before the tremulous herd dared to even contemplate it. While Marshall Field's is vending cheap Taiwanese knock-off fezzes, I will proudly parade my bona fide Nat Sherman creation down Michigan Avenue. Surly teens slouching in doorways, passing around a cigarette, will cast an envious eye in my direction and mutter: "Fresh fez, man."

I Is for Idiot

 Is being normal that bad? Is working at a job, taking vacations, raising your family, watching TV at night, such a terrible fate that the average person will do anything— literally anything—to avoid it, to grab a piece of the pie, a hold on the brass ring, a moment in the sun?

I am thinking of John Wayne Bobbitt. He was in the range of ordinary guys—the low end, to be sure, particularly if you believe his former wife, Lorena. But not a monster. Not Satan.

Then he gets his willie sliced off. The exact circumstances are still murky, but we know that willie ends up on the side of the road, temporarily. Through some quick police work, the judicious application of ice, and the miracle of modern medicine, willie and owner are reunited.

Now, I don't know about you. But if I got my dick cut off by my wife, many thoughts would go coursing through my mind, but "Career opportunity!" would not be one of them.

Bobbitt, however, saw the chance to make a buck. He got an agent. He starred in an X-rated movie, *John Wayne Bobbitt Uncut.* How he didn't also write a book is a mystery—the publishing industry must have been off its feed that month.

He went around the country promoting his porn movie, and the tour brought him to Chicago. Of course a story had to be run in the newspaper. Such an oddity could not be permitted to slink into town unheralded.

My pal, the photographer Bob Davis, took a portrait of Bobbitt—enticing him to pose standing on a stool on the sidewalk, a STOP sign in the background peeking out from the juncture between his legs, one hand tucked demurely into his waistband. Bobbitt also signed a butcher knife for Bob.

Bob excitedly brought the knife and a print of the picture over to my desk for me to admire. I agreed that the photograph was a portrait of rare depth and aesthetic complexity; the knife, obviously a valuable collector's item.

"What?" I said. "He wouldn't expose himself for you?"

"I didn't ask him," said Bob, and the thought that he had been derelict in his professional duty clouded his untroubled, youthful features. But then a comforting realization hit him. "We wouldn't print that," he said.

Not yet, anyway. But the day may come. Society is in the grip of idiots. I don't mean phone solicitors who call you up during dinner, or the repairman who returns your

VCR as broken as when it was brought to him. I'm referring to the anonymous civilians who, through some bizarre twist, suddenly find themselves glistening in the spotlight, like it, and decide to milk their situation for all it is worth.

"Idiot" is just one of many words that could be applied. It happens to fit into my schematic and has a nice trace of irony, since the original Greek word, *idiotes,* meant a private person, someone who had removed himself from public life. At that time, citizens had a responsibility to help run the government, and failure to participate was seen as a detestable lapse. Nowadays anyone who withdrew from the public eye would be viewed as heroic, if only such a person existed.

We could also call idiots "mopes," or "freaks," or "nine-day wonders," a term from the 1920s which has the hopeful element of finality embedded within it.

Those 1920s temporary celebrities—the flagpole sitters and channel swimmers and wrong-way fliers—seem quaint and anonymous compared to today's frenzy, stoked as it is by the media's insatiable demand for fresh fuel to keep their fires roaring. And once people enter the celebrity stream, they bob there forever, it seems.

I hate to argue for loss of innocence, but the idiots of today do have a certain premeditation that the notorious of the past seem to lack. Sure, those involved in famous criminal cases long ago might have eased themselves into vaudeville, but one got the sense they did so gradually, out of expediency, and not after performing the full jackknife-with-a-double-twist dive that people take into publicity today. Whoring oneself never seems far from the back of anyone's mind—tap any man on the shoulder, offer him a hundred grand, and he'll make a porn film too, right now, before lunch. No one involved with the O. J. Simpson trial seemed to have the slightest hesitation about making money off the tragedy. Nicole Simpson's erstwhile friends fell over themselves to calumniate her in print for money. Jurors at the trial were straining like Dobermans to cash in. The lawyers all lined up with their palms out afterward, but I suppose that's to be expected. I'm certain that Judge Ito would have posed naked astride a mule, if the check was large enough.

Contrast this with Charles Lindbergh who, upon arriving at Paris, asked for the name of a cheap hotel, not quite realizing that what he had done had projected him beyond all that.

For every national idiot there are hundreds of local idiots straining to break through into wider obloquy. Chicago has had some doozies. My favorite is the pair, Scott Swanson and Carolyn MacLean, a couple of Wheaton College sweethearts whose particular brand of twisted interior life kept them, apparently, from jumping each other's bones without first staging their own murder, leaving their red BMW running in an alley in Chicago while they jetted off to "find the perfect love," as they told investigators when they were finally tracked down and dragged back home to explain why they shouldn't be stuck with the bill for the thousands of hours of law enforcement effort expended trying to find them.

As a reporter, I'm always astounded by the sudden air of false dignity assumed by such momentary figures of fame. Mayfay Melton, the junkie lowlife whose Keystone Avenue apartment injected the phrase "living in squalor" into the Chicago media vocabulary after nineteen kids belonging to her and a variety of relations were removed from its filthy environs, later held forth in the press, laying out the parameters of the police/judicial/Masonic conspiracy against her, airily holding court as if she was Princess Margaret denying tales of mismanagement in the British Red Cross.

Most local idiots stay local, thank God, but sometimes, after an idiot's fame saturates a particular locality, the idiot jumps into the national spotlight. Less than a week after some moron leapt out of the stands at Soldier Field to catch a football while plummeting twenty feet to the concrete floor, he was chatting with David Letterman, explaining that, why, yes, Dave, he *did* have a couple beers before hurtling himself over the railing. The prototypical minor idiot—famous for a week, then dropped back into obscurity.

The polar opposite is the permanent idiot, as best embodied by the aforementioned O. J. Simpson, who it can be argued is a contender for the title of Idiot of the Twentieth Century. People always refer back to the Lindbergh kidnapping as a rule of measurement; well, Simpson is Bruno Richard Hauptmann, had he beat the rap, moved to Los Angeles, and started dating Carole Lombard.

Society seems to have recovered a bit now. But for a while—like the scientists who worried that the first atomic bomb would set off a chain reaction and ignite the atmosphere—I was concerned that O. J. Simpson news would achieve some sort of critical mass, collapsing into a cultural black hole where every magazine and television show would devote itself completely to O.J., 100 percent, every day, and lock there while public concern about all non-O.J. events withered away to nothing. Food would start being shaped like Simpson's head—otherwise people would lose interest in eating and starve.

So many words have been expended on him that I shudder to add any more, except to say that one can only pray he finds the obscurity he so deserves, and is tracked down every few years by an enterprising reporter, and found laying out towels in the bathroom of a second-rate restaurant, or dancing naked in some seedy Manila club.

Fat chance. Nobody goes away. That's the tragedy of our current situation—there is so much media that people like O. J. Simpson, who should ideally be dropped down an oubliette and forgotten, instead remain jangling before our horrified eyes. The stars who slipped from the top—or never attained it—scrabble over each other in celebrity limbo, churning out infomercials, slipping to ever lower rungs of endorsements, but never disappear. I particularly shudder to catch a glimpse of a porcine Sally Struthers, leering out at me from the racks of fliers at supermarket entrances. Has she no pride? Didn't she save any money at all during "All in the Family"? Jesus, go to Rob Reiner—he's directing movies, he's flush. Hit him up for a handout. (Maybe there's a curse among "All in the Family" alumni. Sherman Helmsley, who played Mr. Jefferson, was on TV last night, as "Entertainment Tonight" dissected his descent into failure and bankruptcy. You'd think that would happen in private, but no, the report couldn't have been more comprehensive if Helmsley had joined the Peace Corps and gone to Kenya to fight river valley blindness.)

Idiots are an indulgence that must be resisted. The

dilemma is that they are interesting, fascinating even, and the tendency is to want to collect information.

The slope is a treacherous one. The ball starts rolling with legitimate interest—*"What?* Tonya Harding was the one who had Nancy Kerrigan bopped on the knee—you're kidding! Tell me more!"—but quickly tumbles into overkill. Before you know it, you find yourself absorbing the biographical details of Harding's trailer park mafia or flipping the pages of a dirty magazine, looking at stills from the video Harding ill-advisedly made on her wedding night, her sad little breasts flopping around as she cavorts with Jeff Gillooly, her husband, who not only peddled the video to the magazine but then expressed surprise that as a result his name should be so closely welded to the idea of craven mopery that he would eventually need to legally change it.

Gillooly should have done much more. The Japanese—so convinced of the superiority of their culture—actually only top us in one important area: they know when to kill themselves. Countless hours of waste could be avoided if idiots such as Gillooly or Simpson or Harding had the good grace to commit suicide when the moment cried out for it. If a writer of Yukio Mishima's talent can disembowel himself, why can't Brett Easton Ellis? If Vince Foster could shoot himself, then why couldn't Bob Packwood?

Simpson nearly did it—he wrote the note, he got the gun—but self-regard got the better of him. Ditto for Susan Smith. Had she left the kids on the shore and stayed in the car herself, the world would have been a far better place.

But they fall down on the job. That's what makes them

idiots. And that's why it's up to us, as individuals, to screen them out. TV, after all, will present anything it thinks will keep people watching commercials.

The strongest image I have of the entire O.J. mess was the night he went on his famous Bronco chase. The World Cup was in Chicago, and the Spanish government was sponsoring a fireworks display downtown. A friend was having a fireworks party at his fifty-third-floor apartment. It was a warm, beautiful night in Chicago. At the party, people were gathered in front of a big TV, staring at the white Bronco, which at this point was parked in a drive-way. We watched for perhaps an hour. The car didn't move. Nothing happened. Then the Spanish government's fireworks show began—huge explosions, right outside the window, it seemed, starbursts of green, golden spheres, bursts of red and blue.

Glorious. Edie and I walked over to the window to get a better view. A minute passed, and we realized we were alone. Everybody else was still watching the television. Nobody could look away. They didn't want to miss any-thing.

Simpson can't be formally credited with snuffing out the lives of the two victims but he certainly wasted millions of collective lifetimes the world over, the years of living that were spent absorbing his pathetic spectacle. If I had the past two years to live over, knowing what I know now, I would have tuned the whole thing out. Just ignored it. Skipped the articles; turned away from the news broad-casts. Or at least tried to. I don't know if I have the requi-site iron will. But I'll find out. Next time, and there most assuredly will be a next time, I'm going to refuse to play along. If I can.

J Is for Journalism

Maya Angelou is filled with *joie de vivre*. She strides onto the podium of the Hyatt Regency Hotel and begins to sing. "I shall not be moved. I shall not be moved. Just like a tree that's planted by the water, I shall not be moved."

Her voice is deep and strong. She then begins to talk, telling stories, reciting her poetry. You are powerful, she tells her audience. You are beautiful.

The crowd eats it up. They roar, these two thousand women attending a national women's conference. They applaud.

Sitting in the back, hunched in a dark corner of the huge ballroom, I scribble a few of Angelou's more succinct comments onto a narrow pad. I didn't want to come here—had felt that sinking sensation I get when given an assignment I consider to be a dog. But now that she's up there, singing, reading, speaking, laughing, the whole process is so skilled, so entertaining and, yes, so uplifting, that I am having a good time.

Maya Angelou is finished. She is escorted from the stage. The two thousand women finish clapping and make for the exits. I have one more task. Journalism has conventions as strict as kabuki, and a story of this sort, the "Famous poet speaks here" story, must end with a blurt of audience reaction: "It was great," said Jane Doe, dabbing a tear from her eye. "I greatly enjoyed the greatness of the great Maya Angelou."

I pick a woman at random—somebody pausing, a straggler from the herd. "Hi, I'm Neil Steinberg," I say. "I'm a reporter from the *Sun-Times*. I'm writing a story about Maya Angelou's speech and I wonder what you thought of it?"

She flees without a word, just turns and rushes away, as if I'm a panhandler. So does the second woman I ask. This leaves me frustrated and a little angry. There is an inverse law in reporting—the more benign the information you are seeking, the more difficult it will be to get. When I stopped hookers on Cicero Avenue, every single one, without exception, told me anything I wanted to know—about their neglected kids, their raging drug habits, how much money they charge for sex.

But these professional women at the Hyatt don't want to talk. I have no idea why. Overeducation? They know what happened to outspoken people during McCarthyism. Prudence? They see the villains who unwisely consent to be grilled like burgers by Mike Wallace on "60 Minutes" every Sunday, indicting themselves, babbling, ruined. Professionalism? They are trained not to speak to the media—"Call public affairs; they'll answer your questions."

Or maybe they're just struck dumb by Maya Angelou's eloquence. The third woman I approach and ask about the speech doesn't run away, but she doesn't answer either. She just stares at me, with the startled expression a frog must give a swooping raptor. So much for Angelou's brave words about romance and beauty and power.

There is a pause, the woman and I looking at each other. Then I do something I haven't done before or since in my entire professional career. I raise my hand into the gap between us and snap my fingers three times in front of her face.

"Hel-*lo!*" I say, and she unfreezes, utters a syllable or two, then runs away.

That's it, I figure. I'll do without the quote, or use the woman's monosyllable. I tried, which is the important thing in journalism.

Outside, a lovely autumn day. I stroll west on Wacker Drive, toward the newspaper. On a corner I encounter a knot of three women, talking to each other, still holding programs from the conference. Okay, I decide, the full Boy Scout try. I whip out my notebook, uncap a pen, present myself to the group and utter my burning question. There is a pause.

"Do you have any identification?" one of the women asks.

Everybody hates journalists. Why wouldn't they? The very things that people dread most—accidents, calamities, disasters, riots—are the bread and butter of reporters. We love them. We might pretend that we don't, particularly the TV people, who like to get in front of the cameras, all grim-faced, and pronounce the horror and tragedy of wherever they are. But it's a lie. As soon as the cameras shut off, they let out a whoop, high-five each other, and go scuttling after fresh tragedies.

Not that journalists *wish* tragedy on people. Not that they sit around saying, "Gee, I wish a tornado would wipe out a school someplace so we wouldn't have to run this boring story on the water reclamation district." But under the skin, subconsciously, that's what goes on. The size of tomorrow's newspaper, the length of this evening's news, remember, is not dictated by how much worthwhile information there is to report. It is dictated by ad sales, or programming. You can't publish a big empty white square with the caption: "Slow news day—use your crayons to color this page." You have to come up with something or, better yet, hope that something exciting presents itself.

A breaking story is pure adrenalin. Why else would Dan Rather, happily playing cowboy on a dude ranch the day of the Oklahoma bombing, immediately get on the phone and start screaming at his producers, begging them to cut short his vacation and rush him to the scene? Because his heart is so big? No, because he loves the process. We all do. Getting on the plane in a hurry. Hustling to the scene with the photographer or cameraman. Surveying some ruin, getting good quotes, then hightailing it to the local Hilton for dictation and cocktails. Great fun, and a feast for one's sense of self-importance.

Not that, as a reporter for a provincial publication like the *Sun-Times,* I ever get much chance to go anywhere south of Kankakee, north of Kenosha, east of Gary, or west of Wheaton. Sometimes, on rare, cherished occasions, when whatever six or seven reporters currently basking in the editors' favor are busy someplace else, I might get the nod. As spring melts into summer, I find myself idly wondering, "Wouldn't it be nice if the Mississippi floods again this year?" A terrible thought, yes, but sincere. After the Mississippi flood of 1993, the newspaper sent me to the river four times looking for flood stories. It was great. Volunteers filling sandbags. National Guard helicopters clattering overhead. Entire towns turned out, fighting madly to save their levees. Fists of water boiling through fissures in the street. And me, roaring around in a rented car, trying to get from point A to point B, dodging roadblocks and washed-out bridges. Knowing that the evening would bring a free meal, a fresh hotel bed, and drinks.

Heck, none of the places was *my* town. To me it was just a gripping scene. It was *interesting.* In Grafton, Illinois, where the river flooded much of the town, a bar called Stenger's stayed open, even though the river came up to the front doorstep and put about an inch of water on the floor. I approached the bar in a motorboat, docked, then went inside and had a beer. After I passed the entrance exam of good-natured ribbing, the guy on the stool next to mine said he'd pay for my beer, and took his wallet out— the wallet was in a Baggie. You couldn't make up a detail like that in a million years. The beer was really cold, too— they had to ice it, since there was no electricity. When I went back the next year, to see how the town had recovered, the beer wasn't quite so cold. The second time around, it never is.

Most people's towns never flood, however. They never

meet a murderer or look at a corpse. But the media do, and bring the terrible details to their homes every day, like a not too bright cat dragging something horrible up from under the house and leaving it on your pillow as a gift. Day in and day out. After a while the process gets bothersome, and people start to resent it.

"Why don't the newspapers ever write about anything *good?*" they complain, as if they would read it. As if they would plop down thirty-five cents for a paper headlined: "CITY SWELL!" or stay tuned to a news report about a bunch of handicapped children visiting the zoo.

So if the public resents us, we resent them right back. Hate them, really, at times. At least I do. The popular term is "cynicism," but I see it as something closer to "revulsion." The worst part of my job, bar none, is trying to get the *populi* to pry open their yaps and let a little *vox* out.

On rare, isolated occasions a reporter will encounter a friendly, intelligent person who has an interesting point of view and expresses it. But that is a signal exception. In general, the public is divided into two groups: the first are fearful, tremulous people who have never appeared in a newspaper and aren't sure how they work. The women at the Maya Angelou reading fall into this category. I am certain that the group I approached on the sidewalk outside of the Hyatt thought that I was coming on to them. I know this because I asked, while digging out my press card, if their organization had perhaps experienced some sort of difficulty with reporters. They said they thought I was trying to pick them up—they feared I was some creep with a notebook routine who would romance them for three weeks, then empty their checking accounts. I'm lucky I didn't get a face full of Mace.

These are the passersby encountered at large public events who say things like, "I am enjoying myself today at the Jazz Festival," and then goggle their eyes in terror and uncertainty when asked for their names, as if they've made bold political pronouncements which will later be thrown back in their faces. "Simpkins, get in here! I notice that you told the newspapers that you not only frequent the public library, but that you on occasion will check out books, which you then read. You are relieved of your position; here is your final paycheck. . . ." I've had people at demonstrations, standing on the sidewalk and holding signs, refuse to be quoted. "I don't want to get involved," they say.

Or, if they do say something, they bleat a few words, struggling to dredge a coherent thought out of the muck of their consciousness and present it, naked and wriggling on a platter. This is bad enough from laymen, but it often comes from professionals, who should know better.

God bless phone mail. I don't know how many hours I have added to my life by being able to dump story pitches that clueless flacks have left on my machine. "Hello, Neil, this is Ellen Kerschmatzgin from Kerschmatzgin Communications. I have your name on a list of people interested in foundation work, and I am calling to follow up on the fax I sent to you about the awards dinner for the community outreach program of the Neighborhood Alliance of Network . . ."

This second group is even worse. These are the people who lunge to get themselves in the media, from the kids hopping up and down between TV reporters, smiling and waving and grinning as the reporter reads the death toll, to their spiritual equivalents, the savvy businessmen offering neckties and skybox seats and their slick PR handlers.

I've noticed that plastic surgeons have a certain genius for this. I once did a story on Dr. Marc Karlan (his registered trademark, "The Facial Architect") simply because I could no longer stand his PR agent, striding into the office, looking to press some gewgaw on me and pitch his client. "How would you like to crew on my yacht?" Karlan asked, upon meeting me. Another plastic surgeon opened with the greeting, "You know, I can suck that fat out of your cheeks if you'd like, gratis." I responded with a mumbled "My wife loves those fat cheeks . . ." eyes downcast, crushed.

At least both these groups are sane. Newspapers also attract lunatics. It seems every day I walk into the paper, there is a new eccentric—a man with plaster casts of aliens, a gaucho in a four-foot-wide sombrero, a stern delegation from some imaginary nation—negotiating to see one reporter or another.

Most are benign. A few aren't. The *Sun-Times* installed security doors after one visitor walked up to the receptionist and, without saying a word, punched her squarely in the face. Then there was the psychotic who slipped back into the features department and cornered food writer Sharon Sanders. Displaying a gun, he started dictating an editorial about politics and God. Sanders, in what I've always felt to be one of the great moments of grace under pressure, told him he had the wrong department. "This is features," she said. "You want cityside."

These are the crackpots who write certified letters crammed with single-spaced, no-margin texts and photocopied evidence. In later letters they send photocopies of the certified mail stubs, to show they have written to me before. I always write back, commiserating, apologizing for not being able to help them battle their enemies, as I am occupied full time fighting my own, grappling with the entrenched conspiracy and intricate web of lies arrayed against my own ambitions. They always understand this, and sometimes send me replies of fellowship and encouragement, though these invariably contain photocopies of my earlier letter, as more evidence.

To close the circle of annoyance, not only does the public hate the media, and the media hate the public, but the media also hate each other, out of envy, or malice, or just for the fun of it. In this sense, being a journalist is even worse than being a cop—cops are loathed by a wide swath of the population and certainly the feeling is mutual, but at least they have that wall-of-blue fraternity thing going—as long as you're not black, gay or a woman. The more cops on the scene, the easier it is for them to do their jobs. With reporters it is exactly the opposite: the more of you, the more trouble you'll have. The grieving widow who gratefully talks to the first two reporters will sic her dogs on the next ten.

We're all envious of one another. The TV people disdain the print media because they aren't on television, their lone yardstick of reality. But TV people still recognize that newspaper reporters often enjoy the advantage of having lived in the city for a while and thus perhaps know what's going on.

So the TV guys gingerly mince up and try to be pals and get the information that they don't have since they just got to town from Minneapolis and don't know anything and haven't made any effort to find out, other than read a Mike Royko collection on the plane on their way in. The TV gals arrive at the scene, their cameramen and producers in tow, glance around, puff their bangs into the air, then flounce up to the first person they see and start to dig.

Sometimes they start interviewing *me,* with my reporter's pad hanging out of my pocket and a look of practiced indifference slapped across my mug. I've not only given interviews to television reporters whom I've met at a half dozen previous stories, but those interviews have run on television. (I once watched Rich Roeper, a columnist whose picture is in the newspaper and on the sides of delivery trucks, a fixture on radio and television, interviewed by an oblivious TV crew at a story we both were covering. Asked his name, he replied, "Hunter S. Thompson." The TV reporter looked puzzled, then asked: "Could you spell that?")

The blow-dried condescension that television reporters show newspaper reporters is only matched by the unalloyed contempt that flows back the other way. God knows it burns in my veins. I've never met a TV reporter who could tell you his name if it weren't monogrammed on his shirt cuff. And the ego, neatly displayed in a diamond setting of ignorance. Walter Jacobson, at one point a prominent name in Chicago television, showed up at one of my book-signing parties, invited by a mutual friend. I was standing in the doorway, and he blew by me, oblivious, grandly announcing, "Where am I? What am I doing here?"

A creed for television reporters if ever there was one, and doubly ironic, given the low quality of what television does.

The cold comfort we print journalists grasp is that, no matter what depths newspapers may sink to, television journalism is worse. Immediacy and quality are almost always opposing values. Ever since the Gulf War, such a high premium has been set on instantly covering breaking news stories both live and extensively that the medium risks becoming a sort of national security camera, displaying static images of a scene—the Baghdad skyline, O.J.'s Bronco, the shell of the Murrah Building—for hours on end, while the anchors tap-dance and time-fill and tell us what they just told us sixty seconds ago. They do it because they have learned that people will watch it.

No banality is beneath television news, from the soft porn of sweeps week (one Chicago station squeezed a fetching lady reporter into a bathing suit and sent her to Florida to caper with dolphins; the exposé, literally, ran not one but two nights) to the fawning reports tied in with network sitcoms to the unbearable shots of sobbing mothers and unfiltered horror. (I think the worst thing I ever saw on TV news was a scene shown on the local Cleveland news maybe ten years ago. Some star-crossed lover had killed his girlfriend and her parents, and the bodies were being brought out the front of their drab suburban dwelling. Police were milling around, and suddenly the youngest daughter of the slain family, unaware of the crime, pulled up on her banana seat bike and fixed a look of boggled horror at the camera, a second of dumb shock before being packed off by police.) I'm sure there's some glib rationalization for it—"We're just showing the human effect of crime" blah-blah-blah—but the truth is it's just invasive sensationalism. Why not position a camera at the morgue too? Catch the autopsies. I suppose we can look forward to that.

TV is part of the decline of journalism. It is the primary source of news for most people, the thin straw through which they chose to breathe the air of their knowledge, and it has stunted their brains. Many times the person I am interviewing will ask, "When am I going to be on TV?" I raise my pen and pad to eye level and display them, carefully, then look over my shoulder, slowly, searching for the camera which isn't there. "Never," I explain, with mock patience. "This is the *Chicago Sun-Times.* The *Chicago Sun-Times* is a newspaper."

This information invariably disappoints them.

K Is for Kin

We picked our spot for lunch carefully. Soft pine needles, shielded from the wind whipping over the mountains, yet with a commanding view of the curving trail we had just spent an hour hiking up, the hillside sloping down sharply below us, and the stunning, snow-peaked Rockies in the distance.

Mom handed out the goat cheese and bagel sandwiches. Earlier, at the house, I had expressed a polite skepticism about goat cheese, but my father insisted. He sang the praises of the goat cheese—mild! fresh! wholesome! Cheese lovingly crafted by a local goat rancher and trucked in every weekend to the farmers' market in Boulder, Colorado, where my parents live.

The sandwich was actually quite good. The cheese, rather than the strong, pungent, goatish taste I had expected, was indeed mild and savory. As I chewed, my eyes lovingly took in the view, and my ears strained to pick out the murmuring wind and twittering birds under the stream of constant narration from my mom and dad. I'd need to have brought a tape recorder to recount it accurately here. Just look out a window and try describing everything you see, the only rule being you can't stop talking: "Here's a tree and there's a bush, oh, a couple bushes in a row like that, right above where the grass rolls up to meet them, and isn't that a bird in the bush, no, it is a pine cone, no, it *is* a bird . . ." Very much like that.

I love my parents. That's why I go visit them a couple times a year. When they visit me in Chicago, I take days off work to squire them from one entertainment to another. I'd hate to fall out of touch, to become strangers, which is always a risk when you live so far apart.

On the other hand . . .

I wondered if there was a polite way to suggest they stop talking for a bit. When I was younger, I might have said it directly. "Hey, guys, quiet down a sec. . . ." Then we would have an argument and now, at thirty-five, I could see that pitfall ahead of time and maneuver around it. Or try to. My central goal in my visits to my parents is to avoid incidents. Play Scrabble, drink cocktails, don't fight. Keep my head. Be an adult. All the while I'm telling myself this, repeating these concepts like a mantra, I know there will always come one awful moment in the visit when I will be on my knees, clawing at my face and screaming at my mother while she cries and my father stares straight ahead as if looking for answers, somewhere in the far distance.

Still, if a subtle artifice could be found . . .

"Listen to those birds," I said wistfully, pleased at my cleverness. "Listen to that wind cutting through the pass. Wonderful!"

My parents grew quiet and I, rather than savoring the

moment, started counting off the seconds, military style, silently to myself. "One-one-thousand, two-one-thousand, three-one thousand . . ." At this point my mother began furiously inventorying the items in her backpack, rustling and clattering with the urgency of someone looking for the anti-venom kit after being bitten by a rattlesnake. At the same time my father started up with an audible sigh, the kind Willy Loman mutters at the beginning of *Death of a Salesman*—"Oh boy oh boy oh boy . . ." Five seconds after that they were talking again.

I gave up and didn't say anything, but it bothered me for a few minutes, and I brooded unhappily as we clomped down the trail after lunch. Immediately the paradox of the situation presented itself to me. Yes, my parents had been annoying, a fly in the ointment of enjoying this natural setting. But on the other hand it was they who had taken me up the trail to begin with, and so without them I wouldn't be here to enjoy the view. Or anywhere else, for that matter. So perhaps it was my problem too. I should not be bothered by their chattering. The Zen man would have accepted the sound as part of the natural setting, as pleasurable as the birds. And someday, of course, I will sorely miss those voices. I was being ridiculous, like those surly teens who make their parents walk ten steps behind them. I was wrong about the talking, just as I had been wrong about the goat cheese. I need improving. . . .

I was filled with such charitable thoughts, of gratitude to my parents, humble recognition of my own inadequacies, and general contemplative serenity, when we reached the car, and my mother turned to me and, out of the blue, asked me if my wife loves her as much as she loves her own parents. My guard down, I answered candidly, "No,

Ma, of course not. . . ." Like a fool, blundering into the trap.

Families are a minefield, a leg snare, a box propped up with a stick. They demand careful consideration. They require premeditation, planning, diplomacy. You can sit down with friends and be yourself, joke and laugh and blurt out your opinions. You do that with your parents, however, and you'll quickly find yourself in Big Trouble, mister. Go to your room and stand with your nose against the wall. Tap-dance and back-pedal and smooth things over. "No, no, Ma, that's not what I meant at all. I meant 'castrating' in a *good* way. . . ."

At least that is how it is with everybody I've ever known in my entire life. Even friends whose parents are lighthearted millionaires, whose mothers call them up and propose impulsive jaunts to London to see what's playing in the West End, whose fathers show up in tool belts to make household repairs. These fortunate souls still find themselves needing to *manage* their families, to balance the fragile lattice of their own desires, their own outlook, their own *will,* or what's left of it, against the crushing, trumping demands of kinship.

Families are terribly difficult to generalize about. "Happy families are all alike," as Tolstoy observed. "But every unhappy family is unhappy in its own way."

The sticking point, which Tolstoy leaves unsaid, is that there is no such thing as a happy family. None. Oh, sure, there are happy family *members*—dictatorial patriarchs, beloved great-grandmothers, cooing infants, and the like. But the idea of a family generally being "happy"—for

111

everybody, all the time—is an obvious impossibility. Any family with teenage children, for instance, cannot be happy, since teens are never happy, not while they are being forced to spend time with their families, at least.

Some families look very happy, on the outside. These are the families you see at the end of the evening news, holding their giant summer reunion barbecues, all wearing identical orange T-shirts with "The 79th Macfarquar Family Camp Out—August 12–14, 1997" printed on them.

From the inside is another matter. The problem is the gulf between ego and reality. Who has the parents they feel they deserve? Your mom and dad could be Grace Kelly and Prince Rainier of Monaco and still, on slow days around the palace, they would grate on your nerves. "Oh, Imperial Dadhood, you aren't wearing *that* crown again today, are you? It's so *démodé.*"

Or, to flip it around, who has the children they feel they deserve? Parents are proud, sure, but they are also frequently disappointed. My brother and I once drove from Chicago to Cleveland to surprise my mother on her birthday. She was happy to see us, but we ended up being the ones who got the surprise. "What, no gift?" she said, genuinely hurt. We tried to explain that we thought our presence there *was* the gift. No dice.

No scientific evidence exists as to how many people consider their families an asset, how many a liability. You'd think, with all the meaningless polling about the status of transitory political figures, somebody would think to ask: "When the phone rings, and it's your mother, are you glad?" or "Are you happy you have a brother, or is he just a pain in the ass?"

If anybody has done those surveys, I've never heard of it.

But I could take a guess as to how the answers would run.

The first aspect of families which makes them so annoying is you are stuck with them. That is their glory, of course. Other people were present the day you were born—a doctor, a nurse, a cabby, perhaps. But only your parents can tell you about it, usually, because of the people present, only they have hung around. I talk to my parents all the time, for several reasons, the primary one being that, of all the people I know, only they are guaranteed to be always eager to talk to me.

But just as consistency is a glory, it is also a curse. Being ever present, even at a distance, the faults of your relatives—and, God, they have faults—are magnified through repetition. There is a certain sense of inevitability to dealing with family. Bad as being hit in the head with a hammer is, it's much worse to know the hammer is coming, to expect it, perhaps to try to avoid it, and still get hit anyway.

That's family. And, if you are any sort of decent person, you have to deal with them, like it or not. Because you owe your family, don't you? Big time. A central aspect to the annoyance of kinship is recognition of a gigantic debt that never goes away. Your parents gave you life and a supporting cast of supernumerary relatives who have been around for as long as you can remember, and—good or bad—you've got to make nice with them until one of you is in the grave.

Only a person with a heart of stone rejects his family,

however horrible. Your dad could be Eichmann, your mom Lady Macbeth, and you're still supposed to remember to send cards on their birthdays and chat on the phone now and then. Society wields a powerful taboo against rejecting your family. It has to. Without a strong taboo, who wouldn't wash one's hands of the lot of 'em, sometime around the age of twenty-five, flee and be done with it?

A young person—or a naive person—holds out hope of changing his or her family. To soften Dad up a bit. To make Mom realize the error of her ways. Years can be wasted like this.

The general rule that people do not change their personalities after the age of five is magnified and hardened into unalterable, universal law when it comes to your family.

The story is an old one. Kinship relations are probably the original annoyance of humanity. Before there were cities, before agriculture, before fire, there were families, dragging themselves across the savanna in search of a better patch of scorched ground. Piled together in a cave at night. They had to get on each other's nerves.

Suffocating as those primitive familial relations must have been, they had the advantage of being rigid. Many a mother-in-law made many a bride's life a living hell after she moved into her husband's household—"No, Hannah, pound the grain like *this!*" "What's the matter? Zeus! Haven't you ever skinned a camel before? Start at the ears and go *back!*"

You couldn't really question the system, however, and that made it easier to accept—situations are much more tolerable when there is no choice in the matter. Ancient times didn't have some families who were headed by the father, some by the mother, some by nobody at all. There was a code, a system.

Nowadays, nobody knows what they are supposed to do. Modern families are composed of blind people feeling their way through a foreign land. Fathers can no longer rule, if they are indeed even around. Mothers can no longer concentrate on housekeeping and rearing children; they need to go to work to keep the family off the street. Parents are too busy to pass anything of value on to their children other than the benefit of using a Filofax to schedule your play week. *The New Yorker,* in its special issue on women, spotlighted a Type A, dress-for-success mom who drew up lists for her children. Included was: "13. Observe stars."

No doubt her kids will turn into vagabonds—hobos and drifters who fail to find employment because the very idea of doing something according to a schedule makes them twitch. Children invariably spend their youth carefully attending to their parents' ideals and aspirations, then, as soon as they are able to act independently, do exactly the opposite.

For every pianist who follows in his musician father's footsteps there are a dozen aggressive businessmen who sire shiftless lazeabouts. For every prim socialite whose daughter becomes Miss Tea Rose there are twenty poor, shocked women who wonder what use those expensive manners lessons were when their daughters start rolling around in public, nude and covered in molasses as part of some fourth-rate performance art piece.

My son will be forbidden to read books, encouraged instead to devote his time to video games. If all goes well, he'll end up a professor of classics.

But reverse psychology is no guarantee. In fact, the only guarantee is that, after loving me for a while, he'll spend a few years intensely hating me and, perhaps, if my luck holds, end up appreciating me again before I shuffle into the tomb.

I'm not looking forward to that final period. There is something terribly sad about the parents of grown children. Like deposed royalty, they find themselves in exile, their tiny state-owned apartments crammed with double-headed imperial eagles and golden orbs, the trappings of lost power and faded authority. They cling to their few remaining prerogatives, demanding the ceremonial falcon be delivered promptly at noon each St. Swithin's Day.

The children, grown, are the victorious revolutionaries, still a little shocked to find themselves in power, squirming uneasily on the throne, glancing guiltily back at the exiled king and queen while they rule for a time, until they, too, are overthrown by the next generation. Thus is the way of the world.

My wife's family are very nice people. Warm, loving, uncritical, supportive. I dated Edie for seven years, and her mother never once asked me what my intentions were toward her daughter. Not once.

My family, on the other hand, like nothing better than to sit around and criticize anybody who doesn't happen to be in the room. That's fun for us. We sneer and swill and laugh, our bitter chuckles and cynical guffaws exploding into the yawning chasms between us. And when we've exhausted the list of available victims, we turn on each other, sniping and arguing and insinuating until it becomes unbearable and we pause, apologizing, to wait a respectable interregnum until we begin again. I'm not complaining—I'm part of them. I *like* it.

But my wife—whose family I compared, in print, to *The Peaceable Kingdom,* that famous painting of Eden—sometimes finds it difficult to pass time with my family, whom I have compared, in print, to the court of the Medici.

I'll never forget the first weekend she spent at my parents' home. We Steinbergs were our old selves, laughing and drinking and damning humanity. Edie put up a good front. But the first moment we were alone together, in my car going to a restaurant, she burst into tears. I was shocked. Everything had been going so well. I asked what was wrong. It took her a moment to compose herself. "You're all crazy," she finally sputtered, half crying, half shouting. "I feel like a prisoner trapped within a nightmare."

I looked at her, teary-eyed in the passenger seat, with renewed appreciation, sympathy and love. Finally I had found someone who understood me, who understood my entire family, and who could summarize our essence in a single, elegant synopsis. We were on the road to marriage.

L Is for Litter

The deepest impression Paris made on me was not the treasures of the Louvre; not the rail-thin French ladies linking arms on the Champs Elysées. Not the Eiffel Tower, Notre Dame, or the Jardin des Tuileries. Not the grandmothers bringing their dogs to dinner at restaurants. Not the alligator act at the Moulin Rouge.

Not, even, the hot Nutella-filled crepes served at outdoor carts.

No, the most fabulous thing I saw in Paris were the garbage cans in the Métro system. They were little. They looked like they held about a quart. And they were empty. Always empty. We traveled by subway everywhere we went, and each time we got off at a Métro station, we would notice the garbage cans—these pristine little round metal oatmeal boxes, stuck on sticks, their brown plastic garbage bags primly inserted inside, awaiting their first crumpled pack of Gauloises.

As a patriotic American, I hate to yield the upper

hand to other nations, particularly to the French, who are stuck on themselves as it is. I can explain away the fact that Paris, a city of comparable size to Chicago, has one tenth the number of murders. I can shrug off their thrice-daily mail delivery, their outdoor cafés, the rubber-wheeled, graffiti-free subways, their beautiful money, their spanking clean automatic public pay toilets, their chocolate shops so elegantly immaculate they look like jewelry stores. A city can do a lot with the national government pumping billions of francs a year to prop it up and a 12 percent unemployment rate to provide eager street sweepers and gum-removal squads.

But I am haunted by the vision of French garbage cans, particularly as I pass the inevitable rusty 55-gallon drum overflowing with rubbish at Chicago train stops and street corners. Each drum is surrounded by a penumbra of litter created by those who either tossed and missed, or who could not quite balance their contribution atop the pyramid of trash rising above the rim.

I am mixing my metaphors here. Garbage, rubbish, trash and litter are all slightly different things, technically, varying in wetness, content and the like. Potato peelings are garbage; crumpled-up newspapers are trash when you put them into a can and litter when you toss them into the street. Rubbish is, inevitably, what you read in the newspapers before you throw them away.

Sorry.

Of the various classes of society's rejectamenta, litter is especially loathsome because it marries the distastefulness of somebody else's by-products to the idea of social disintegration—you expect garbage, back in the alley, hidden in dumpsters, under control, out of sight. Litter is a surprise, when you notice it, a hearty punch in the nose, delivered by the uncaring or the careless to those who cling to the faded notion of an ordered society maintained by concerned individuals.

Litter is a true modern annoyance, in the sense that it just didn't exist—as a concept—until very recently. It couldn't. For a place to be littered, it first has to be generally clean, and the level of filth associated with most human activity before our century was so tremendous as to defy modern imagination. Any trashed vacant lot or cluttered modern road (the Highway Research Board found that a typical mile of American highway is graced with 710 beer cans, 143 soft-drink cans, 227 glass bottles and jars, 155 pieces of plastic, and 1,605 magazines, newspapers and bits of paper) is immaculate by historic human standards. For tens of thousands of years, people just pitched their refuse out the window, if they had a window, or else dropped it right in their place of habitation. This was not a big problem when humanity gathered in small unnamed bands of scavengers and hunters, who could move their huts a hundred yards down the veldt when the smell around camp grew overwhelming.

Not too long ago, historically, people even argued that garbage-strewn streets were *good*. In 1892, Chicago editor John McGovern claimed that filth helps keep city life economical.

"Perhaps the reason for the inexpensiveness of life here is the low state of municipal cleanliness," he wrote in apparent sincerity. "Purity is never a bargain. Filthy streets, black buildings, unswept gutters and walks, careless raiment—these matters unquestionably make life easier, just as a soiled child in an alley has a much happier life than little Lord Fauntleroy, and lives longer."

Chicagoans were debating the price of clean streets in 1892 because the World's Fair of 1893 was looming and, like any anxious host, Chicagoans worried that the place was a mess.

The City Council created a Department of Street Cleaning—the first in the nation—which managed to clean the downtown area but petered out when it came to the rest of the city. What the Department of Street Cleaning lacked was a leader as zealous as Colonel George E. Waring, Jr., who became the New York commissioner of street cleaning in 1894.

Waring not only dressed his street sweepers in white uniforms and had them march in public parades, but made disposing of garbage into a measure of humanity's ascent from the beasts.

"There is no surer index of the degree of civilization of a community than the manner in which it treats its organic wastes," Waring said.

Waring also organized thousands of children into the Junior Street Cleaning League. They also marched, and monitored their neighborhoods, upbraiding litterers, singing songs and reciting pledges ("I will not throw any paper into the streets, because I want our streets to be clean. I will take my own drinking cup to school with me. I will not bite anyone else's apple . . .").

I sometimes think of Waring's high-stepping, white-uniformed sanitation army when I see the typical Chicago street-sweeping detail, a trio of slouched Shakespearean clowns, dressed in a close approximation of rags, moseying along a quiet thoroughfare, laughing and shouting dirty slogans among themselves, scraping the gutter with shovels, occasionally worrying at some stray piece of paper with their pointed sticks.

Not that I expect to find regimented cadres from the Island of Doctor No jogging along the roadway, catching garbage tossed from cars before it hits the ground. But just as one delights in finding a waiter who is even nominally interested in serving food as a profession, so it would be pleasant—if only as a novelty—to occasionally stumble upon some public employee actually concerned with the execution of his or her duties.

While Waring did have an impact across the country, attitudes toward litter still depended on the efforts and energies of isolated local officials. National campaigns against litter didn't begin until the mid-1950s, when the Keep America Beautiful program tried to prick people's consciences through advertising. This was followed by Lady Bird Johnson's highway beautification program in the 1960s, which raised public awareness, if not dramatically changing the behavior of people, who seemed to have some sort of inborn desire to litter.

"Few Americans under the age of thirty-five remember the casual abandon with which many of their fellow citizens threw garbage from car windows as they drove," writes garbologist William Rathke.

Actually, Rathke might be overoptimistic in his use of the past tense. Many still litter. A survey in Oklahoma in 1982 found that nearly 40 percent of people there said they expected they would litter in the future. In 1989, two years after the state began a vigorous anti-litter campaign, the figure was still above 30 percent.

It is the "casual abandon" mentioned by Rathke, rather than the physical presence of litter itself, that makes the problem so vexing. A Coke bottle is certainly more aesthetic than a deer turd, as an object, yet the former is a blight and the latter a natural marvel. The thought behind the litter—the uncaring brainlessness of it, the utter lack of alibi—is what is ugly. You can murder your parents and have a reason, maybe even a good reason. But why does someone toss a paper cup on the train tracks rather than into a nearby garbage can? Laziness? Indifference? Ignorance? Some blend of the three?

Academic studies of litter tell us that litterers tend to be younger rather than older, men rather than women—the same group that commits crimes in general and keeps car magazines in business. Much as I loathe littering now, I do seem to remember racing my parents' 1975 Dodge Dart Special Edition at eighty miles an hour down Fair Street in Berea, Ohio, and pitching a Ronrico rum bottle out the window, laughing hysterically as it shattered across the pavement. Not among my prouder moments, but germane to the topic at hand nevertheless.

It may reveal something about the American national character to point out that we pay the greatest attention not to urban litter, or to preserving natural splendor, but to highway litter.

Massive government attention—most of it on the state level—analyzes what gets pitched out of cars traveling along highways. Generally, these studies do not make for captivating reading. The most comprehensive and noteworthy of them comes from California, naturally enough, which not only broke down roadside clutter into such typical categories as bottles, cans, paper, etc., but took the time to include the *brands* of the littered material. The reason apparently being that any deviation between a product's market share and its representation in California roadside trash might indicate something worth knowing about why people litter. For example, the preponderance of beer cans underscores the obvious point that people driving and drinking beer are more inclined to toss their cans out the window than those drinking soda. Other observations are less illuminating—for instance, Coke drinkers tend to litter slightly more than their statistical share would suggest, Pepsi drinkers slightly less. Draw your own conclusions.

California also took the time to estimate how many people are injured by litter—a whopping 300,000 each year in the state, by their count, from people who step on a piece of broken glass at the beach to those who kill themselves driving over a stray muffler at seventy miles per hour. (Paris, to be fair, reports that 650 people a year are injured slipping on dog turds, which might not be so large a number, given the glut of Parisian dogs.)

The most distinctive detail gleaned from roadside litter studies is that several states hit on a characteristic approach to the problem: combating litter by letting the grass grow on the side of the road. "This offers the immediate or short-range solution of hiding the litter, but it does not offer a long-range solution to reducing litter," helpfully observed a U.S. Department of Transportation Report to Congress.

Studies find that people litter more in places that are already littered. This makes sense. Not all of us can just cavalierly fling away our garbage; many require the tacit social approval implied by an already messy area. Littering can be seen as sort of a reverse looting—an exploitation of mob approval, not to take something, but to give something up.

Some settings actually invite litter—movie theaters, for example. One academic team hit on the clever approach of testing out anti-litter campaigns at children's matinees, taking advantage of a captive audience certain to litter—left to their own devices, children in some groups dumped nearly 90 percent of their trash on the floor of the movie theater instead of tossing it into a garbage can.

Certain areas of a city can also exude that type of unspoken approval, a comfortable and expected level of crushed cans and shattered bottles. City dwellers hardly notice it. Walking down the street in Chicago, I don't think twice about tossing my toothpick or cigar butt into the gutter, which might horrify some litter purist. To me they are *de minimus*—too minor to be of concern in the general clutter. Beside, they're both organic—back to nature, and all that.

But even in a city, context is important when it comes to litter. One's reaction differs depending on whether X amount of litter is scattered in an alley glimpsed from the train or piled before your front door. There is a certain proprietary care extended toward even the grittiest city block, if you yourself happen to live on it. Should too much litter accumulate on the blasted and barren patch of dog-piss-murdered grass in front of my building, I start to worry that the entire neighborhood is deteriorating. I fret about the number of vacant storefronts. I balance the squad of babbling lunatics and glowering drug addicts against the platoon of oblivious jogging professionals and shuffling grandmas. And I wonder . . . is it time to go? Will I end up one of those defiant old people, shaking my fist at the cocky gangbangers? Standing on my stoop in a strap T-shirt, my white tufts of armpit hair showing, bitching to TV reporters how this used to be a nice place to live, back in the nineties.

Just as the city inspires laxity, so nature demands higher standards. I would never toss a toothpick in Colorado. Litter in nature is a much crueler blow than urban litter. A single cigarette butt at your feet on the rock outcrop overlooking the scenic vista in a national park is as bad as someone pouring a pot of old coffee grounds on your pillow at home. In the city, someone would have to dump a skinned goat carcass on my doorstep to have the same effect as a crushed beer can found along a pristine lake shore, a sight vile enough to plunge me into the most gruesome Jacobean revenge fantasies. (Arnold Schwarzenegger and Sylvester Stallone are wasting their time battling drug kingpins. They should do a film in which they skulk around a national park, expertly camouflaged, rearing out of duck blinds and from behind trees to blow away thugs who have pitched paper bags filled with wine cooler bottles against the sides of rock formations. It would make a fortune.)

The comedian Rick Reynolds has a bit where he postulates an apt punishment for littering—whatever a person is caught discarding must then be shoved up the perpetrator's ass. "Cops should carry rubber gloves and Vaseline at all times," he muses. "It would really cut down on people littering those big two-liter plastic bottles."

I myself don't think harsh laws will cut down on littering, just as the death penalty doesn't cut down on crimes of passion. Litter is a crime of passionlessness, which is in its own way a strong force. I suppose if the police had the power to kill a person on the spot for tossing a cup, and did so, often, it might have an effect. But the policy would cost a lot of lives, and the resultant neatness would itself be something dire—the eerie cleanliness of Singapore, with its anti-chewing-gum laws and its jackboot democracy.

A devil's advocate might suggest that the easiest way to combat the annoyance of litter would be to end all public anti-litter campaigns. Given the intractability of the problem, perhaps it would be better to recast litter as a source of comfort. Grow the mental grass tall, as it were. The Ad Council TV spot would open with a shot panning slowly by a stand of aspen trees, the sun sparkling through the white trunks, finally settling on a clump of discarded fast food wrappers at the base of a tree. "People have been here," Patrick Stewart intones. "The warm welcome of a fellow human being, peeking out from amid the harsh indifference of nature . . ." and so on until the tag line: "Please litter—and leave a bit of yourself behind."

Such spots would come too late to help me. The anguish is that, once you are attuned to litter, you see it everywhere. I wouldn't mind having my own vehemence against litterers toned down a bit. In my mind people who litter are equally capable of any crime conceivable. The cops might as well shoot them, because they have removed themselves from the family of humanity. If you can pitch a beer bottle at the scenic overview, you can just as easily burn down an orphanage, humming happily to yourself as you spread gasoline over the back stairs, genuinely shocked when the police arrive, sincere when telling the judge you never meant any harm to anyone.

I worry that someday I'll do something rash, impulsively strangling some poor old lady for tossing her Dentyne wrapper. Trouble is brewing. I was walking down the street this week when a crude-looking fellow in a workman's outfit drained the dregs out of his can of Old Milwaukee beer and chucked it into a bush. Perhaps because I had just finished writing about litter, or trying to, and was taking a walk to clear my head, the little action enraged me. I grabbed the can out of the bush and turned, intending to—what? Run after him? Throw the can at the back of his head and scream, "Hey, buddy, you dropped *this!*" But the self-preservation subsystem so carefully hardwired into my psyche took over at that critical point, and I meekly deposited the can in a nearby official trash receptacle. My easygoing mood, the whistling insouciance vital for a pleasant walk, was spoiled, however, and I ended up trudging through what seemed to me an endless landfill populated by menacing characters out of a Da Vinci sketchbook, all of them gleefully cackling as they emptied their pockets into the street.

Do people, I wonder, have this kind of problem in France?

M Is for McDonald's

 H. L. Mencken once wrote that supporting Calvin Coolidge for President, out of a nation of millions of potential candidates, was like a starving man set before an immense, sumptuous banquet, turning his back to the table and slaking his hunger by catching and eating flies.

That's my view on McDonald's. Given that the experience of eating is one of the primary pleasures of life, and given one's span on earth consists of only a finite number of meals, it is a source of constant wonderment to me that people would choose to consume even one meal under the Golden Arches, never mind make it the most popular restaurant in the history of the world.

The problem isn't just that the food is bad, though that is a good enough place to start. Greasy, lukewarm burgers; napalm-hot fruit pies. Ominous, artificial-tasting frozen substances known as "shakes."

People claim to like this stuff, and certainly eat enough

129

of it. But does anyone really prefer these simulacra to the real things? Is there anyone who would turn down a hot-from-the-backyard-grill hamburger on a fresh-baked bun in favor of a Big Mac? Anyone who wouldn't lunge for a slice of actual apple pie over the lozenge of superheated glop encased in a crusty husk McDonald's uses to defame the word "pie"? Who wouldn't prefer a genuine milk shake, made from genuine ice cream? A real french fry, not quite so far removed from the paternal potato as the predigested sliver of a McDonald's fry?

It isn't as if real food were unavailable.

The urge to eat at McDonald's might be seen as a form of pica, the compulsion to eat odd substances, whose victims can't stop themselves from gobbling handfuls of dirt or starch or flour. I must admit that I myself have been occasionally unable to resist the impulse to visit McDonald's. Usually the urge is directly connected to having a hangover and wanting something comforting. Indeed, if nothing else, McDonald's fare does have a certain regurgitated, baby-food quality to it. The burgers almost do not require chewing, but can be sucked through clenched teeth, like strained bananas.

The connection with hangovers may have a deeper, psychological element. A friend claims there is an aspect of self-punishment to going to McDonald's, and finds himself seeking out McDonald's after collapsed love affairs or other personal calamities. He attributes this to a subconscious attempt to further debase himself, like a Hermann Hesse character, as a way of reaching rock bottom and thus hastening personal redemption.

While the theory of eating at McDonald's as a way to nuzzle oneself deeper into the mire does have definite appeal, I don't think it fully explains why people eat the food. Sometimes the desire for my yearly visit seems to well out of nowhere, a bubble that forms in my brain and lingers until I've broken down and gone in and consumed. Perhaps the urge is the cumulative effect of a lifetime of being exposed to McDonald's advertising. The food looks so good in the ads—perfect burgers, straining the thumb-and-forefinger capacity of ecstatic diners—that one easily forgets the deformed mass inevitably unwrapped at a real McDonald's: skewed bun hiding the grayish beef patty. The entire affair crushed and vaguely alien-looking; one of the dead Martians hanging out of their spaceships at the end of *War of the Worlds.* You eat the thing just to get it out of sight.

No matter how unappealing the reality, one moment I have this irrational want, and the next I am running my tongue along my slick, oily front teeth, feeling the noxious foodstuffs coursing through my system, and wondering how much vague nausea I'll have to endure before my body metabolizes the offense committed against it. The fact that there was a fleeting moment of genuine, undeniable pleasure—a primal, onanistic satisfaction during the moment when the McDonald's meal was actually in the process of being chewed and swallowed—only makes memory of it worse.

The food alone would be reason enough to loathe the place, even if it were served on fine china by a Frenchman in a tuxedo while a string quartet played in the background. The food is not the entirety of McDonald's offense, however, only the beginning. One must also consider the astonishing context in which McDonald's ladles out its fare.

Walk into any McDonald's. They dot the countryside like a pox. The building—a low, industrial-looking bunker with a mansard, tiled roof. Bright, nursery colors—yellows, blues, reds—predominate. McDonald's prefers not to identify its restaurants while they are being built—no HOME OF A FUTURE MCDONALD'S signs on the plywood fencing around construction sites. The better to forestall the frenzied protests by neighbors horrified to find a McDonald's restaurant blighting their vicinity. In the upscale suburb of Bexley, Ohio, in 1994, neighbors protested the planned construction of a McDonald's on a major street; they felt it wouldn't contribute to the status of the neighborhood as much as the business being displaced: an adult video store. The village of Lake Forest, Illinois, spent $150,000 in legal fees to keep McDonald's away.

Stealth is about the only defense the corporation has. Otherwise, words fail them. When *Fortune* ran an article, years ago, complaining that McDonald's signs were marring the American landscape, a McDonald's executive wrote to the magazine arguing "uninterrupted scenery, too, can get pretty monotonous."

McDonald's is opposed even more fiercely in Europe. When the first McDonald's opened in Italy in 1986, thousands of Romans jammed the Piazza di Spagna to decry the "degradation of Rome." A fashion designer whose headquarters was next to the new restaurant sued McDonald's, alleging his workers were forced to endure "an unbearable smell of fried food fouling the air." McDonald's responded by opening restaurants in the heart of other Italian historical treasures, sticking one in front of the San Carlo Opera in Naples, another in the ruins of Pompeii.

McDonald's met the wild protests against the "infamy" at Pompeii by claiming that the restaurant was designed to blend in with the two-thousand-year-old site. In America too, many of the restaurants make a wan attempt at a theme: paintings of ducks, or cheap memorabilia, stuck in a display case, decoration often connected to the historical charm of the area before it was displaced and despoiled by a McDonald's (in Cambridge, Massachusetts, McDonald's razed one of the city's two surviving pre-Civil War Greek revival landmark buildings to build an outlet).

Certain McDonald's have become known for their décor. In St. Louis there is a McDonald's riverboat moored on the Mississippi. In downtown Chicago the "Rock and Roll" McDonald's covers an entire city block, is open twenty-four hours a day, and has become one of the most popular attractions in the city. About as many people visit it each year as visit the Art Institute.

Many McDonald's, however, have no greater decoration than the image of the chain's scary mascot, Ronald. For all the hundreds of millions of dollars spent sandwiching his image around every minute of TV time devoted to children, Ronald is still sort of a marginal, shadowy figure in the pantheon of product mascots. You seldom see a child hugging a Ronald McDonald doll. At first this seems a mystery—Ronald is idiotic enough to be popular; indeed, his mien makes Barney seem like Bill Moyers. The problem, I believe, is a simple quirk of poor conception; clowns are frightening enough, as a class, but Ronald is particularly repulsive: his round, sex doll mouth; his form-fitting, yellow-banded Uriah Heep outfit; his red harridan's wig; his band of deformed followers.

A newcomer to McDonald's wouldn't be blamed for

assuming that Ronald and his henchmen were placed at the entrance of the restaurants, Cerebus-like, to scare people away, perhaps as a service of the government. (As if such a thing as a newcomer to McDonald's could be possible anymore—overfamiliarity with the chain arriving nowadays in infancy, along with language.)

McDonald's is revolting in ways beyond either taste or aesthetics. Even if McDonald's were serving my mother's home cooking in the garden at Versailles, and the leering Ronald face were replaced by Vermeer's *The Lacemaker*, I would still have a hard time walking into the restaurants, just out of reluctance to witness the grueling plantation of minimum-wage slavery across the stainless steel counter. There are always forty or so teenagers, joined by the occasional senior citizen and displaced housewife, scrambling desperately over each other, dropping wire baskets of fries into sizzling oil, jamming cups under the teats of shake machines, sliding multicolored clumps of burgers down metal chutes. Their actions are closely monitored by one or two managers—grim, set-jawed martinets, watching eagle-eyed over their charges, making sure that the supply of Filet-O-Fishes heaped under the heat lamp does not dwindle. The teens are too harried to speak. There is no time to fully articulate the Proustian greeting, "Hi, welcome to McDonald's. May I take your order?" So it is compressed into: "Hiwelkm t'McDonal. Mayie t'ky-order?" I'm surprised that more of them don't kill themselves, right there on the job; just squinch their eyes shut and plunge their heads into a boiling french fry vat. I would.

Take your tray of food and stumble into the holding-pen dining room, where you join the steerage cast of lunatics, impoverished old people, and the homeless, either shouting to each other or staring fixedly at a point on the floor. A few mothers and children out on a lark might be thrown into the mix, hunched over, whispering to one another, ashamed, trying not to attract attention. Avoiding eye contact, you grab a seat, bolt back your food, and race outside, which is the entire point.

Perhaps it is inevitable, given the deteriorating economy, but most McDonald's do resemble soup kitchens, with bundled women frantically inventorying their shopping bags filled with dirty towels, and unshaven men in watch caps, eyes blazing, conducting intense conversations with themselves, jabbing their fingers at the air to drive home their points as their small cups of coffee go from boiling to hot to cool to cold.

This might be more of a city phenomenon, now that I think of it. Suburban McDonald's tend to be jammed with the unlettered children who make up such a large percentage of McDonald's business: Little League teams being rewarded for finally winning a game; clusters of belligerent teens, gathering at the only place in town that won't roust them along if they loiter.

Of course, you never see these typical customers in the company's omnipresent TV ads, just as you never see the grimy, overlit and depressing interior of an actual McDonald's. On TV, the restaurants are always basked in a warm morning glow, Arcadian greens and golds filtering in from the rustic lanes outside. Gleeful, multinational professionals pour into the TV-fantasy-McDonald's and begin ordering, raising the food to eye level, the better to stare delightedly agog at their sandwiches for a moment before eating them with a grand, eye-popping relish that would look exaggerated in a silent movie.

I always wonder: while the commercials are being made, what do they do with the Edward Hopper bums and low-income clans who normally occupy any given restaurant? Kick them out, I suppose, force them to huddle out back by the dumpsters, eating discards, waiting for filming to end.

Doesn't pooh-poohing the economic status of people hanging around McDonald's point to the disturbing possibility that this is a class issue? That, like so many clammy intellectuals blowing off our big bazoos in our marginal publications, our *Commentary,* our *National Review,* I am just another pampered sophisticate, squinting through my monocle to pick the pin bones from my $30 squab, mocking the poor people whose only option for a night on the town is Mickey D's?

The fact is, however, eating at McDonald's is not that cheap. You can buy a bowl of lobster bisque at Shaw's, one of Chicago's best restaurants, served with a loaf of hot fresh bread and crackers, which taken together make a satisfactory lunch, for $3.45. The waiter may give you a disparaging look, but nothing compared to the wet-lipped gape of deficiency you can expect from one of the galley slaves at McDonald's. The $5.00 you spend for a Big Mac, big fries and a Coke would also buy the unlimited lunchtime buffet at half the Indian restaurants in the country. Of course, many people don't want ethnic food, no matter how cheap it is. That is exactly the reason for McDonald's success—while it isn't necessarily inexpensive, it certainly is bland, and the vast majority like that.

Urbanites, steeped in the swirl of imported cuisines and cultures of a big city, forget just how basic the palates of most Americans can be. Whenever our friends Jim and Laura visit from Ohio, my wife and I struggle to present fare that is plain and acceptable. But we always seem to screw up. Spice creeps into the chicken. Novelty insinuates itself onto the menu. Last time we really thought we had succeeded. We served mostaccioli—those simple cylinders of pasta—covered in tomato sauce. Laura speared a single cylinder, lifted it up, examined it closely, and flatly observed that she had never seen anything like it before in her entire life. It was not a compliment.

This is not a mistake McDonald's would make. Nothing on the menu has any sort of spice, the overriding flavors being salt and grease. Nothing is unusual. The idea of dining, of exploration, of discovery, is entirely foreign to the McDonald's experience. At McDonald's, introducing pizza to the menu in selected cities thirty years after it became a staple in the diet of every person in America was a wild departure into gastronomical experimentation.

The implication is that McDonald's is not so much to blame for its success as we are ourselves. I can endorse that. The greatest marketing genius could not have infected the planet with 19,000 McDonald's restaurants had not huge segments of the public been eager for a source of bland, cheapish, identical burgers.

Did I forget "hurried"? Another key attraction to McDonald's is the idea that you are eating quickly. Even though nobody's career ever foundered because he or she ate lunch, many people at my office are afraid to take their hour lunch break. So they hurry over to McDonald's to fetch their lunch, bringing it back to eat at their desks, in

137

some sort of public display of efficiency and self-denial. There is a McDonald's next door to our building (next door to most buildings, now that I think of it) and some coworkers go there nearly every day to pick up food. I don't scorn them. I feel sorry for them. There is a guy at my office, Don Hayner, whom I pass in the hall all the time. I am on my way out to lunch at Shaw's. He is quick-footing it back from McDonald's, carrying his little brown sack (a couple decades after the first Earth Day, McDonald's learned about environmental correctness; now their corporate graphics look as if the company were run by Pueblos).

Don eats at his desk, while working, his cheeks bulging with burger as he stares at the computer screen. I eat at my table in Shaw's. His meal takes ten minutes. Mine takes an hour, at least. If alone, I read the paper, occasionally looking up to signal a waiter, or nod and smile at passing acquaintances. If with others, we talk, gesture, joke, marvel at the quality of the food, the freshness of the hot loaf of bread. Sometimes it is the best part of the day.

Sure, Don is heading to the top—the glass office, the monogrammed cuff, the cherished skybox invitation, the chance to tell other people what to do. But he is a smart guy, and a good editor, and he would get there anyway, I think, even if he ate a real lunch. And is the loss worth the gain? I'd say that being a manager is not worth missing lunch, but then I think being a manager is not worth missing a cup of coffee. Good coffee, I mean, not the scalding, old-woman-maiming stuff they serve at McDonald's.

The past ten thousand years of civilization have been a struggle against eating on the run. To no longer be forced to gnaw on a shank bone while fleeing from wolves, but to be able to sit, to relax, with friends, and eat, good food, maybe a little wine. Maybe a cigar after. That is the joy of life.

And the polar opposite of the McDonald's philosophy, the eat-it-and-get-out mindset, the order-it-in-your-car-and-gobble-it-at-stoplights attitude. The very concept of McDonald's is a screeching 180-degree turn away from progress, an elephant step back toward Hobbes's feral and hectic world, of lives and meals "solitary, poor, nasty, brutish, and short."

For the millions duped into believing in the value of this pointless brevity, it is their misfortune. But few ills are entirely without positive aspect. McDonald's does give unsavory elements a place to congregate off the street, and draws the masses away from eateries of quality. If everybody valued eating and cherished mealtimes, think of what the lines would be at finer restaurants.

So that leaves McDonald's as an annoying, yet perhaps necessary, evil. A necessary and, one might be forgiven for hoping, impermanent evil. In my heart, I confess, dwells the sincere belief that the monster may one day disappear. Growing old would lose its sting then. Watching my face dissolve into wrinkles and spots, my faculties shutting down, one by one, would be much more tolerable, if at the same time the McDonald's Corporation was also shrinking, shriveling, enervating, falling out of favor. It is possible. It could happen. Look at Sears. One day astride the world like a behemoth, sending the tallest building in history shooting toward the heavens, dry goods merchant to the world. The next day—*piffft!*—all gone, nearly, the catalogue a memory; the tower, sold; the stores, shut down or ailing. That could happen to McDonald's. Tastes change.

Time marches on. The power and the glory that were Rome transform slowly into the *opera buffa* that is Italy.

McDonald's in decline would be very entertaining. Think of the desperate measures the corporation would take in its death throes—Ronald McDonald replaced by a tart, her heaving bosoms barely concealed by strategically placed pickle slices. Weird product mutations—burgers the size of derby hats, the size of nickels, anything to draw people in. McBeer. Finally, after the company contracts with a mighty shuddering groan, the sight of boarded-up franchises, abandoned, rotting, decayed. The burst of renewed public interest and nostalgia—too late!—as the restaurants dwindle down to a mere handful, then none. Wouldn't that be great?

Of course, one atrocity gives way to another, and McDonald's would no doubt only be replaced by something blander, faster, cheaper—Gruel on the Go. Papstop! Bunn-Run. The mind reels.

N Is for Noise

The sun has just set over the Chicago & Northwestern Railway tracks, momentarily tinting the sky a luminescent, Maxfield Parrish blue before dwindling into dusk. Across Ravenswood Avenue from the tracks, the Freedman Seating Company is well into its evening shift. From the alley out back, you can hear a gentle hum of muffled industrial noises.

"Even though this area may be zoned for manufacturing, as soon as it goes across into that residential area, it's a violation," says Joe Pratt, an inspector for the city's Department of Environment. He is parked in a dark blue city van in the alley between the factory building and a strip of modest, three-flat apartment buildings.

The "it" Pratt is referring to is noise. A woman in an apartment across the alley from the factory has besieged the city "for months and months and months" with calls complaining that the noise is bothering her.

"This lady, she would call us up and say, 'I hear hammering. I hear compressed air,' " says Pratt. "Every time we come here—and sometimes we come three times a week—we only hear a little *tap,* a hammering noise here, *pffft,* compressed air every once in a while, but never enough to get a level we need to nail them with."

Chicago has six noise inspectors for a city of three million people. And noise is not their only concern—they also respond to hazardous material spills, fly dumping, and a variety of other code violations. "We're supposed to enforce the ordinance against spitting on the sidewalk," says Pratt, though not as a complaint. You get a sense that Pratt *wants* to enforce the no-spitting law, only he doesn't have time. He brings a solemn, Joe Friday kind of determination to his job despite the impossibility of rescuing distraught citizens from the noises all around them, sometimes in reality, sometimes only in their imagination. Pratt was once summoned by a woman who pointed to a bug zapper hanging from her neighbor's porch, the kind with a purplish light to attract insects. "She kept saying, 'Did you hear that? Did you hear that?' " Pratt recalls. "I said, 'What, the zapper?' And she said: 'No, the *bugs.*' She was complaining about the noise the bugs made."

Pratt gets out of the van and, pacing off ten feet from the factory, takes a decibel measurement with a foot-long sound pressure meter. Sixty-eight decibels—about the loudness of ordinary conversation.

"It has to be eighty decibels, so she'll just have to put up with the noise," says Pratt. He gets into his van and drives away.

———

Noise. You just have to put up with it. All the attempted remedies—complaining to the city, summoning the cops, calling up the hotel manager, turning around in your seat and going "Shhhhh"—are to many people as unpleasant as the problem itself, maybe more so. Those who complain rarely find satisfaction anyway—after countless petitions and public meetings the planes may be diverted, for a while, but they still keep coming in. The chattering gossips, hushed for a few moments, return to their whispering, this time about you.

More than any other irritation, noise illustrates the complete divergence between the design of a person's natural senses and the cramped purposes to which those senses invariably find themselves applied nowadays. Hearing is the sense intended to convey the first warning of danger. You cannot close your ears at night the way you close your eyes. Ears are always on, always listening, so they can jolt you awake, ready to fight or flee, at the snap of a twig or a distant growl.

That was vital five thousand years ago. A person discovered he was hard of hearing when a tiger sank its teeth into the back of his neck. Today for every noise conveying actual danger there are thousands that just deliver unnecessary shots of adrenaline, putting your systems on alert because a car backfired or some kid tossed an M80 into a dumpster or a door slammed. Even noises that are still intended to convey warning—sirens, car alarms, shouts—are invariably intended for someone else in our crowded world, or are just a mistake, an artifact.

The fear response lurking behind noise makes unwanted sounds all the more annoying, as shown by the countless studies of aircraft noise. People are bothered far more by aircraft noise than by road vehicle noise, even when the volume of the noise they make is the same. A house that suddenly becomes part of a noisy aircraft pattern will depreciate more in value than a house near a newly built and equally noisy highway. Some of this may be due to the greater falloff of traffic noise (which is louder in the front yard than in the backyard, assuming a house faces the street, while the noise of passing airplanes is the same front or back) but some of the special annoyance extended toward airplanes is thought to be due to fear of having one crash into you. This was shown elegantly in a study that found people were more annoyed by the sound of a plane passing directly overhead than an equally loud plane passing off to one side.

Psychologists and social planners love to study noise—asking what sorts of noises are annoying? What frequencies? What volume? Intermittent or regular?

Despite a rich academic literature, annoying noises are hard to classify. Loud noises are generally bothersome, but rock concerts are very loud, and people seek them out. Irregular noises are often annoying, but few people complain about erratically twittering birds. In studies of certified noise nuisances—airports, factory machinery—there is always some considerable percentage of people living nearby who don't mind the noise at all. Some small fraction even claim to *like* it. I grew up a few blocks from an interstate highway, and at night would hear the distant roar of the trucks as I fell asleep. Now a busy highway—provided it is removed at just the right distance—is a soothing sound to me, associated with rest, night, home.

Each individual is bothered by his or her own personal thumbprint of particular noises. For instance, as I write this, the children who live next door, a pair of energetic young lads named Christopher and Alexander, are screaming as if being flayed alive, pausing only to hurl their bodies against the wall. Their mother yells, louder than both, for them to be quiet. Such shouts and thuds and piercing sobs break out every two or three days. But I would never dream of asking their mother to have them pipe down, since my aversion to the unneighborliness of complaining is greater than the annoyance caused by these periodic eruptions. First, I know that the noise will end shortly—always a great comfort when dealing with annoyances. And, second, I'm sure the poor woman would quiet them if she only could, short of murder. Instead, I tell myself that the caterwauling is a reminder to cherish my otherwise placid life.

I can shrug off howling children bouncing off my door, but I've almost had to give up going to classical music performances. I settle into the red plush seat, happy and expectant, flipping through the program. The music begins. And suddenly the realization strikes me that the city's entire population of asthmatics and tuberculosites has been gathered together and quarantined here in Orchestra Hall. They rasp and hack and cough, synchronizing their phlegmy explosions with the quiet passages of the music. I want to kill them.

There is always some man breathing as if on a respirator, or some lady s-l-o-w-l-y unzipping what I hope is her purse, under the misapprehension that it is somehow less bothersome that way. My mind is taken away from the fawn entering the glade and begins furiously deliberating whether I should turn around in my seat and snarl, "You rattle that program one more time, Granny, and I'll snap your neck like a breadstick."

I understand that classical music patrons are old, in many cases, and their systems are failing them. Still, I believe that I would first strangle and die in my seat before I would let fly a rasping, ropy cough in the middle of the slow movement of some Mozart concerto. Worse are the people who start to whisper to one another, or unwrap what sound like Christmas presents but are probably mints.

Eventually I do whip around in my seat and shush them, though in truth at that point I might as well get up and go home, since Yo Yo Ma could have stopped playing Dvorak, set aside his cello, picked up a kazoo and begun happily piping "The Rooty-Toot Song" and I wouldn't have noticed.

I truly believe that disruptive noise is the reason orchestras and opera companies sell their tickets by series, in hopes that you will get used to the distractions or, at least, be forced to come back a few times more than you normally would.

You can, after all, get used to any noise. Some expensive real estate in Chicago abuts the elevated train tracks. I ran into a casual acquaintance who told me, with surprising candor, he had just spent $419,000 on a townhouse located three doors from the Ravenswood el line, which runs all night. He seemed like a man stunned. "It has Thermopane windows," he said. "I'm sure I'll get used to it." He waited for me to agree with him, and I did so, out of politeness. But in truth I couldn't see paying an other-worldly sum of money in order to spend the next decade or two listening to the el train rumble past every seven minutes, twenty-four hours a day.

"Getting used to it" isn't the answer. You can get used to anything. If somebody came into my office each hour, on the hour, and hit me on the head with a croquet mallet, I suppose I'd get used to it over time. Heck, I might even grow to like it. Maybe the Republican platform would begin to make a little sense to me. Provided, of course, it was a really big mallet.

Indeed, the entire history of noise shows that humanity has gradually raised its tolerance level as life has grown louder. Seneca wrote an essay about people being bothered by the splashing noise from a Roman bath. Sei Shonagon, writing a thousand years ago, included a creaking carriage in her list of "Hateful Things." John Donne complained about the "noise of a fly." Sounds that we would consider pleasant were once maddening—a flock of sparrows were excommunicated by the Bishop of Dresden in 1559 for "their unceasing and extremely vexatious chatterings and scandalous unchastity during the sermon."

Whether splashes or birds or sonic booms, the root of the problem of noise seems to be control. A song coming through the wall is far more annoying than the same song, played at the same volume, on your stereo, because you can't reach through wall and shut it off if you want to.

Psychologist D. C. Glass and his associates illustrated this in a clever experiment twenty-five years ago. Two groups were given paragraphs to proofread while hearing the same loud, randomly occurring noise. One group, however, were given a button and told they could press the button and stop the noise whenever they wanted to. The other had no button.

The group that could stop the noise both did better on the test and found the noise less objectionable, even when they didn't use the button to stop the noise. Just having the ability was enough.

Perhaps that is why noise can be so maddening when we can't control it—not the ordeal of hearing a particular sound itself. The sound could even be a pleasant one, the song, one that we like. No matter—it's still annoying because it is a reminder that we are in close proximity to someone else, and that person is doing something loud, regardless of us. A loud party is much more annoying if you haven't been invited to it.

People who complain about the noise *you* make, remember, seem petty, peevish. I used to live in an apartment on Logan Boulevard. The apartment had beautiful wooden floors. Our downstairs neighbor, Gail, would complain of the noise our cats made running on the floors. This we dismissed, laughingly. What could be quieter than cats? "The fog comes on little cat feet" and all that. Our landlady offered to carpet the floors, but we declined. Tough luck, Gail.

Soon Gail moved away, and some young guys I came to refer to, collectively, as "Gail's Revenge" moved in. We greeted them in neighborly fashion, showing up with pleasantries and a plate of sweets, and so had every reason to hope, when they threw their first loud party, that they would comply with our polite request, delivered humbly, about 2 A.M., to please quiet down.

They didn't, and they continued to throw riotous Bacchanalias, which we would have happily attended, had we been invited. I found myself exercising greater and greater efforts to calm them. Eventually it got so bad I would just walk into their apartment—the door left unlocked to more readily admit whooping guests—turn the stereo down, then walk out. Once I unplugged it.

Oddly, I would never call the police. That seemed too extreme. I worried about being embarrassed. There is a definite feeble quality to presenting oneself publicly as a person bothered by noise. Such sensitivity seems like a personal weakness. The irate neighbor, pounding on the wall and screaming, "Will you turn it down in there!" is viewed as somehow weak. Obviously a lonely, unhappy man. Elmer Fudd, in his nightshirt and cap, desperately trying to rest. "I've got to get some *sleeeeeep*. Please, let me *sleeeeeep*." Pulling the big white pillow over his head while Bugs Bunny marches by with one of those bass drum/one-man-band getups. Pathetic.

The police, busy fighting criminals, could not be counted on for sympathy. Maybe they'd arrest *me*. Take me down to the station. "Yeah, Sarge, we got another one of them *sensitive* fellahs. Mebbe we should put him in the Hole. Awful quiet down there. He'll probably like it. . . ."

So I faced the menace alone. Once, at about 4 A.M., I went into the basement and popped the fuses for their apartment. This struck me as a clever and completely non-confrontational approach and I was quite proud of myself. Back in bed, savoring the sudden stillness emanating from below, I castigated myself for not stringing a few trip wires across the basement stairs.

By the end, I had spent a lot of time thinking up novel ways to chastise our noisy downstairs neighbors. My favorite, inspired by the fact we lived in a Hispanic neighborhood where alarming ethnic foodstuffs were on sale at the supermarket, was to take the skinned sheep's head sold for soup, and, picking some moment when the nightmare beneath us wasn't home, nailing it to their front door with a big finishing nail. Perhaps it would require a leap of logic for them to realize the sheep's head meant they should pipe down, but I thought that being confronted with the dripping, gory, odorous head would almost certainly have a humbling effect.

I never got the chance to deploy the sheep's head, however. Constant pressure on our landlady inspired her not to renew their lease and, after a year, Gail's Revenge were gone, replaced by a man without arms. He would sometimes call me downstairs to open a storm window or tie his shoe, but I found this far, far less intrusive than the noise had been.

Of course I did. Because control had shifted back to me. People making noise always have the advantage. They are the ones in control, and there is something in noise itself that suggests power. Which is why society was slow to recognize noise as a problem and regulate it. In the relative quiet of earlier days, noise was considered a sign of vitality and strength. O. Henry praised the hum of the elevated and the clang of the city. Ambrose Bierce, while citing noise in his *Devil's Dictionary* as "a stench in the ear," adds that it is also "the chief product and authenticating sign of civilization." Manufacturers of steam engines rejoiced in their mighty roar, and silence was associated with provincialism—and thus a veiled criticism for a city.

"How quiet the streets are!" a visiting Charles Dickens marveled of New York in 1842, noting the absence of London's clanging urban entertainments. "Are there no itinerant bands; no wind or stringed instruments? No, not one. By day, are there no Punches, Fantoccini, dancing-dogs, Jugglers, Conjurers, Orchestrinas, or even Barrel-organs? No, not one . . . nothing lively; no, not so much as a white mouse in a twirling cage."

People still associate noise with power, as seen by hot rodders installing glass packs and muffler cutouts (which, indeed, do increase an engine's power, by not forcing it to push exhaust through a muffler). This connection is best illustrated by the difficulties encountered by companies that manage to silence noisy products. When Hoover engineers introduced a quieter vacuum cleaner in the late 1960s, customers rejected it as underpowered, even though it sucked up dirt as readily as noisier models. Quieter lawn mowers have had the same problem.

Society has disintegrated too much for noise to get much attention anymore—fighting noise has acquired too much of an arranging-the-deck-chairs-on-the-*Titanic* aspect to it, compared to the crushing problems of violence and poverty and the like.

But for a few brief years earlier in the century noise control had a moment of popularity. In 1929, New York City established the nation's first official body devoted to fighting noise. The New York Noise Abatement Commission attacked the problem with the sort of confident, can-do attitude that brings a pang today, in light of the general paralysis of government. They thought that just by addressing the problem it was half solved.

"The city can well congratulate itself that the complex noise situation is in the hands of such distinguished specialists in whom the public has an abiding confidence," wrote Dr. Shirley Wynne, the commissioner of health, in announcing the effort.

The noise commission was a blue-blood group, as such bodies inevitably were at the time. One commission member showed his hand a bit when he let slip that a negative effect of city noise was the need for "frequent recuperation in the country."

In spite of this, or perhaps because of it, the commission threw itself into its mandate, battling noise on all fronts, from installing "silencers" on noisy subway turnstiles to convincing garment district businesses to put rubber wheels on rolling clothing racks, to having radio stations broadcast a reminder at 10:30 P.M. that it was late, people were trying to sleep, and radios should be turned down "as an act of good sportsmanship."

One of the first things the commission did was publish a survey in all metropolitan papers, attempting to rank annoying noises.

"We were convinced that the noisy condition of the city constituted a kind of emergency situation, calling for a speedy survey of the more preventable and diminishable noises in order that New Yorkers may as soon as possible begin to enjoy the fruits of the Commission's efforts," wrote a member.

More than 11,000 responses were received. Most are still familiar today—truck noises and car horns were ranked numbers one and two in annoyance. The commission expended much effort on the latter, seriously considering at one point a total ban on the "various squawks, hoots, shrieks, and trumpetings" of car horns. Thirty-three different types of car horns were submitted to scientific testing, not only for volume and frequency of sound, but for "objectionableness" and "frightening effect."

A relic of this dim view of horns is the ordinance, enacted in New York and widely copied, against blowing the horn of a car while not in motion. The law is still on the books in many cities, though hardly ever enforced.

Despite the familiarity of most noise annoyances listed in the survey ("roistering whoopee parties" was my favorite) other irritants have ceased to be considered problems, from "the noises from milk wagons and pie trucks" to "newsboys' cries" to "youths and maidens grouped on front stoops sing[ing] in close harmony at unreasonable hours of the night," an image that makes one positively pine for the past.

Needless to say, the commission did not end the problem of noise in New York City. It did temporarily improve things, if nothing else by raising awareness among New Yorkers. Shortly after the commission's very public formation, builders erecting a skyscraper at Broadway and Wall Street sent engraved apologies to five hundred neighbors, requesting their indulgence while the fifty-four-story structure was riveted together.

"May we hope," the apology read, "that you will bear with us as patiently as possible during the unavoidably noisy weeks that lie just ahead while the steel frame of our headquarters building is going up?"

Such apologies were in vogue for a while. Another construction site bore the following sign: "Our sincere apologies to our neighbors for the unavoidable annoyance this hammering must occasion."

Campaigns against noise reappeared in the ensuing decades, but with less ambition and less brio. New York's

1971 campaign, Project Quiet City, only covered the area from Fifty-ninth Street to Seventy-Fourth Street between Central Park West and the Hudson River, and took a survey of just several hundred residents to find which noises afflicted them.

Many noises combated in 1929 were still there in 1971, including honking horns. Under Project Quiet City, a fine of $50 a toot was imposed on drivers who honked their horns except in cases of "imminent danger."

This time, as everyone knows, the plan worked, making New York City the oasis of quiet and calm it is today.

O Is for Oprah

 When I first set out to try to express my deep visceral dislike of Oprah Winfrey and her wildly popular program, I began by wondering if I should at some point actually sit down and watch a show, beginning to end, something I had never done and had no desire to ever do. Bits of the "Oprah" program, caught accidentally in passing, plus what I knew about it from the media, were enough to inculcate within me a powerful aversion to this froglike dominatrix presiding over her Theater of Pain.

I told myself that watching the show itself was superfluous. An unnecessary display of self-flagellation, akin to Bill McKibben's watching 2,000 hours of television—one day's worth of cable broadcasts on all channels—in order to ascertain, in his book *The Age of Missing Information*, that massive television viewing is a less spiritual experience than hiking alone in the woods. You have to wonder what kind of person undertakes such a conspicuous ordeal to confirm the blatantly obvious. A masochist, I imagine.

"Happy is he," wrote Kierkegaard, "who did not need to go to Hell to see what the devil looked like."

The beauty of television, after all, is you never have to watch it. This fact is lost on many people, who complain bitterly about the content of TV, or lack of which, never quite realizing the power of liberation is in their own hands. This freedom is what keeps television from being a true annoyance. Nobody forces you to watch. In fact, I find more than a little unconscious self-indictment in those who gripe about the quality of television—akin to someone praising his host's cooking as a whole lot better than the stuff served in prison.

But Oprah Winfrey's fame, bordering on omnipresence, transcends television. You don't have to watch Oprah's show to be smothered by her. She is in movies, and on the covers of magazines and books, and salted liberally throughout the pages of newspapers, especially in her hometown of Chicago (it almost seems an inversion to say that Chicago is home to Oprah, instead of Oprah being home to an appendage city of Chicago). Thus a person—me, for instance—who never watches her show, and takes active steps to avoid all references to Oprah, still finds himself apprised of her every move: her latest weight fluctuation, the state of her perpetual engagement to Stedman Graham, her newest tinkering with the show to draw in viewers, her most recent televised confession. (Unlike most celebrities, Oprah only enhances her status by admitting to crimes and moral lapses, as long as they are safely in the past. I imagine her sneaking out at night to commit furtive acts of minor illegality, so as to replenish the stock of undisclosed misdeeds to confess to on future shows.)

Because of her fame, Oprah is even more bothersome than the legion of talk show hosts who imitate her—the Lizas and Sallys and Jennys and so forth. These imitators might outdo Oprah in terms of sensation, focusing on the sex perverts and teenage sluts whom Oprah now professes to avoid. But Oprah packs the wallop of notoriety, making her offerings, though theoretically milder, even more grating and unavoidable. No matter how horrible her rivals are, we know they are nobodies who will, sooner or later, disappear. Oprah, on the other hand, has the air of permanence about her.

The show's moderation actually puts it on a level where it can more easily breach our defenses and cause annoyance. Geraldo Rivera, for instance, is far more odious than Oprah—so much so, in fact, that the mind rejects him, hurrying on to more pleasant thoughts like a villager fleeing a leper. We are protected from Geraldo by a sort of mental gag reflex. I couldn't write two coherent paragraphs about him because I couldn't force myself to watch his show for ten consecutive seconds. The moments I have seen, through splayed fingers, in the brief span between the time my mind registers what I am watching and when my hands can fumble for the remote control to change channels, are enough to convince me that Geraldo would let Satanists feed a baby into a grinder on his show if it would boost ratings. Perhaps he already has.

Oprah also has a cult of self thing going that no other host enjoys. Sociologists studying talk shows found that Oprah talks more often during a program than does any other host. Her staggering financial success has made her an object of veneration among the many who grant their esteem based on wealth, and a lot of Oprah's shtick consists of springing the golden calf of her physical entity suddenly upon her startled fans. Oprah is forever bringing hot coffee to surprised commuters at bus stops, or showing up at their homes to baby-sit their kids, or flying her audiences to distant cities at a moment's notice, or guiding cameras through one of her many grand residences.

Given this ubiquity and the massive, fanatical adoration, or perhaps just insatiable curiosity, that Oprah inspires in the mob, I realized it would be foolhardy to dare speak of her shortcomings without first subjecting myself to the scourge of witnessing an entire program, or several. If nothing else, I would then have concrete proof of what I already know to be true.

So, after working my way through the traditional Kübler-Ross series of denial, bargaining, anger and acceptance, I sat down one Monday morning and began a planned week of Oprah watching.

With a burst of light jazz, a glimpse of pounding surf and sparkling sunlight, festooned with Oprah's laughing face and a trio of violet-tinged graphic "Oprah"s sweeping by, Monday morning's show begins. Oprah announces that the show isn't live—the latest publicity gimmick, after years of being prerecorded—but a taped continuation of Friday's discussion of the then ongoing O. J. Simpson trial, a session so riveting they must go at it for another hour. The guests are four network TV trial commentators, plus *Vanity Fair* pet author Dominick Dunne, hovering in the background on a giant video display, like Big Brother in a starched white shirt.

Oprah casts a cool image—trim, in a pearl-gray suit and delicate Armani eyeglasses, she spends most of the show curled catlike on the steps leading up to her guests, turning sometimes to face them, sometimes to her bumptious studio audience.

As soon as they are given a chance to speak the audience quickly establishes themselves as a band of village idiots, whiffing conspiracy on the breeze, howling their opinions. They are passionately in support of O. J. Simpson, shouting "Liar!" when a videotape of Los Angeles police officer Mark Fuhrman is shown (rather presciently, as it turned out). "All the evidence was planted," states a woman confidently, a sentiment heartily applauded and repeated by others. The real world and assorted private fantasy worlds mingle freely within the audience's heads—one woman suspects that house guest Kato Kaelin will soon be implicated in the murder, since he once wielded a knife in a movie role. A man in an improbable bowl haircut insists, in a high-pitched voice, that Simpson would be judged "at the pearly gates" and, if found guilty by God, would "spend the rest of his life in Hell."

Oprah sits between the guests and the audience, as a filter, or more like a bridge, between the gross public, whose thought processes border on pure hallucination, and the measured, sensible opinions of the commentators (well, sensible except for the speculation from CNN's Roger Cossack that interest in the O. J. Simpson trial could only have been equaled in history had the assassin of Lincoln been caught and tried, the statement is not only an exaggeration, but ignorant too, since there was a Lincoln assassination trial involving Booth's supposed accomplices, who were hanged).

The other exception to the general sensibility is, of course, Dunne, who flaps his French cuffs and recycles stories that he has already published in *Vanity Fair*.

"I don't think there has ever been a trial like this," Dunne ventures, a statement which, while technically true, could also be applied with equal accuracy to absolutely anything.

A pair of obese women in the audience, who seem to be twins—distaff Tweedledum and Tweedledee—most passionately support O.J., and the camera keeps returning to their contorted, puffed faces. Tweedledum gets up and says that she once called the 900 number of Simpson toady Al Cowlings, at $2.99 a minute.

"It is so sexy," she gushes. "It is great. He just keeps talking to you and telling you stuff." Oprah asks what she learned for the $10 or $12 spent on the call. "I learned he was a really nice guy," the woman says. But nothing, Oprah points out, about the drive in the Ford Bronco. Nothing, Oprah asks, about what you wanted to know? The woman's face twists into a stricken look, as if she is being assailed by concepts too deep for her to fathom.

It is during this line of questioning that I begin to hope Oprah might not be the foaming cheerleader I had imagined her to be. Later, when Tweedledum shouts that they want the truth, Oprah retorts, "Do you expect to get the truth from a 900 number?" Impressive.

My hope is strengthened when a woman in red vehemently explains that O. J. Simpson is covering for his son Jason, who killed Nicole because she dumped his father. Others in the audience voice their assent. "You think O. J. is covering for his son Jason?" Oprah says slowly, incredulously, her eyes lowered, as if fighting the urge to scream. A moment later she leads into a commercial. As the camera lingers on her face—controlled, expressionless—she gives a little disgusted shake of her head, as if she herself can't believe the stupidity of her audience. As if she, like me, just can't wait for this thing to be over.

I find myself actually eager for Tuesday's show. Is Oprah a soul in pain, forced to endure the unwashed blather of her public in a Faustian bargain for riches and fame? Or was that little shake of the head a fluke? Something unique to the grating, inescapable shriek of the O. J. Simpson case? After all, Oprah is always going on about how she and her audience are one, a united whole bonded together by empathy and understanding.

Tuesday is affirmative action, and Oprah has about a dozen guests, onstage and salted throughout the audience, who feel affirmative action is either racist discrimination against white people threatening to Balkanize the United States or a necessary tool to correct historic wrongs and address inherent bigotry.

They argue their points, a babble of voices, sometimes drowning one another out, sometimes straying into the trivial or the plain meaningless. Nikol Alexander, a black law student from the University of Texas, her voice sodden with incipient tears, speaks so fast that her words become a confusing spout of verbiage. "You can talk really fast," marvels Oprah when the young woman pauses for breath.

Cheryl Hopwood, a white student denied admission to the University of Texas, argues that, despite her color, she too is a bona fide member of the victim class and thus deserves to go to law school. "I'm the mother of a severely handicapped child," she says. "How many students going to school can say that?"

Still, as a discussion, it isn't bad. I admire the fact that Oprah's producers don't stack the deck one way or another, going so far as to invite Larry Elder, the outspoken black radio host, who stands up and denounces affirmative action as promoting the "notion that blacks are victims, that they can't compete, can't cope unless there are set-asides."

I am almost worried that Oprah has gone cerebral—that her professed reform is real—and should Wednesday's show be a debate on the essential nature of justice ("How does it make you feel when Thrasymachus says justice is the advantage of the stronger?") I might have to reconsider the entire thing.

But, to my relief and dismay, Wednesday's theme is "Daddy has AIDS," featuring *both* a Norman Rockwell family afflicted with the dread disease *and* a guest appearance by victim du jour, Olympic diver Greg Louganis.

The "Daddy" is Andy Lipschitz, a cardiologist who infected himself with HIV, he says, by an accidental needle stick in 1986. Joining him on stage is his wife, Judy Stein. A videotape, accompanied by sad music, shows them frolicking with their two children in their lovely home. "They were the perfect family . . ." Oprah intones.

Lipschitz tells his story: though a doctor, he never thought to get tested for AIDS in the six years after he jabbed himself with a needle he knew to be tainted with HIV-infected blood. Even when he had pneumonia in 1992, it took other doctors to urge him to get the HIV test. In the meantime, he didn't tell his wife, and they had a second child.

Oprah, sitting on the stage for the first time this week, seems hushed, reverent. She never presses the most obvious questions. Why didn't he consider the possibility that the needle stick had transferred the virus to him? How could he put his wife at risk for six years? Instead, she focuses on the miracle that the wife and child were not infected. Oprah wants to know how each of them "feels." She teases from the mother the entire story of how she informed her son that "Daddy has AIDS," flashing big pictures of the bespectacled lad while his mother describes the poor boy's heartbreaking, horrified reaction to the news.

I wonder what urgent message the parents are trying to get across that is worth their exposing their children's private agony on national TV. The girl is about five years old, the boy, maybe ten. I can understand what makes some transvestite in a trailer park want to fly to Chicago to tell his story. But what motivates a doctor and his wife to risk turning their children into objects of pity, at best, and at worst into objects of ridicule?

Nothing, as far as I can tell. To get on TV. On the show, the father's central point is the clichéd, palpable untruth that only massive government effort stands between AIDS and its cure. "If we can send a man to the moon, if we can harvest nuclear energy, we can come up with something to prevent this disease," says Lipschitz, perhaps forgetting that many other diseases, affecting far greater numbers of people, have so far thwarted intense efforts to cure them. Just because we cured polio does not mean, prima facie, that we can cure cancer or, for that matter, AIDS.

The wife's opinions are even more ludicrous. "You know what this disease has done?" Stein says. "It has empowered me to stand up and fight."

She never explains what she is standing up and fighting against. Clumsy doctors? Deceitful husbands? For the elusive cure? For "education," the rubric under which all manner of victims spout their tales?

But the content of the message doesn't matter—a nod to Marshall McLuhan. What's important is to go on TV and deliver a message. To raise awareness, whatever that means.

Balancing what slim good might come from their appearance is the potential harm of adults trotting out children's inner pain in order to entertain viewers. The phenomenon reaches an epitome later in the program, when a fourteen-year-old girl named Laura Campbell reads the letter she sent to the show, addressed to Greg Louganis, who had also appeared a few weeks earlier to promote his tell-all book. Oprah begins to read the letter, has second thoughts, and abruptly hands it to the girl and tells her to read it herself. The girl reads a painful missive about diving being her only possible ticket to college because she isn't very smart. "I, too, have considered suicide," she reads.

The moment she finishes the letter, Oprah shifts to a buoyant sixty-eight-year-old grandmother, sitting next to the girl, who reads a gushing love note to Louganis. The diver is then brought out from the wings—the "surprise" these shows repeat again and again. He hugs the girl and the grandmother, mouths some platitudes, and is gone. The show ends, never returning to the teenager or addressing her wrenching letter. She is packed off from whence she came, presumably to cope in her own fashion with this latest twist in her sad life.

No headshaking now, no distancing herself from her audience. This is Oprah Winfrey's meat and potatoes, and the true horror of her show, the stench I had been reluctant to inhale.

I reassure myself that at least the classmates of the doctor's kids and this girl are in school. Perhaps word won't get back to them. What do kids care about Oprah Winfrey?

As if a rebuke to this cheery thinking, Thursday's show is devoted to letters from children. The thought occurs to me that, just as the *New York Times* crossword puzzles start out easy on Monday and get progressively harder as the week goes on, so perhaps Oprah's show starts mildly on Monday, then builds, growing more invasive and awful as the week progresses. Who knows? By Friday, she could have a show on dying people begging for a last sip of water.

The audience for Thursday's show is packed with children, and volunteers are shown sorting through brimming cartons of letters. Oprah does not wear a rough cloak or carry a crooked staff, but every other indication shows that she has assumed her St. Oprah pose. "Sometimes I feel really helpless," Oprah admits, in the requisite initial display of humility. "There's no way I can reach out to every child who writes."

But she tries. Oprah's idea of reaching out and helping is demonstrated when three very obese girls, among the many who wrote in pleading for help, are displayed on-stage. One, who reads in her letter that she is twelve years old and 246 pounds, begins weeping the moment the cameras turn on her. The second, also twelve, reads her letter, telling of the anguish of being close to 200 pounds, of suffering low self-esteem, in the shadow of a beautiful sister, of being teased, called "a fat whale." The third watches, her mouth clenched.

Just bringing out these unfortunate people, spotlighting their woes, then drop-kicking them back to their dismal lives would be too bald, the cruelty too transparent. So Oprah, the secular saint, must feign some sort of attempt to heal them.

Oprah utters the ritual admission that in the short moment together she is not going to help anyone, then proceeds to pretend to do so anyway. "You can stay heavy, but if you want to lose it, I can give you a plan," says Oprah, holding a girl's hand. The plan isn't revealed on the program. Perhaps because it involves a private chef, a personal trainer, and lots of down time at expensive spas. Oprah promises to explain her plan to the girls after the show, and vows to follow up on their cases. It's not hard to imagine Oprah following up—if the plan for some reason works. I can see svelte teens being paraded on some future show, amid film clips of heavy former selves, much applause, and hosannas to the power of St. Oprah. I can't see the girls ever returning if they fail. ("Fat Girls Who Weren't Helped by Celebrities—Next on Oprah!")

Oprah is not satisfied with this little tableau of ailment and proffered cure, however. As if to top herself, she manages an even greater distillation of everything obscenely wrong with these shows in general and hers in particular. A quiet, fourteen-year-old girl named Chaka materializes, with *her* letter to Oprah.

"My life is pretty messed up," she reads. "Mom died when I was ten. Dad is in jail. I sit and cry every night. Sometimes I wake up and I feel dead."

Quite a job for Oprah, who again begins with the initial show of modesty, almost a legal caveat. "We're not going to solve her problem in the few minutes we have," Oprah says, then, as always, gives it a go. A surrogate

Oprah is brought in—therapist Christine Honeyman, planted in the audience. On cue, Honeyman rises to utter a few meaningless phrases of therapist's gibberish.

"You will never lose your relationship with your mother; it's an inside relationship," she says, then adds this helpful suggestion: "Imagine your mom tucking you in at night."

That grotesque trivialization still hanging in the air, Oprah wades in with her wisdom. She skews the problem of a dead mom and a felon dad into hormones. "This four-teen, honey, it whipped my butt," she says, citing her own history of abuse and promiscuity. To Oprah's surprise and evident disappointment, however, Chaka does not warm to this pair of momentarily concerned adults and their television advice. Her face remains flat, she responds to Oprah's demand to know if she's feeling better by whispering a crushed little "Yes." Oprah leans forward, staring hard, wanting better evidence than this that the girl's woes have been lightened, goddamn it. She begins to turn the screws.

"I hope it helped a little bit," she coos. No answer. "I hope the airplane ride helped," Oprah adds hopefully. Still nothing. "Hope the hotel helped." Still nothing from the little ingrate, and Oprah gives up, her patience at an end. She looks at the audience with a "Can you believe this?" shrug and indulges in a bit of sarcasm. "Hope something helped," she says.

No matter. The intransigently dour girl is whisked away and the carnival continues. That Oprah Winfrey, her-self a victim of abuse, should be the ringmaster in this me-dieval spectacle of torment is ironic but then, I suppose, fitting, since the abused invariably go on to become abusers themselves, though not typically in such a public fashion. Perhaps in twenty years Chaka, in keeping with the looser standards of the day, will host a TV show on which kids are tied to radiators and beaten with electrical cords.

It continues. A girl reads a poem critical of her delinquent dad, who, of course, is there, and Oprah extracts a promise from him that he will mend his ways. No stubborn clinging to one's problems here—adults know when to fake reform. Two teenage friends who had been separated for almost an entire year are—surprise, surprise—reunited. Oprah hugs them as they hug: a happy, hugging threesome to bring the show to its final segment, where Oprah is surrounded by kids, answering their questions about her first "official" kiss and whether the studio has ghosts.

One girl almost spoils it. She floats her "theory" that talk shows are the spiritual heirs of circus freak shows. "Why are people obsessed with seeing deformed people?" she asks, catching Oprah off guard—the peril of live television. "You can think about it if you like," the girl suggests helpfully, filling time for her flustered host, who of course cannot think about it. These shows are, if nothing else, a running affront to thought. Pause for five seconds to form an answer and you might as well go home.

Oprah, ignoring the substance of the question, addresses instead its implicit criticism of her program.

"I think our show over the years has evolved," she says. "I've gotten older and matured. I have grown." Sadly, Oprah notes, the rest of the industry has not followed her example.

"I think television is bad for the most part, don't you?" Oprah says. "It's really bad."

Friday's show is about miracles, according to the dramatic promo. A Virgin Mary is shown weeping "real tears." A crucifix turns to gold. "A teenage girl is cured of leukemia," Oprah Winfrey says.

That's what years of evolution, maturation and growth will do to the quality of a television show, I suppose.

A week after I sent the above to the publisher's, I found myself appearing, irony of ironies, on the "Oprah Winfrey Show." The show's theme was "Second Chances," and one of the producers knew somehow that I had written a book on failure, and decided I should be brought out at the end of the program to dispense some sort of wisdom.

They screened me well. A producer spoke to me for probably an hour on the telephone, over three separate conversations, wanting to know how I would respond to a variety of questions and situations. She never asked if I disdained Oprah or loathed her program, and I, visions of sales figures dancing in my head, didn't volunteer the information.

I was told to arrive at the windowless, fortresslike Harpo Studios three hours before the program began. It would be taped—live television must not have boosted ratings enough to counterbalance its discomfort. To my surprise, I had to go through two metal detectors—first the regular, airport-type walk-through, then a personal pat-down by a lady with an electronic wand. Standing with my arms straight out, being frisked, I wondered, "Did

Michael Jordan go through this?" There was no body cavity check, however. Careless.

I found myself in one of several Green Rooms which, contrary to everything I had heard about such places, actually was green—the walls, the carpeting, the furniture.

To pass the hours, I made small talk with the other guests in the room. The couple sitting across from me were from Alabama. "We live in a double-wide," confided the husband, a tall, gaunt fellow, referring to a type of house trailer.

"Of course you do," I thought, and almost said aloud.

Slim young women in brightly colored mini-skirt suits came charging in every few minutes, eyes wild with suppressed panic, clipboards clutched to chests. They were producers, and would usher in a new person, or take somebody away, or simply introduce themselves and disappear, never to be seen again. One brought a form which, as far as I could tell, gave Oprah possession of the copyright to my book and forbade me from ever mentioning her name or describing my experiences on her show. I crossed out the lines of the form that I felt might cause trouble later on, guessing correctly that none of the harried young women would check to see whether I had amended the document before signing it.

We on-deck guests were all too wound up about the prospect of appearing before millions of viewers to touch the unappetizing pile of cellophane-wrapped muffins that had been kindly heaped into a basket by representatives of the richest woman after Queen Elizabeth. Like any strangers, we talked about the weather and, as talk show guests, we compared the perks that had lured us onto the show—airplane rides, hotel rooms, free meals. I was definitely the cheap date of the group—I got nothing. On the phone, I hadn't even had the presence of mind to ask that they pick me up in a limo. Her studio is fifteen minutes from my home. I drove.

In keeping with the show's theme, all the guests had committed some gaffe in their lives and wanted to have another chance. The wife from Alabama had flunked English in high school and didn't graduate with her class. A new bride's wedding had been "ruined" because her father didn't walk her down the aisle. A contestant on "Wheel of Fortune" had blurted out the wrong letter and been eliminated.

I wish I could say that I had mixed feelings about appearing on a show I had just finished castigating. But writing a book does strange things to you. The metaphor I use is that it is like your children being kidnapped and held for ransom at bookstores across America. You'll do almost anything to free them. If the show was on exterminating pets, and I was asked to go on with a few cuddly puppies and drown them in a bucket, I might have qualms. But if it helped sales. . . .

After a three-hour wait I was ushered into the studio, which, to my surprise, was set up in the round—four risers filled with, mostly, women, surrounding a circle of carpeting. A producer took me up to Oprah, who was holding a wireless microphone in her right hand, and introduced us. Oprah stuck out her left hand and, after puzzling a moment over this social quandary, I too stuck out my left. When in Rome, as they say. We shook hands in reverse fashion.

"Wrong hand," Oprah said as we shook. I indicated the mike in her right, and she transferred it to her left hand and we shook again in the proper style. This bizarre bit of business out of the way, a technician brought a single stuffed chair and set it at the center of the circle. I sat in the chair, alone in this ring of carpet, and regarded the bank of bright lights overhead, Oprah Winfrey directly in front of me and her audience of fans all around. For a panicky moment I convinced myself that Oprah had somehow found out about this new book, and that I was about to be subjected to some sort of trial, an auto-da-fé where I would be forced, on national television, to fall to my knees and recant my writings. Well, if it helps sales . . .

Instead, everyone got a second chance. A church wedding, complete with father, had been arranged for the disappointed bride. The Alabama woman got to wear a cap and gown and receive her diploma from her high school principal. The friends of the woman who blew her game show chance threw a "G" party to help her get over her trauma.

Watching the little tableaux of renewal, I couldn't help but reflect how lucky we Americans are. No graduation. A wedding glitch. A game show blunder. These are the regrets we weep over for the rest of our lives, the tragedies that cause us to pound our chests. Not quite Andromache watching her son Astyanax hurled off the walls of Troy. Not quite wishing you had built a stronger boat before setting out for the refugee camps in Thailand.

I tried, when I could wrench a chance to speak away from Oprah, to politely point out the falsity behind the entire premise of the show, to explain that one should not think of "second chances" but should view life as a steady chain of effort and, regularly, failure. Neither Oprah nor the other guests seemed to hear a word.

It was all over very quickly. Oprah, shadowed by big bodyguards, worked the crowd a bit. People seemed to be thrusting notes at her and pleading special little cases. I half expected someone to hold up a crippled child, but nobody did. Perhaps they cull them out at the door.

Usually on TV shows the host will come up afterward and say something about how the show went. But Oprah and her entourage merely worked their way to the studio exit and were gone. Perhaps she was in a hurry to go explain her diet plan to fat girls. I was left to find my own way out. At the street door, a smiling woman gave me a special signature "Oprah Winfrey Show" mug and herded me toward the limousines, waiting to ferry guests in luxury to the airport. It took a moment for me to convey the fact that I had driven myself—my car was parked across the street from the entrance. Perhaps I imagined it, but the woman seemed a bit shocked—maybe I was the first guest on Oprah's show to arrive under his own power.

What surprised me most about the entire experience was how many people watch and are impressed by Oprah's program, which is broadcast three times a day in Chicago—literally morning, noon and night. A reporter from my alma mater's newspaper—whom I had sent my book to months earlier and never heard from—called within days of the broadcast, eager for an interview. Several high school acquaintances whom I hadn't spoken to in years called up—more than had phoned regarding the publication of any book I had ever written. One high school friend, who had last called me after an appearance on "Good Morning America," left a brief, gushing message on my voice mail. "Cathy," I admonished the telephone receiver, while deleting the message and hanging up, "you watch too much television."

P Is for Politician

Ralph J. Perk was mayor of Cleveland during its nadir in the mid-1970s. The city was a laughingstock. The budget was hemorrhaging. Cleveland had to sell its own transit and sewer systems in order to raise money.

And Perk was not exactly the dynamic man of the hour. One of the few Republican mayors at the time, he had a definite mini-Nixon thing going—baggy gray suit, widow's peak, funny nose.

Perk's Republican connection helped siphon federal dollars to the city. But what made Perk famous in Cleveland was his setting his own hair on fire during the opening ceremony of a steel plant—they handed Perk a running acetylene torch to cut a ribbon and he scratched his ear, or something, and set his head on fire. For years, news photos of the event were clipped to bulletin boards all over Cleveland. They might still be posted, for all I know.

The burning hair episode meshed well with the then

recent ignition of the Cuyahoga River, and while Perk might have been a loving father and grandfather and a skilled mayor, Perk's setting his hair on fire is his entire legacy in Cleveland—it's all I remember about him and, I would wager, all anybody remembers.

Politicians had it all. Money. Power. Prestige. The fawning press would wink and raise a glass as they filled their pockets with boodle and their beds with eager paramours.

Then they blew it. Whether you trace the change back to Nixon or to Boss Tweed, the proverbial camel's back was at some point snapped, irrevocably, and what had once been a love feast turned into a gynecological exam.

Oh, sure, they still have some money. And a measure of power. Occasional prestige. And the eager paramours, they're still around somewhere, back in the shadows.

But politics has changed. Fifty years after the American public was politely screened from even glimpsing their President attempting to stand on his crippled legs, the current President is commonly portrayed as a disgusting species of damp pervert, a soulless, amoral monster whose only immutable quality is a fierce, animalistic instinct to try to get himself reelected, something base and primeval, like a salmon fighting upstream to spawn.

And that is what his *friends* say. . . .

I can't comprehend why anybody would run for office. Nobody who watched Mel Reynolds go down could consider it. The Chicago congressman, who went to prison for having sex with a sixteen-year-old campaign aide, expired like an animal caught in barbed wire, writhing and thrashing and emitting horrible cries. Just when you thought it was finally over, he would let out another whimper and thrash around some more. Awful.

Politicians have always had enemies, of course. Congress has been viewed as a nest of vipers and crooks since its inception. Jefferson was tarred as a pervert, too, creeping into the slave quarters at Monticello at night.

But the damnation of politicians always had a sense of outrage to it, of exception. Now there is a sort of weary indifference, an expectation of venality, corruption and incompetence, that is somehow worse. I can't think of a politician alive whom I admire—and I bet you can't either. People who believe in politicians are either zealots or dupes. Either a fiery-eyed fanatic backing one of his own to promote the policies revealed by God Almighty, or one of those obese boobs with the Styrofoam straw hats plastered with little flags and bumper stickers. Swell choice.

I'm used to holding my nose and voting—anyone casting ballots for both Michael Dukakis and Walter Mondale has got to have developed a pretty tough hide by now. But still, I'm planning to go into the voting booth in one of those full body radiation suits this year. Holding your nose just won't do the trick anymore.

Of course, I'm assuming that I will vote for Clinton again. I may not. I'm tempted to vote for Dole, who has the benefit of being a figure of pathos. A twisted survivor, both physically and mentally, staring out from behind the bars of his self-constructed cage. So old. So out of it. The grim, scary uncle, leaning on the bar at the family reunion, watching the light refract through his glass of scotch and railing about how his business went belly up and his kids hate him.

I feel real affection for Dole—half sympathy, half

pity—the same emotion eventually extended toward his mentor, Nixon. After the loathing subsided, that is, once Nixon was humiliated one last time, finally hounded from office, declawed and hung up on a nail. That Steve Martin line about him at San Clemente—"walking along the beach in San Clemente, all by himself, with big old shorts on, a metal detector"—was not only funny but sad and true.

This book goes to press long before the November election, but if Dole somehow wins, I can't say I'll be sorry. Poor old guy. Let him be President. What does it matter? That was the liberating glory of Ronald Reagan. When he was elected in 1980, I fully expected the world to end. I was definitely, sincerely convinced that Reagan would kill us all. I fully and honestly thought he would wake up from his nap one day, order martial law, and then fire the missiles toward Russia, thinking he was in a movie. If we can survive eight years of *him,* we can survive anybody (assuming we have survived, assuming the debt-burdened economy doesn't collapse around our heads about 2025—Ronald's Revenge, they'll call it).

The horror of politicians is that, when you finally do get a good one, they go away. Chicago's Mayor Harold Washington was like a figure from fiction—an outsized, good-humored, tough-minded man whom people loved, really *loved.* Aside from his good qualities as an individual and a mayor, he also represented something symbolic to every single black person in Chicago—that the power structure, the good life that had been denied to them for so long, that they had been forced to stare at through the kitchen window for decades, shut out and trumped, could be opened up. All it took was guts and brashness and cunning, with which Harold Washington was amply endowed.

Then he died, in 1987, three years into his term, at age sixty-three, of a massive coronary. It would have been better if somebody had shot him—an embittered white precinct captain who lost his patronage job, for instance. That would have provided some tangible focus of hatred and grief. As it was, his death seemed the malevolent work of a cruel and capricious fate. For several years after he died, Harold's supporters grabbed wildly at the air, hoping to extend his legacy without him. But he was gone.

Of course, it might be argued that premature exit is exactly what makes politicians beloved. Had JFK stuck around, he might have been known as the guy who embroiled us in Vietnam, then embarrassed the nation by resigning in 1967 to marry Mia Farrow.

Try to think of a politician who was both beloved *and* long-lived? Difficult, isn't it? Winston Churchill got the big boot right after winning World War II. Harry Truman hung on long enough to become a saint, but it was popularity he never enjoyed while in office. Thomas Dewey is still pinching himself, somewhere in heaven, wondering how he lost in 1948.

One comes to mind: Paul Simon. Not wildly popular, but certainly respected and, in my house, loved. The senator from Illinois was so wholesome that he seemed a throwback to another age, as if Lincoln turned up, alive in the Rose Garden, paring an apple with a pocket knife and asking, laconically, what some red-nosed gazoo was doing in his office.

Simon was the only politician I ever bumped into in

the city, like a regular human being, without coat-holders or security men or supernumeraries carrying standards proclaiming "SPQR." Once I ducked into the Executive House Hotel to buy some cigars at the gift shop. Simon was there, standing behind a pillar, gazing anxiously out at the street. He was waiting for a car, he told me. The other time was at the Auditorium Theater, during intermission at a concert. He and his wife were mingling with the other patrons. As if they were real people.

Of course, Simon too is ducking out, part of the massive bolt for the exits that is one of the most vexing developments on the political stage in recent years. Dinosaurs like Strom Thurmond cling to office with all their preternatural might, waiting for Death to pry their clenched fingers off the fasces of power. While basic honest legislators like Simon simply throw up their hands and walk away. Like the captain in that classic *New Yorker* cartoon, tossing a leg over the rail of the sinking ship and telling the startled second in command, "Congratulations! You're captain now."

I only saw Ronald Reagan once. He was speaking before a huge throng of cheering students at the College of Du-Page in 1984. I was covering the speech for a newspaper. The COD band played a variety of rousing songs to crank up the crowd while we waited for his arrival. Reagan showed up onstage, unexpectedly, right in the middle of that song from *Flashdance,* "Maniac." The band segued smoothly from "Maniac" into "Hail to the Chief." Certainly a coincidence, but one that has given me comfort over the ensuing years nevertheless.

I was not always such a cynic about politics. In fact, for one season I was something of an idealist. In the autumn of 1972, almost every day after junior high school I would go to the McGovern headquarters on Front Street in Berea and stuff envelopes and make phone calls and practice defacing Nixon bumper stickers. I got quite good at it—a single snip could transform a NIXON NOW sticker into a NIXON NO sticker.

The election was very simple in my mind. Nixon was evil personified, a demon who would ruin the country utterly. There was no policy motive behind this—I wasn't anti-Vietnam, or pro-pot, or anything like that. I hadn't inherited the position from my parents. My father, in fact, refused to put a MCGOVERN/SHRIVER sticker on the bumper of the station wagon, saying that it was against the law for government scientists to publicly declare political positions. I think he was afraid of vandalism.

It was just a conviction I felt. I had known Nixon was bad since the time he ran in 1968, when I was in second grade. Our teacher let us watch his inaugural speech in school, and I came home and told my parents that I was surprised how well Nixon had spoken, despite my reservations about him. My father told me I should write him a letter and tell him—maybe the President would write me back! I made a face and declined. Even at seven, I knew better than to suck up to Nixon.

My current political outlook was formed the night McGovern lost. My father and I went to hear a lecture by Russell Baker at Baldwin-Wallace College. When we went in, the polls were still open on the West Coast. When we came out, McGovern had lost forty-nine states. I remember standing in our living room, with my coat still on, watching Walter Cronkite read the tallies, and crying—me, not him. It wasn't that McGovern had lost. I knew he was going to lose. But forty-nine states. It seemed like the country had gone mad. They had not simply elected Satan, but reelected him. I realized then that the general population is a malleable mass that will go anywhere, given the proper herding techniques, and nothing I've learned since then has caused me to question that understanding.

Years later I met George McGovern. He was on the SALT 2 hearings committee, and I, by merit of sort of dating a senator's daughter, momentarily, attended one of the hearings. After the session adjourned, I went up to McGovern and babbled about how important he had been to me in 1972. He was very gracious.

I prefer to think of him that way: tall, august, with the marble and velvet edifice of the Senate committee room behind him, driving the Democratic spear up the butts of the missile mongers, and not the glimpse I had of him, years later, on "Saturday Night Live," dressed as a general and playing with army men. I stood frozen in front of the TV set, flashing back to Walter Cronkite and 1972.

I'm not sure why he did it—maybe he was trying to impress his grandchildren, or earn a little pin money, or spit in the eye of his legacy of failure and defeat.

But all I could think of was the tragic Emil Jannings character at the end of *The Blue Angel,* having ruined himself over Marlene Dietrich, now part of her cabaret act, dressed as a chicken, humiliated, emitting pathetic little clucking noises onstage in front of his jeering former academic colleagues.

Why do they do that? Why do failed politicians drop their last shred of dignity in defeat and hawk Doritos and pizza and Diet Pepsi? How can they? Don't they realize that people—poor dumb, duped people—believed in them? When third-party candidate John Anderson, immediately after the 1980 election, dropped all pretense of caring about the future of the country and became a newscaster, I wanted to track him down and scream in his face, "You *cocksucker! I voted* for you! It was my first presidential ballot and I cast it for *you* and now you're going to read the news in upstate New York!?!?!"

Perk's successor in 1977 was Dennis Kucinich, the youngest mayor, at the time, ever elected in a major American city. Youngest, but not most popular. Taking the reins of a faltering city from Perk, Kucinich presided over Cleveland's slide into financial default and, one year into his term, was challenged with a recall vote mounted by his enemies, who argued that Kucinich was an incompetent.

He sure looked the part. Maybe five feet six, red hair, freckles, ugly, Kucinich was Howdy Doody without the strings. The already grim self-image of Clevelanders was exacerbated by the conviction that our mayor was Huck Finn, leading us on a poorly constructed raft down the river and toward the waterfall.

In the midst of his troubles, Kucinich visited my high school. His wife, Sandy, was an English teacher there, and active in the theater department. The mayor stopped by after a performance of *The Wizard of Oz* to congratulate our junior thespians and press the flesh.

I was a munchkin in Oz, sitting in a far corner of the

cafeteria that served as our backstage, watching the mayor work his way across the room. What astounded me, then and now, is how students—gangly teenagers, just learning about civics and Democracy's fierce torch—turned away from the mayor as he approached, busying themselves straightening makeup boxes, tying their shoes, coughing into their shoulders, or just walking away from Kucinich as he approached, as if he were diseased.

Q Is for Quackery

When my wife became pregnant with our first child earlier this year, I thought I had better get myself tested for Tay-Sachs, the genetic disease prominent among Jews. Ideally, I would have reversed the order—got the test *before* she became pregnant. But that would have required the intense Ninja discipline and long-term planning abilities of a better man than I. One does not tend to enter into a pregnancy saying: "Hey, honey, hold on, first let's see what horrific, fatal genetic disorders we might be carrying."

Also, I don't have a doctor and had no idea how to go about getting one. We have insurance, of course, but I can't imagine how it works. My wife knows—she's an attorney, after all. They teach them these things.

Normally my wife would have taken care of getting the test set up, since she knows that I'd be overwhelmed at the prospect. But I didn't want to leave it to her, this time. Perhaps inspired by the impending responsibility of fatherhood, I decided that I, myself, personally, would roll up my sleeves and handle the situation. Tay-Sachs would be my department. *I,* myself, personally, would make what I imagined would be countless phone calls to insurance agents, *my* ear would be pressed against receivers squawking endless hours of burbling Muzak. Who knows—maybe they make you stand barefoot overnight in the snow, like Martin Luther, before they give you permission to take a test nowadays. It wouldn't surprise me.

The first step, of course, was to determine the identity of our insurance company and seek out its phone number. It's in our files, somewhere, I know. I stood, poised at the precipice, ready to act. But at the last minute I chickened out and cheated. I instead phoned Children's Memorial Hospital, in Chicago, which I knew had invented the test for Tay-Sachs. I asked how much the test cost. They said $86. A chunk of change. But I figured, if I went through our insurance company, by the time the test was administered, I would have blown more than $86 worth of my time and the kid would be in kindergarten. I had already waited longer than I should, so immediacy seemed important.

Fine, I said. I would like to set up an appointment for a Tay-Sachs test. Do you take MasterCard?

When I showed up for my test, there was a little problem—a line on the form demanded the referring doctor's name. Yet no doctor had referred me. The admitting clerk was loath to leave the line blank. Nature hates a blank line. I explained that a referring doctor wasn't necessary, that I myself knew I should have the test. My wife and I are both from Eastern European Jewish stock—the mother lode of Tay-Sachs. My wife is pregnant, I said. One of us needs the test so that, if nothing else, we'll know to order a tiny coffin along with the layette. Here is my MasterCard. No doctor—or insurance necessary.

Paying directly for a medical procedure felt both quaint and invigorating, like baking bread. The admitting clerk looked befuddled, but he eventually issued me the proper blue plastic card and ushered me into the hospital.

This completely bollixed the system, and I was shifted from one department to another, from hematology to genetics to obstetrics, for about an hour. I worried I would feel a prick in my shoulder and wake up with a leg gone.

At one point a young Indian doctor walked into the waiting room and called my name, never looking up from the fat sheaf of papers attached to a clipboard in his hand. "Who's your physician?" he said mechanically. I went into my spiel, for the third or fourth time.

He looked at me, finally, his face slack with stupefaction, as if beholding a wonder. "You mean," he said, boggled, "you ordered your own *bloodwork?!?*"

That was worth $86 right there. Well, that, and finding out I don't carry the disease.

I won't attempt to explain how, in the span of my lifetime, the American medical establishment has managed to utterly ruin itself. I don't understand it myself, really. Money was involved, I'm sure, and expensive advances in technology, too. Beyond that, all I know is when I was five years old my family had a doctor, Dr. Joseph Hadden, a kindly, skilled man, who would come out to our house when I was sick and sit at the foot of my bed, rummaging through his big black doctor's bag for a toy to give me before checking my infected ears.

It is a recollection so out of keeping with the rest of my life that at times I wonder if it could be some sort of static —somebody else's memory, perhaps from an Ohio farm in 1905—that somehow bled into my consciousness through that great psychic ether that everybody seems to believe in but me.

When I think hard, I realize that it really was me in that bed, under the red toy soldier bedspread (made of *burlap,* for God's sake, Ma, what were you thinking?).

Dr. Hadden was our family doctor for twenty-five years. He did well for himself, despite sometimes coming out to our home, despite being pleasant and competent, despite having an office without a dozen waiting rooms each with a color-coded flag system over the door, so more patients could be herded through at peak efficiency. When my sister had pericarditis, a serious heart disease, we even went to his house to have her examined, because it was an emergency. We found he lived in a sprawling country residence, complete with stables and horses. So he did okay.

In my adult years, I have rarely seen the same doctor twice. They seem to be constantly cycling through a game of musical chairs—perhaps they are always on the move to escape prosecution. None of them act like they ever want to see me again. Maybe that's my fault. I once told a doctor that I wasn't living right, I was eating too much, drinking too much, and I hoped he would help me get my life in order. I liked the thought of being "under a doctor's care." He looked at me as if I was crazy. Maybe I was.

The difficulty of receiving legitimate medical care has stoked the fires of quackery—which burn consistently throughout history—into a white-hot flame in recent years. While cost and paperwork push real treatment out of the reach of more and more people, cut-rate cures of dubious efficacy seem to be sprouting everywhere. You can't turn on the TV without seeing some mumbo-jumbo shouting swami, or herbologist, or chiropractor, or health guru outlining his particular shortcut to eternal health.

The connection was pressed home to me after an editor at the *Sun-Times* got the idea of Chinese herbal medicine into her head. I don't know how. Maybe she went down to Chinatown for dim sum and noticed a box of ginseng tea. Maybe she rented *Gremlins*, with its opening scene of a gnomelike Chinaman pharmacist and his dark shop filled with odd boxes and mystic powders. She liked the thought of such a store being found in Chicago, a place where ancient Chinese ladies—perhaps still hobbling on bound feet—would mince in to purchase their tiger root balm and ground elk antler.

So I was dispatched to Cermak and Wentworth, to Chicago's Chinatown, to hang out at the half dozen herbalists and Chinese pharmacies. Since reality rarely conforms to uninformed preconception, there was a story, but not the one my editor had anticipated. The customers, every single one, were African-American women, double-parking their cars on Cermak and running in to pick up boxes of Pain No More and Female Relief and Healthy Brain. The only Chinese ladies were behind the counters.

Here was a genuine mystery. Why were African-American women journeying to Chinatown to buy Asian folk remedies? The answer was not obvious but made perfect sense when it was explained to me. Chinatown is on the South Side, near depressed areas where the only access to health care for many comes from the scant mercy of the county, which generally means sitting for six hours in the lobby of Cook County Hospital, sometimes only to be turned away. Better to drop $10 for a Chinese remedy that also may or may not help, but at least is quicker.

And some "herbal" remedies, it turned out, contain a wallop of prescription narcotic (for instance Cow Head Pills, for a while a national fad, were found to contain that ancient curative, Valium, which did not prevent aficionados from protesting the government's banning import of the pills, claiming the feds were in cahoots with the medical establishment conspiracy, trying to hobble superior Chinese pharmacology).

The Valium tucked into the Cow Head Pills points to another tradition in quack medicine. In earlier years they might not have cured your tuberculosis, but they gave you enough alcohol or opium or whatever that, for the moment, you didn't really care.

Is it any surprise that patent medicines were and are so popular? It was patent medicine vendors, after all, who struck upon the idea of sugar-coating their concoctions, the better to go down paying customers' throats. Medical doctors, on the other hand, thought the more vile a substance, the better it drove out disease, and were not reluctant to administer dung or urine or worse to their patients.

In fact, solicitousness and quackery so often go hand in hand, while true medicine has developed such a thick crust of indifference, they seem the natural assignment of those qualities. So even if I met a modern-day Dr. Hadden, who was really, really worried about me, and was heading over to my house right now with his black bag to check me out, that alone would be enough to make me doubt his competency. "If you're a real doctor, then why do you care about my health?" I would say, barring the door.

Let's not go overboard. Since our baby was born, we've found a very good pediatrician—Dr. Janice Salem—who always returns our frantic phone calls with a dollop of soothing advice: "No cause for alarm. The yellow liquid dripping out of your baby is urine. Completely normal. Just change his diaper and he'll be fine."

So there is at least one good doctor, and I'm sure there are others, lone warriors struggling against a system gone mad. Any doctor who paid full price for this book, for instance, I assume is extraordinarily skilled and compassionate. Those who checked it out of the library, perhaps a little less so.

And while I am backpedaling, I do not want to completely equate quackery and modern medicine. Taking penicillin is not the same as swallowing a crystal. But I do want to recognize a porousness to the border between them, a shifting of qualities. Much of what strikes us now as the most obscene and medieval malpractice—bloodletting and such—was at one point an accepted standard of medicine. And at the same time standard medicine once shunned and abhorred what we now consider good care, sometimes in the very recent past.

In the early 1960s the American Medical Association blasted those who sought to lower their cholesterol by reducing their intake of fats, warning "the antifat, anti-cholesterol fad is not just foolish and futile," but "it also carries some risk." They collaborated with the cigarette companies at one point, too. The entire history of the AMA, in fact, reads more like a medieval guild hall trying to suppress competition than any sort of ethical professional organization trying to rein in dubious practices.

I collared Howard Wolinsky, the medical writer at the

Sun-Times, and asked him about quackery, figuring he would direct me to the freshest and most fantastic excesses currently on the health care scene—the most obvious fake remedies, the most wildly popular frauds and delusions.

Not quite.

"Well," he said, scratching an ear. "If you define quackery as promising something you can't deliver, or charging too much for what you do deliver, then about 85 percent of current medical practice is quackery."

Then he walked away.

Quackery is one of those annoyances that you barely notice until you look for it. Then suddenly you see it everywhere. A few blocks from my house is a Barnes & Noble bookstore, whose shelves contain more patent medicine puffery than a dozen Victorian tent shows.

A quick scan of the store's "Health" section underscores the argument that, if there has been one central development in twentieth-century quackery, it is the driving of dubious cures into the realm of nutrition, where law has a harder time reaching them.

Some books, just by their titles, put themselves foursquare into the realm of quackery. How can *Stop Aging Now* by Jean Carper deliver, unless it instructs you how to kill yourself? I don't care what Deepak Chopra tells you to do in *Perfect Health.* The result is guaranteed to fall short of the title's promise. How could it not?

Earl Mindell's Food as Medicine starts out, as most do, with a base of sound dietary and nutritional ideas—eat roughage; don't drink liquid butter; that kind of thing— then lets loose a blizzard of dubious claims, all based on trends and studies and couched in enough qualifiers to render them meaningless anyway.

When Earl Mindell writes, "A tomato a day may be the difference between developing cancer and living cancer free," he is of course technically correct, but the eye of the careful reader will zero in on the word "may." Conditional qualifiers—"may" and "might" and "could"—have let slip more questionable medical data than an army of top-hatted patent medicine barkers.

Earl Mindell would be equally correct writing, "Twirling around three times and shouting, 'Cancer be gone!' may be the difference between developing cancer and living cancer free." The question is, do we want to take his advice and eat our daily tomato, religiously, while Earl Mindell slips out the back door of that convenient "may"? He cites as evidence the ubiquitous "recent studies" that the lycopene in tomatoes will "lower the risk" of cancer, which already undermines his previous claim, since lowering the risk of cancer and "living cancer free" are two entirely different creatures. I "lower the risk" in Russian roulette by using a revolver with six chambers instead of five; but that doesn't guarantee that I am going to live bullet-in-the-head free.

The key when reading these books is to take a good hard look at the disclaimers in the front. Earl Mindell's says, "The ideas, procedures and suggestions contained in this book are not intended to replace the services of a health professional." Could he be suggesting that you might want to check out those mysterious lumps *despite* your daily tomato? Richard Gerber, M.D., starts his *Vibrational Medicine* with the caveat that the book is not "meant to give specific recommendations of advice for the treatment of particular illnesses," or "intended to be a replacement for good medical diagnosis and treatment." Could he somehow be suggesting that you shouldn't stake your life on the efficacy of the "flower essences, crystal healing, therapeutic touch, acupuncture, radionics, electrotherapy, herbal medicine, psychic healing" and other mystic hoo-ha delineated in his book?

I wish just once somebody would write, in the small-print warning by their book's copyright information: "None of the cryptic bullshit contained in this book is intended as anything beyond a pretty fantasy designed to occupy the credulous and desperate." Sales probably wouldn't be affected.

It gets worse. Right next door to the Barnes & Noble is a sprawling marketplace called Sherwyn's Health Food. Sherwyn's has a full supermarket of organic beans and violence-free apples, plus a huge pharmacy-like area filled with bottles of medicine . . . excuse me, *vitamins* and *supplements,* all claiming to help prevent any medical malady possible.

Sometimes the fakery is subtle. You have to read the bold guarantee of Nature's Plus Source of Life a couple times to realize what they're saying—"Guaranteed burst of energy within two hours or your money back on your unopened bottle," may sound reassuring at first. But how can you try the pills without opening the bottle?

The books at Sherwyn's make those at their neighbor seem as grounded as *The Joy of Cooking.* I could not stop myself from purchasing *Sharks Don't Get Cancer* by Dr. I. William Lane and Linda Comac, just so I could study it leisurely at home.

My first thought was that the authors would be encouraging people to eat raw, living sturgeon and old tires and whatever else it is that sharks subsist on

The reality was better than that. Eat the sharks—shark cartilage to be precise—and you too can be cancer free. I particularly relished this advice since the idea of imbuing oneself with the attributes of a particular animal by eating it is among the oldest mystical notions of mankind. Ancient kings ate lion flesh to assume the courage of the lion and, to this day, rhinos are threatened with extinction because old gentlemen in Singapore are convinced that, by eating ground rhino horn, their Little Wee Kim Wees will be blessed with a rhino horn's arching, rock-solid tumescence.

And by the way, sharks *do* get cancer, something that even the authors admit, explaining that *Almost No Sharks Get Cancer* would have been "a rotten title."

After reading the book, I searched out shark cartilage, huge bottles of which just so happened to be on a nearby shelf at Sherwyn's. The first bottle I picked up, Cartilade, cost $89.95 for 300 capsules, or about 50 days' worth. After I caught my breath, I picked up an even larger bottle—$279.98, for a brand called BeneFin, again with about a month and a half's worth of dosage. A note on the BeneFin label read: "Compassionately priced," a claim whose bold hypocrisy I had to admire, since it both implied the crap was not only economical but was kept so out of basic human mercy for the desperate user. Some $2,000 a year, with tax, for something which will keep cancer away as well as Ovaltine.

And excuse me, but aren't sharks *fish?* Nuzzling their young with a humanlike affection, blah blah blah? Sherwyn's is a vegetarian store, filled with tofu burgers and soy protein chili and animal liberation magazines. How come running tests on animals is bad for cancer research, but you can pitch them into the grinder if your crazed belief system suspects their bones will keep cancer away? (I noticed, next to the shark cartilage, "100% pure bovine cartilage"—$159.95 for 375 capsules. How does that differ morally from steak? The label made the amusing claim that the cartilage came "from range-grown, certified hormone-free cattle." Range-grown, as if they were corn.

Around the corner from Sherwyn's is a General Nutrition Center—sort of a health food for the bulked-up set—hawking its "Alive Total Wellness Program," whose literature is filled with gnostic imprecations, no doubt written with one eye toward obeying the letter of the law regarding the Food and Drug Act. "The energy formula uses herbal ingredients such as Ginkgo, Bilba, Garlic, Echinacea, and Guarana to naturally lift the spirits and boost energy levels," it cries.

And I hadn't even gotten off one city block in Chicago.

I can't address quackery without pointing out that I am fortunate enough not to be sick. These cures are craved, in part, by people who are desperately ill, and it is not good poker to laugh at sick people.

But my time will come someday. It comes for everybody, though admittedly not in the same fashion. I am hoping that I follow in the footsteps of my grandfathers, who both took sick and died very quickly—my father's father in the span of time it took him to hit the sidewalk; my mother's father within two hours of feeling ill. Such a rapid, unexpected end is harder on the surviving family, but in the end a blessing for all concerned.

Should I not be lucky enough to get it quick, and instead it comes on slow, I hope that I have the fortitude not to zip off to Mexico to grovel in the entranceways of peach-pit clinics. I hope I don't blow my kid's inheritance by journeying out to some mesa in Arizona so a dimestore Hopi shaman can smear guava jelly on my afflicted areas.

The key is to live your life well, so that when the end comes you're ready, and you don't go freezing your amputated head in a ridiculous and vain effort to wring more years out of life, a final gesture of ingratitude in the face of a world which, after all, had the good grace to put you here in the first place, albeit for a shorter time than most would like.

Of course you never know how you'll behave when the crunch comes. Maybe I'll panic too, and rush out to build a pyramid the moment the first lab reports come back.

Situations tend to cloud your mind. While I was in Kyoto, visiting the shrines, I studiously avoided participating in the Buddhist rituals—lighting incense, kowtowing and such—because it wasn't my gig, and seemed disrespectful, touristy.

Then I found myself in front of what was described to me as the Fountain of Eternal Life and Health. No kidding. People were lining up to drink from it, reaching over to its trickling waters with metal dippers which, in true Japanese form (and in apparent contradiction to the promise of the waters), were then passed under a disinfecting ultraviolet light. I figured, "Heck, I'm here," and lined up to drink. I mean, what if it worked? I'd hate to be on my deathbed, I later told my friends, screaming and straining against the straps while the doctors shrugged and puzzled, my final, desperate thought being: "I should have drunk from the goddamned fountain!"

The water was indeed cold and sweet. But on the other hand, it was free. I wouldn't have paid $279.95 for it. Not yet, anyway.

R Is for Rude

Thirty-five suited me fine, so far. My wife had slipped downstairs, prepared a delightful birthday breakfast, set out on the good china, and brought it up to me on a tray. Then came presents, a whole stack. The presents fit, and looked good, too. Showered and dressed, I thought I would celebrate such a propitious start to the day and year by lighting up one of the Cuban cigars I had smuggled out of Canada and taking it for a stroll down the street. I had never done this before—cigars before noon seemed, I don't know, decadent.

But heck, it was my birthday.

After several blocks, the calm that can emanate from a good cigar descended around me. I admired the full green leaves on the trees. Summer was just beginning. I thought about recent problems—they seemed so small, so far away and manageable. I brushed them from my mind with the back of my hand and smiled. Life was good. "Just maybe," I said, out loud, softly to myself, "maybe every-thing is going to be all right. . . ."

"STINK!" The shout was muffled, behind me, in the distance. But I could hear footsteps flapping up to me. A middle-aged woman came running, a jogger. "Stink!" she shouted. "That must be a cheap cigar—it stinks!"

I was caught completely off guard. "This is a Cuban," I said dully, looking at the cigar in my hand as if noticing it for the first time. "It wasn't cheap. You just don't know the difference because you're stupid."

"No, you're stupid, because you're smoking," she said, passing me now. We carried on in this embarrassing vein, calling each other stupid until she jogged past, down the block, and out of sight.

The exchange lingered with me, a foul taste in my mouth, for the rest of the day. Several days, really. I wasn't upset that I had discomfited the woman by smoking a cigar. I was outside. Smoking a cigar is not, as yet, illegal. It isn't even rude, to my knowledge. She could have crossed the street if it bothered her so much. Instead she ran up to me.

What annoyed me was the encounter. First, for its complete lack of the sort of Oscar Wildean wit I like to think I possess in my marrow. "You're stupid," while dis-playing a certain economy of form, is not exactly a riposte of Churchillian elegance.

Second, I was irked that the woman obviously felt she enjoyed license to criticize my behavior. She wouldn't go up to a city bus belching out smoke on the corner and start upbraiding the tailpipe—buses are our friends, and what would be the point? Nor would she approach some mas-sive, bearded gang member sitting astride his motorcycle, smoking a giant doobie. But because my behavior was voluntary, and something of a vice (vices being anything that both creates pleasure and is not essential to life), and because I am a doughy, bespectacled guy, someone open to her suasion, she felt free to attack me in any way she saw fit.

I am lucky she didn't shoot me.

What really bothered me, most of all, was the rudeness, on both sides. As the initiating, aggrieved party, she had an obligation to find some polite, clever way to upbraid me. "Such a fine day," she would say, wistfully looking at the treetops, "a shame to spoil it with a cigar." And gone. I, on the other hand, should never have snapped at her bait. "Or without one," I would reply, my eyes twinkling. We'd both feel better.

But comebacks are easy, after the fact, what Diderot called *l'esprit de l'escalier,* or staircase wit, for the good lines that come to you after an exchange, too late, on your way down to the street. Ingenuity wasn't even necessary. A startled, injured "I beg your pardon?" accompanied by a taken-aback fluttering of fingertips at sternum would have done more than all the hurled "stupids" in the world.

Whenever anybody writes about rudeness, the first, obvious temptation is to declare the current period in history a nadir of unprecedented incivility, the low point reached by society after years of tossing standards and values over the side like passengers hurling ballast off a sinking ship.

And there certainly is an argument to be made for that.

Nobody knows how to dress. They tumble into the streets, fresh from bed, it seems, wearing sweat pants, pajamas, bras, anything they like or practically nothing at all. They attend the opera in T-shirts, go to elegant restaurants in tank tops, wear cutoffs to court. I wore a suit to a funeral recently and found I was the only person to do so other than the funeral home employees—even the widower wore a sports shirt.

None of my friends can write a decent letter. They scribble postcards of thanks, jot notes in the margins of articles, write condolence letters on yellow Post-It notes.

Honorifics have faded away. The years when society agonized over "Ms." seem quaint now because the idea of calling anybody "Mister" or "Missus" or indeed anything other than "Motherfucker" is pretty much dead. Teenage store clerks read your first name off your credit card and address you as if you both were going to Riverdale High together.

The flip side of the rudeness caused by this creeping uninvited chumminess is the cold wall that technology often drops in front of people's brains. Countless salespeople have served me without ever taking their eyes off the computer screens in front of them—I want to reach over the counter, hook my fingers into their nostrils and angle their heads up thirty degrees or so. "Look at me, kiddo, not the computer," I'd say. "I'm the one paying for this."

On the other hand, much rudeness, such as that of the jogging woman, stems from the popularity of altering other people's behavior, or trying to. People feel free to violate any norm if they think it will lead to someone else's edification. Strangers will gladly step up and lecture you on your child-rearing abilities, your eating habits, your exercise posture. I'm amazed to see this again and again at restaurants, where the wait staff, freshly scrubbed and new to the working world, think nothing of critiquing your order. My brother and I sometimes drink wine at lunch, and while my request "We'll have a bottle of the Pinot Grigio" has not yet been met with "The hell you will," it's only a matter of time, what with all the startled looks and arched eyebrows and sly statements we usually receive. (One waitress asked breezily, "What are you celebrating?" to which I should have answered, "Finding a waitress who does her job—now get the wine.")

This tendency is a descendant, I believe, of the culture of protest and social action. What worked so nobly for civil rights or against the Vietnam War is now applied to every fanaticism and fringe fixation. The jogging woman obviously felt she had the moral high ground to handle me in any way she saw fit, since I was a polluter and a health criminal and thus had already removed myself from the fold of humanity.

The impulse baffles me. If, in her passing, the cellulite porridge at the back of the jogging woman's flabby thighs had sickened me, I would never scream, "Hey, porker, put on long pants!" That would be rude; we exist in the same world, particularly in cities, and it is the mark of civilization that we all try to tolerate and respect one another.

Cigar-hating harridans are only the beginning of the perils on the street, however. You have rollerblading twenty-somethings whipping by like comets, cloaked in the bullets-cannot-harm-us false immunity of youth. Neighbors lead their Great Pyrenees dogs, their Irish wolfhounds and Great Danes to your lawn to relieve themselves. (Unlike most city dwellers, I am not so much bothered by the shit itself as by the dog owners, screaming at 11 P.M. right under my window in an attempt to discipline their pea-brained charges. "Randy! Ran-DEE! RANDYYYYYYY!!! Be good! Sit! *Sit!* Randy! Ran-DEE! RANDYYYY!!!! No. NO! *NOOOOO!!!")*

I have not yet thrown on my pants, gone downstairs, gathered a bunch of somebody's shirt front in my fist and hissed: "If you scream at your damned dog one more time on this block I'm going to follow you home, kill you, kill the dog, and then burn your house down and sow the ground with salt so nothing will ever grow there again."

See what rudeness does? It replicates. I am typically the most courteous of persons, leaping up like a frog on a hot plate to offer my seat on the bus to an old person, reflexively holding doors open for strangers, male or female, offering my wife the larger half of the pie slice.

Yet somehow rudeness throws a switch in my head and suddenly I am screaming, cursing, falling to my knees and waving both extended middle fingers in the air, howling like a beast.

I think, in the final analysis, that is why the jogging lady bothered me so. Nothing angers someone like being lectured on what they already manifestly know. I am excruciatingly aware that most people hate the smell of cigar smoke. My wife hates it. I was walking the cigar outside because I had to. I would sooner melt chunks of tar on the kitchen stove burners than light up in my own home. In a bar, I wouldn't dream of smoking a cigar before taking a poll of the bartender, the manager, and all the patrons within sight, to see if they mind, or know anybody else who might mind. Walking down the street, I palm the cigar, move toward the curb, delay my exhale, so as to minimize the impact on approaching pedestrians. I would climb a tree to avoid antagonizing someone with cigar smoke. That's only right, in my opinion.

Therefore I feel I generate a certain amount of psychic good will. I'm a *nice person,* goddamnit, and for this hectoring jogger not to recognize me as such, for her to handle me as if I were *rude,* is just too much. Gun fanatics like to say that an armed society is a polite society, but I truly believe that, if everyone carried a gun, the population would dwindle down to nothing in six months, as firefights blazed away over who saw a parking space first, over which person was next in line at the deli counter, over whether a cigar should or should not be smoked on Oakdale Avenue. If I had been carrying a revolver, no question, I would have pumped six bullets into the back of this woman and then gone to prison for . . . gee, what is it nowadays? . . . four and a half years.

On that note, with the dripping beast of human competitiveness, hostility and violence in sight, the pulsing pathology gilded with a thin and oh so delicate tissue of quavering courtesies, I'll end with a positive observation: despite everything rude and wrong and getting worse in society, we still expect to be treated with respect. I've never met anyone who didn't. Beggars in rags, groveling for change in the gutter, demand a certain level of politeness from passersby. The bedrock is still in place.

You don't see it much—covered as it is with the muck of reality. But it's there, supporting us all.

I was hoofing down Michigan Avenue a few years ago when a swarthy, mustachioed man in a suit—he looked like an Iranian or an Iraqi—stopped me. He held out a photo album, filled with atrocity pictures: butchered families, maimed survivors. He turned a page or two—horrible images—which he proceeded to try to show me while launching into some sort of spiel about a relief fund.

"I'm sorry," I said, and I moved off. If I stopped to extend pity to everybody who asked for it on the street, it would take an hour to walk a city block. I would have instantly forgotten the man, but he called after me something that has stuck with me ever since, making me just a little more sympathetic to people accosting me for causes, pushing me a few notches toward generosity, patience and politeness.

It wasn't a biting insult. It wasn't some cleverly worded put-down or compound obscenity. He said, in a genuinely aggrieved voice, not so much indignant as puzzled: "But I haven't finished yet."

He must have been new. "But I haven't finished yet." I kept going, but I regretted it almost immediately. That naiveté, that surprise, the expectation that his plea would receive a full hearing from a busy pedestrian in front of the Wrigley Building, was touching to me. Haunting really. The *expectation* of being treated in a certain way. Rudeness can wax and wane with the times. And politeness can easily be just a mask for cruelty. But so long as we expect a little courtesy, a little consideration, some kindness from strangers, there's still hope for us all.

S Is for Self-help

 I had always bitten my nails. I couldn't remember a time when I didn't. In fact, I'd never needed to trim them with clippers. It was that bad. I'll never know how much biting my nails kept me back in life. It isn't as if a prospective employer will snap your file shut and say, "We'd love to hire you, but those cuticles . . ." I'm sure people must have noticed, and judged me harshly. People can be so cruel that way.

Princess Diana was on the tube last night, talking about her bulimia and the maelstrom of personal problems that come with being one of the richest and most famous women in the world.

Her interview was quite well received. Feminists applauded her candor. The British public crushed her even harder against its ample bosom. Nasty old anal-retentive Charles, who would never dream of confessing his gastrointestinal peccadilloes to the general public, seemed even weirder and more repellent by comparison.

Diana was only undergoing what has become a public rite in modern society—the venting of sins and afflictions, the airing of laundry. No autobiography is deemed honest unless the stained sheets are held up for display, unless a few syndromes and addictions are ventilated. These lapses—infidelities and cravings and crimes—become the focal point of the life in review, and the accomplishments that supposedly gave merit to a person and made the story interesting in the first place fade away into insignificance.

When those two boobs came out with their book spotlighting the poor parenting habits of Albert Einstein, I wanted to scream, "So what?" It's not as if he's famous for his discovery of the Theory of Daditivity. There is something terribly beside the point to such efforts; akin to some naturalist writing a book about fish and emphasizing that they are wet, cold creatures and don't learn tricks easily.

It is a closed circle—the person with problems feeding to the receptive public, which applauds and sympathizes and claps its flippers together for more. No one is permitted to wedge in between and deliver a dissent. A hearty, arm-spread cry of "Did we *ask?*" is seen as cruel and hypocritical, since the vast majority of the population does indeed want to know, though God knows why. I suppose it's *interesting*.

So I will dissent. I didn't want to know about Diana worshiping the porcelain god, just as I didn't want to know Bob Packwood was "a binge drinker" or Mary Tyler Moore tried to help her brother kill himself or Grace Kelly was a whore or any of the other back-room bilge spooned about the famous and near famous.

First, these private ticks are not my business. None of anyone's business. That's a quaint concept, I know. But there's a defense for it. Private afflictions are so riveting, they have a way of overshadowing everything else in that person's life. Ask anybody about Joan Crawford and I guarantee you he or she will utter the words "coat hanger" long before they ever get to *Mildred Pierce*. Personal flaws loom so huge, they tend to blot out everything else. Recent biographies of James Thurber have cut such an excruciating portrait of his last few months of illness that one tends to think of him not as the preeminent humorist of the Twentieth Century but as a mean drunk who wet himself at parties.

Thus, in the span of an hour, Diana is no longer a mildly romantic and charmingly dim figure of royalty, but a woman who sticks her fingers down her throat.

Such discoveries are like seeing your grandmother sneeze into the soup. Dinner at her house is never quite the same afterward. Woody Allen can make the greatest movie in the world, but he'll still be the unattractive fifty-ish guy caught popping his not-quite-stepdaughter. Yuck. (Who can enjoy *Manhattan* after that? It's too easy to convince yourself he created the entire movie just to grope Mariel Hemingway.)

This curiosity about the famous is only a reflection of the confessional candor that has crept into private life. What started as a breaking of harmful taboos, the brave women who exposed the trauma of abuse, has deteriorated into a moan fest at which the owners of any quirk or gripe or woe trot them out for the lone reason that it is easier than keeping them private, solving them and moving on.

Not to sound grim and millennial, but this enthusiasm for expressing personal problems is a sign of decay, of societal decline, a luxury wallowed in at the expense of more practical pursuits. Interest in this type of dirt—whether spewing it or absorbing it—shows we have too much time on our hands. I keep thinking of the pioneers, jolting along some dry riverbed in their Conestoga wagons, searching the sky for a cloud. Not a lot of room for indulging internal weaknesses here. Not many farm wives, churning butter, suddenly turning to their husbands and exploding, "All day long it's 'Lucy, the chickens *need* this!' and 'Lucy, the ox *needs* that.' Well, Zebulon, I am a person too, and I have *my* needs."

We have the culture of self-help to thank for this—the I'm-Okay-You're-Okay-Let's-Go-Out-in-the-Woods-and-Bang-a-Drum-and-Talk-About-Our-Fathers pop psychology which descended, I suppose, originally, from psychiatry, and its notion of the talking cure, where you lay on a couch and told Uncle Sigmund all about it.

The beauty of the couch sessions was that the rest of the world did not have to be informed about them. This notion is lost today, when a person who won't confess his darkest secrets on national TV is considered somehow strange. Somehow aloof. Whatsamatter—you think you're better than us? C'mon, tell us. Tell us! Tell Barbara! How do you *feel* when the lights go out?

Jenny Jones can flash a request for sons who slept with their mothers and killed their fathers after encountering them on the road to Thebes, and a week later the men are lining up outside the studio door. Amazing.

Once upon a time just the fact that you were seeing a psychiatrist was something you hushed up, never mind what you said once you were there. Now we have Bruce

Springsteen talking to the newspapers about his years of therapy. Perhaps this is liberating to some people, but to me it's a foretaste of doom. If the Boss isn't happy, then what small hope of happiness can people like myself cling to in this world? Those of us who never climbed atop an amp tower and led the E Street Band in kicking out the stops to "Rosalita"? Or rather, who did so only in our dreams. What hope have we? I like to imagine that Bruce Springsteen is really, really happy, and if he isn't, well, frankly, I don't want to know about it.

Doesn't anybody believe in carrying his or her sorrows in dignity and silence? Whenever there is some high school tragedy—a shooting or car wreck or something—we are immediately reassured that the grief counselors are on their way to make everything okay again. I can't help but think that, in many cases, they only make things worse. If I get blown up by a bomb hidden in a cheese shop garbage can, I don't want my wife reading *Mourn Your Man in 30 Days* and then going out dancing with her new fancy friends before the flowers wilt on my grave. I don't want her joining Widows Holding Hands and sharing and crying and growing and learning. I want her wearing black veils and shattering the mirrors at home. I want her like Carlotta O'Neill, half insane, walking the halls where we once lived, talking to the air, sitting in a darkened room while friends plead with her to take a little broth. Selfish? Damn right. And you know what? I don't want to talk about it.

Do you have any Kleenex? Because this part gets hard. When you bite your nails, well, inevitably, a bit of nail comes off. In your mouth, usually. I suppose a better person

*would spit the bit of nail out, in a handkerchief or some-
thing. But I don't. I just swallow the little bit of nail. There,
I said it. I feel much better now. Thank you.*

The supposed benefit of all this confession is twofold.
First, the victims themselves feel relieved—empowered,
ennobled. Taking control of their vice instead of being
controlled. If nothing else, they no longer have to worry
about people finding out, because everybody already
knows.

Second, the rest of us learn more about the problem—
whether incest, or binge eating, or obsessive-compulsive
disorder, or Tourette's syndrome, or Cri de Chat, or whatever. The untold fellow sufferers, who thought they were
freakish anomalies, are supposedly buoyed by discovering
they are not all alone.

Here seems to be a flaw in logic. Do people really
want to discover that their innermost demons, the problems which plague them in the dark, private midnight of
the soul, are in fact no more than bland data points, just
the vast general trend made specific? Not me. Not this guy.
In my mind, nothing is worse than dragging home late at
the end of an exhausting day, flopping on the couch to eat
leftover Chinese food out of the carton, and flipping open
yesterday's paper to read the headline:

TODAY'S BOOMERS EXHAUSTED
LIVE ON TAKEOUT, COUCHES,
SPEND TIME PITYING SELVES

Now I suppose that liberates some people. They
shovel a garlic shrimp into their maw and think: "Great,
it's not my fault." But it just drives me lower. The last self-

delusion, that little fig leaf of uniqueness in suffering, is yanked away. I like to think my problems are particular to me, not what all the *haut monde* are suffering this year. Maybe that's just a delusion of grandeur. I hear it's a common problem.

Similarly, those self-help books do nothing for me. I tried a few, when I was a teenager, and it was like reading a manual for a car I didn't own.

Researching this chapter, I polished off a handful of the mountain of books: *I'm OK; You're OK* and *How to Be Your Own Best Friend* and *The Road Less Traveled* and *All I Really Need to Know I Learned in Kindergarten* and others of that ilk.

They were a pretty uneven lot. Most were just sort of squishy and mediocre and padded. *Kindergarten* showed its greatest ingenuity in managing to insert, within its 196 wide-margin pages of jumbo type, 36 pages that were entirely blank. By my calculation, if the book had been set in normal type, and the blank pages extracted, it would be about 80 pages long. Nice gig.

Robert Fulghum is the sort of guy whom women who've never dated a man before imagine they would like to date. He enjoys doing the laundry, for instance. "It's a near religious experience, you know," he writes. "Water, earth, fire—polarities of wet and dry, hot and cold, dirty and clean. The great cycles—round and round—beginning and end—Alpha and Omega, amen. I am in touch with the GREAT SOMETHING OR OTHER."

The above statement is a lie. It has to be. Anyone who claims that doing the laundry is a "near religious experience" doesn't do much laundry. Rather, he is gilding his reality with a fake veneer of false enthusiasm, creating a sparkling little world he then dangles before his audience, hypnotizing them into thinking their world can be as pretty if they only will it to be so. Somebody once asked Lord Byron what it was like to live his life in a poetic fervor, and he said: "Nobody lives life in a poetic fervor—how would you shave?"

I suppose it started when I was very young. I was at a party and, yes, I was nervous. Before I knew what was happening, I was chewing on a nail. It comforted me. It made me feel better. It made me feel like a Big Shot.

Looking down the road, I can't imagine how this trend will play itself out. Perhaps with mini-video cameras and Internet access, we'll be able to watch every moment of celebrities' lives. We'll be able to observe Burt Reynolds on the toilet, if we so desire, or sit in on a counseling session with Jay Leno.

I can hardly wait.

This talk of privacy might seem disingenuous from a writer whose stock in trade is distilling tidbits of his own personal life. How does my writing about being fat differ from Di brushing her teeth and toddling off to chat with the BBC?

Well, I guess that leads us to the idea of *context*. Perhaps that best expresses my dislike of squeamish confessions and chirpy self-help books. They're distorting, they grab for the goods too quickly. Remember, Rose of Sharon flops her breast out and nurses the dying stranger at the *end* of *Grapes of Wrath*. There's a whole book in front. Nowadays, the scene would come at the beginning, and we would sail off from there. Or it would be gathered up into some compendium of similarly shocking scenes—"JOLT

POINTS! 200 Gripping Moments in Literature Help You Organize Your Work Week."

It isn't that the self-help tomes I read have nothing helpful in them. They do, but without any sense of process, of journey. The tidbits and witticisms and observations and credos and suggestions rain down, one after the other, like sex scenes in pornography. Cheap epiphanies, quickly absorbed and just as quickly forgotten.

When Robert Fulghum writes: "In deep, spiritual winter, I find inside myself the sun of summer," on page 112 of *Kindergarten,* it is just another positive platitude in a forgettable string of same. On the other hand, when Albert Camus wrote: "In the depth of winter, I at last discovered that there was within me an invincible summer," it had the benefit of being both original and within a piece that is not just a smug bleat of good-thinking. Instead, the line is part of a brief, rain-soaked reflection on the sorrow of aging and the sweet tortuous tug of memory. In fact, had Fulghum actually read Camus's 1952 essay "Return to Tipansa," instead of grabbing the quote off a box of tea, or whatever, he might have noticed the sentence "Isolated beauty ends up simpering," which sums up the entire self-help oeuvre in five quick words.

No one was more surprised than I by the success of Bitten No More—the 12-Step Plan to Fantastic Nails. *Critics have suggested that I simply took the 12-step plan from Alcoholics Anonymous and substituted the words "biting my nails" wherever the word "alcohol" appears. I say, why parse the fine details of something if it helps people?*

T Is for Traffic

Harlem Avenue—a busy, charmless four-lane commercial road bordering Oak Park. I am trying to turn left out of a White Hen parking lot. To my left, a nearby stop-light has turned red, and cars are accumulating before it. A break in the traffic, and I pull gingerly forward and begin my turn, intending to make a quick left and squeeze behind one of the cars waiting at the light. Suddenly a van roars up and blocks me—pulling deliberately into the open spot I had been guiding my car into. I'm stuck, sitting across two lanes of traffic. I'll have to pull back into the parking lot. The driver of the van looks down at me and smiles. The smile has a distinct, unmistakable meaning. It means: "Fuck you, buddy." Something carbonizes in my brain. "No," I say out loud, shifting into low gear and driving my car into the side of the van, "fuck *you!*"

Traffic brings out the worst in people. The absolute worst. You can spend your days working for humanity's uplift—teaching immigrant children to read; helping elderly women relearn the lost weaving skills of their youth; visiting hospitals to share the healing power of poetry with convalescents—but the second you get behind the wheel of a car, whoever you are, you are transformed. Suddenly your meek, deferential skin splits, and a hostile, snarling beast swells up in its place, a harried, foaming, reckless monster ready to risk not only its own life but the lives of everybody around, just to gain a car length, to move a little faster, to get a little bit ahead.

No, I take that back. I exaggerate, grasping at comic effect. Only half the drivers quaver between their normal states and rabid death-dancing mania. The other half are a hairsbreadth away from coma—clueless roadblocks, mouth breathers, singing tonelessly to themselves as they crawl along at twenty miles an hour in a 45 mph zone. "If you knew Susie . . ." they drone, oblivious to the honks behind them, "like I know Susie . . ." Slowing down in anticipation of that green light perhaps turning to yellow. "Oh, oh, oh, what a gal!"

Common wisdom once divided the groups by gender, but that no longer applies. Nowadays a female vice-president is just as apt to be the fiend in the red BMW trying to pass a gasoline truck on a solid yellow line. And a guy dreaming about football might be the driver trying to make a left under a gigantic NO LEFT TURN sign.

Other categories transcend gender. Shriveled old people, sitting on phone books, peering over the dashboards of their Cadillacs. Blockhead parents, turned around in their seats, walloping their wailing brats as their station wagons run stop signs. Tremulous teens, piloting those white sedans with the triangular driving school signs on the roof. Why doesn't the highway patrol ever pull *them* over and beat *them* to a pulp at the side of the road? Heck, string together ninety minutes of *those* videos and people will pay $8.00 to go see them in premier movie houses. I would.

Driving is not just getting from place to place—that should be obvious. It is not a physical act. Driving is about transportation as much as baptism is about getting wet, or as much as sex is about reproduction.

The problem of traffic is not just the inconvenience of having your smooth routine interrupted. Even with the jams, backups and delays, we still get from point A to point B faster than anybody, ever. Not only does Ma Ignotus, with her swollen, arthritic feet, wedge herself behind the wheel of her Buick and head to the video store at a speed that would astonish every fleet-footed courier who ever lived. But we also get around quicker than 99 percent of the people alive in the world today.

In most other countries, citizens grinningly hang off the chicken coops lashed to the tops of antiquated buses, reflexively apologize to each other as they are packed armpit to nostril into bullet trains and balance bundles of sticks on their heads and sing as they walk the six miles to town down shimmering asphalt.

Only in America can a driver throw an outraged conniption fit while sitting behind the wheel of a $50,000 car, bathed in air conditioning and Bach, cursing out the school bus daring to disgorge a group of kindergartners into his path.

Why are we so spoiled? Why are we not satisfied? What is this psychological thing, driving, and its nightmare twin, traffic?

A big hint, I think, lies in the wheel-pounding, horn-blaring, face-reddening reaction that traffic evokes in so many. Such an exaggerated response is way out of line with other frustrations of life—ATM machines are routinely down, routinely deny money and eat cards. Yet you never see people going berserk at ATM machines, stamping and screaming and flailing their arms. They curse softly under their breath and silently shuffle away.

No other activity, outside of perhaps drug dealing, inspires so much impulsive gunplay as driving does, or sees so many people who send themselves to prison over tiny incidents. One car dings the other, somebody cuts somebody else off, and suddenly people are killing each other.

Deep psychological factors must be at play. Traffic punctures a cherished fantasy. The romance of speed and power, the unconquered frontier. We are car people, we Americans. We are mobile. We have a right to jump in our cars, get on the roads whenever we damn well feel like it, and *go*. That reality often does not comply—that the stage is too littered with supernumeraries to properly enact our script of solitude and freedom and speed—wrecks things. It makes us mad.

Traffic shouldn't be such a surprise. The Kennedy Expressway snarls nearly every day between 4 and 7 P.M., Saturdays and Sundays included. Yet hitting that traffic, the quick deceleration from 60 miles per hour to zippo miles per hour, still comes as a shock. "What's happening?" people marvel. "Why, the traffic is *jammed.*"

The daily surprise of traffic is testimony to the fantasy's power. Car manufacturers portray their products, invariably, in splendid isolation, rocketing unimpeded down country lanes. Roaring up the 45-degree incline of deserted mountain trails. Churning up secluded, lovely beaches.

Doing their damnedest to distract us from "the sordid reality of the crawl to work," car makers offer instead "the sex-laden imagery of freedom, mastery and power," to use British sociologist John Whitelegg's apt phrasing.

Our expectations are raised to unreal levels, levels where we are willing to put ourselves into hock to buy that rocket sled. We don the cool shades and set out searching for precipitate adventures.

They are seldom found. Traffic interrupts the little automotive drama running in our heads, stops the music, pulls back the camera and reveals ourselves as we really are: tiny, frail, ridiculous creatures, puffing out our cheeks and drumming our leather-driving-glove-clad fingers against our sport-grip steering wheels, craning our necks, trying to see what the problem could be, our massive engines idling, useless.

Once, through an incredible quirk of fate, I was given a brand-new Chevrolet Corvette to drive for a week. Midnight blue. Electronic dashboard. V8 engine. Fat tires. It was a great car, for the rare stretch of open road. I got it up to 104 miles an hour on a city street in the dead of night. But generally, in the daytime, driving the car in city traffic was like trying to ice a cake with a shovel. The engine howled in agony below 25 miles an hour, and my heart, my *soul* screamed with it.

That scream was the frustrated urge to move quickly, what Nietzsche would call the Will to Go. Unprompted as it may be by necessity, it is what makes traffic an annoyance. We aren't upset because we're going to miss the last train out of Berlin. We aren't panicky because we've got to get serum through to the sick townspeople before it's too late. I would venture that most people, in going from place to place, can take ten minutes or an hour to get there, no matter, and traffic upsets them so because it subtly points this out, drawing rude attention to the cheapness of their time.

The car/speed fantasy isn't the entire story. We know this because people have been complaining about traffic for thousands of years. Traffic was worse on foot. "Hurry as we may, we are blocked by a surging crowd in front, and by a dense mass of people pressing in on us from behind," wrote Juvenal, of the congestion of downtown Rome nineteen hundred years ago. "One man digs an elbow into me, another a hard sedan pole; one bangs a beam, another a wine-cask, against my head. My legs are beplastered with mud; soon huge feet trample on me from every side, and a soldier plants his hobnails firmly on my toe."

Then and now, traffic is a symptom of every social woe—overpopulation, environmental blight, infrastructure collapse, social isolation, urban decay. Every new trend in society, it seems, makes traffic worse, from growing suburbia to increasing prosperity to the entrance of women into the work force and the growth of service sector jobs.

Traffic is the only way most people encounter larger social problems. I can forget about overpopulation, laugh off pollution, thumb my nose at the ozone layer and ignore the growing poverty of my fellow citizens—in my living room, stroking the cat and contemplating my accounts. But step into a car and, boom, there they are, the problems of the nation, of the world, climbing in my lap, or trying to. Traffic rubs your face in the noxious spoor of your fellow humans. No wonder we shoot other motorists so frequently.

As these macro factors boost congestion, congestion in turn affects individual people in direct, physical ways, none of them good. Studies show that, as traffic volume goes up, so do the heart rate, blood pressure and electrocardiogram irregularities of drivers. (Actually, traffic congestion has one positive health aspect—it cuts down on traffic fatalities. Cars are hard to roll at 8 mph.) In polls, a chunk of city dwellers—sometimes up to a third—list traffic as the worst problem they face, beyond crime, or health care, or anything.

Gazing off into the murk of the future, traffic engineers fracture into two distinct schools of thought regarding what will happen to automotive traffic.

One mode of thinking runs ahead of the upward-arching congestion curves and tries to make those regions of unimagined traffic density as comfortable as possible, with advanced computer systems and private roads and double-deck mega-highways. This school has inertia on its side—we are already heading in that direction, full bore, all cylinders firing away, speedometer needle pinned to the right side of the scale.

The other takes the entire sweep of the automobile's postwar predominance and concludes—perhaps wistfully—that it is an anomaly, a historical dead end that will wane exactly because of the multitudinous woes of traffic. These are the people who applaud worsening traffic congestion. Who hope that car travel becomes more time consuming and more expensive, so as to hurry the day when people will return to those Utopian, nineteenth-century towns where you don't have to jump in the car to rush to the All-Night Mart because at any moment the fruit vendor, with his large immigrant's mustache, will push his cart down your block, shouting, "Aaaaaaaa-pulz, nice-a, fresh-a, aaaaaaa-pulz . . ."

On their side, tantalizing possibilities such as how computer networking will ultimately affect work schedules; how many of us indeed will end up doing our jobs while sitting on scenic mountain peaks with our laptops and our Irish setters.

I fear the first group is right, though emotionally I put my hopes in with the latter group, having myself moved to an area of the city so congested that car ownership is impractical bordering on impossible. Within months of moving here I was forced to sell my car, not a complete commitment, since we kept my wife's big green sedan, renting a garage space two thirds of a block away for a price a little more than half of what I paid for my first apartment.

It's amazing how fast you get out of the habit of driving. Perhaps I've always secretly hated getting behind the wheel, because I've found that when the question of what to do in the evening comes up I invariably cast my vote for entertainments within walking distance.

Habitually avoiding the car does tend to add a sheen of significance to the times when I do drive. After leaving the car parked for a week or two, the act of firing it up assumes a certain dignity and drama. "We'll take the car," I announce, as if committing myself to a manned moon landing within the decade. "I will go now and bring the car around."

Public transportation has also proven not as odious as suspected from behind the wheel. When I drove all the time, I flatly refused to take the bus, ever. There was something so dismal, so Eastern European about buses. You would see them on cold, rainy nights, rearing out of the gloom, these big overlit boxes, struggling to navigate a corner, the few people inside, drawn and tired, clinging to straps and lurching toward lives that I knew were desperate and empty.

But then I started taking the 151 bus downtown, owing to my wife's constant lecturing on the topic "The Causal Link Between Taxicabs and Personal Financial Ruin." The bus is actually very nice, if you get a seat, and I try to plan my trips at times when I can always get a seat. Pretty women ride the bus, and you can gaze dreamily at them. Old people ride too, senior citizens raised in an age, before interstate highways, when strangers talked to each other as an enjoyable way of passing the time while traveling. Steeped in this antique practice and liberated, I suppose, by their own pending mortality, they will sometimes speak to me, unprompted, leading to pleasant encounters which can linger for days, if not years.

I had just begun to ride the bus and was sitting alone, in the back, as is my habit, reading a book by James Thurber. An old gent sat down nearby and, after a few stops, leaned forward and said: "My friend was telling me, just last night, that young people don't read Thurber anymore."

I looked up at him. "Tell your friend," I said, smiling, "that he is wrong." I went back to reading, but after a moment the appropriate coda came to me, in real time, for once. "And thank you," I added, "for considering me 'young.'"

U Is for UFO

 Pick a premise: (a) there are five billion people on earth and a surprising number of them are capable of spectacular acts of deceit, gullibility, greed and idiocy; or (b) space aliens have been hovering around the periphery of human affairs throughout history, kidnapping people, conducting strange experiments and delivering messages of monumental urgency and importance.

No one who believes the first statement—and I don't think a more self-evident observation can be made—can possibly believe the second. And anyone who believes the second, I assume, bailed out of this book a long time ago.

The belief that Unidentified Flying Objects are some sort of shy emissaries from outer space—bees from Mars, preinvasion scouts from Alpha Centauri, whatever—is just one of the many clods of pseudoscientific nonsense regularly flung into the face of the public. Time travel, reincarnation, telekinesis, ESP, numerology, astrology, and a variety of other carny tricks and cargo-cult delusions are embraced by an ignorant few and then widely disseminated via the credulous modern media.

Belief in UFOs represents the epitome of these misreadings of reality, however. No other folk belief, except perhaps astrology, gets such serious play in the mainstream press. No other cooks up so much ridiculous nonsense and serves it as scientific method. No other group of adherents is so vigorous in promoting its worldview of unexamination and ignorance.

I was compensated for the chunk of my life wasted studying UFO literature by the number of howling boners liberally scattered throughout it. There was the "noted metallurgist" in Robert Loftin's book, *Identified Flying Saucers,* who examined fragments of a UFO and pronounced them pure magnesium ("a laboratory rarity," Loftin pants). This certainly sounds impressive, and magnesium is used in aircraft parts, because of its lightness. But always in alloy—pure magnesium, just like pure anything, is not structurally strong (that's why you don't see 24-karat gold rings). Pure magnesium also melts at 1200° F. and has an affinity for bursting into flame. All told, probably not the material a clever space alien would use to build a craft to go hurtling higgly-piggly through the atmosphere.

Then there was the unnamed scientist who told Frank Scully, in his *Behind the Flying Saucers,* that the crashed UFO he had personally examined was 99.99 feet long, with all other dimensions being multiples of nine feet. The aliens obviously had a 9-based system, the scientist concluded. Neither the scientist—if he existed—nor the author questions how this alien 9-based system happened upon the anachronism of English measurement, however.

But this is a digression. The danger in dealing with the subject of UFOs is the constant temptation to address specifics, to slip into the mire of UFOlogy, a field as graceful as its name. There are so many claims, each one spurious in its own unique way—whether a vision, a hallucination, a lie or some other thing—that the moment they are challenged, individually, one is overwhelmed and defeated.

"Proponents of such claims compile almost endless files of UFO sightings and other UFO-related phenomena," writes Terence Hines, in his valuable book *Pseudoscience and the Paranormal.* "The skeptic is then told that unless he can explain away *every single* report, the theory that UFOs are extra-terrestrial craft must be true."

No matter how many specifics are disproved, there is always more evidence. Prodded by the persistent, fearful mooing of the public, the United States Air Force examined 12,000 reported sightings in its *Project Blue Book.* Over 90 percent of these sightings were found to be the results of various prosaic causes. Yet the ever expanding UFO community pointed hysterically to the cases that couldn't be readily explained as proof extraterrestrial spaceships are real.

To provide a metaphor: it is as if I set myself the task of finding out what sort of entity leaves behind the beer bottles discarded on my block every week. With hard work, fingerprinting, surveillance and the like, I might be able to track down many of the various bums, college students and bikers who dropped them in a given period. But there would always be a few bottles I could not trace to their source. Would I then conclude: (a) these bottles were left by bums, college students and bikers whose identities I could not discover or, (b) since I could not tie them to human sources, these bottles obviously were not left by earthly agency but must have been planted by the Zygorthian Space Raiders from Rigel 7?

Ironically, the very massiveness of the evidence presented by UFO apologists is what undermines their case. To accept their testimony, the UFOs are spheres, discs, cylinders, doughnuts, cubes, crescents. They glow or are dark. They are any color of the rainbow or translucent. They have jets of flame or none. They roar. They are silent. They are inches wide or hundreds of miles across. Their occupants are short, tall, human, not.

Again, the choice is one of two conclusions.

Perhaps a vast armada of spacecraft of every known geometric shape and possible physical configuration, piloted by a galactic United Nations of infinitely varied life forms, is sniffing about the planet in a way that is both ubiquitous and subtle—the answer the UFOlogists heartily endorse.

Or, gee, maybe people are *imagining* all this. Perhaps the entire thing is due to innocent fantasy, brain fever and mendacity—the answer that makes sense to the rest of us.

UFOlogists howl that this is impossible—that any phenomenon attested to by so many people *has* to be real. But as Hines points out, the millions of children who believe in Santa Claus do not, by weight of numbers, wish him into physical being.

The most annoying thing about UFOlogists is that, even if their premise were true, their approach is moronic. If I believed in the existence of visiting spacemen, I don't think my mind would be absorbed with the specific dimensions of their ships and what color the running lights were. UFO literature might betray a whiff of charm if it occasionally paused to contemplate the stupendous philosophical ramifications of intelligent life from outer space pressing its face against our windows all the time. But instead, the field is given over to paranoiacs and frustrated engineers, conjuring up conspiracies, drawing schematics of nonexistent propulsion systems and compiling pointless data, like those lunatics one sees carrying little pads and writing down the license plate numbers of parked cars. Speculating about the exact form of a spaceship glimpsed in the sky is something like critiquing the plot of a porn movie—a possible path of inquiry, yes, but missing the point entirely.

So we must try to keep to the big picture. Though UFOs are a dry well for scientific insight, they are a rich source of societal study. Just as predictions of the future are valuable, not for their success as augury, but for how they reveal the cultural fears of a given moment, so UFOs are not a view of the galactic but a peek below the rock of humanity.

The current fascination with UFOs began in 1947, when a private pilot named Kenneth Arnold reported nine strange objects he described as flying "like a saucer skipping over water" near Mount Rainier in Washington State. Usually overlooked is the fact that Arnold had penned an article on UFOs for *Fate* magazine the year before, establishing a suspicious progression common to UFO fanatics: (1) first becoming interested in the subject and, (2) then encountering UFOs.

Soon people were seeing UFOs all over the country—

hundreds of reported spacecraft. The immediate dilemma then facing UFO supporters was, given the frequency of UFO sightings, why weren't they being quickly accepted as commonplace normality? Why was something so manifest to those who believed so rebuffed by a chunk of the population?

The answer, maintained then and now by UFO advocates, is a secretive and coercive government. Fearing "panic," the government, in league with the scientific establishment, conspires to suppress and discredit the mountains of evidence proving that UFOs flit about the globe like so many luna moths.

UFO books of the 1950s usually begin with elaborate declarations about governmental conspiracy, a thread that remains unbroken to this day. Five of the six headlines on the cover of the spring, 1995, issue of *Unsolved UFO Sightings* refer to governmental cover-up.

One can only yearn for a government as swift and effective as the one inhabiting the lush dreams of the UFOlogists. The CIA that dithered blithely while Aldrich Ames was spooning Russian caviar from the ashtray of his Jaguar is transformed into a finely tuned Gestapo, dispatching mysterious "men in black" to swoop down on UFO crash sites, confiscating evidence and terrorizing witnesses. NASA, whose top brass can't even work out a system to inform its own upper echelons of the agency's multitudinous blunders before they appear on the front page of the *Washington Post,* suddenly has the discipline of the Illuminati, concealing the ancient ruins discovered on the moon.

And geez, not to get into rebuttals again, but *why?* Given NASA's current state—lashed to the block, listening to the ax being honed—if it had a shred of evidence, a funny-shaped rock, a bit of metal, anything to imply that a civilization had once been on the moon, as many UFO fanatics insist, NASA officials would be in front of the Senate Appropriations Committee in a heartbeat, waving the artifact like a flag.

(Of course, the nimble paranoid mind will point out that these outward signs of incompetence are only further proof of conspiracy. How could such ostensibly vital federal agencies be so consistently inept, if not to conceal their ruthless efficiency regarding their real interest, UFOs? The only cogent reply to this line of thinking is to place your thumb against your nose, wiggle your fingers and go: "Pbbbllffbblft!")

The skeptical UFOlogist, were such a thing possible, might also ask himself why, if the government is so closely guarding UFO secrets, do those secrets always seem to fall so quickly into the hands of *UFO* magazine and its advertisers? Why are they able to hawk costly books, pamphlets and videos exposing the verified reality of literally any insane premise the human mind can conceive? (My favorite is the joint Nazi-Japanese UFO flight to Mars during World War II. As if they didn't have more pressing concerns at the time.)

Given the energy spent debating what the U.S. Government knows about UFOs, I would be so bold as to suggest that it is anti-government paranoia, and not any deep interest in extraterrestrial life, which really is the driving force behind the entire UFO phenomenon. Howard Blum, in setting his premise for his 1990 book *Out There,* unconsciously reveals his priorities when he asks: "Was the government back in the UFO business? Had they found anything? Was there life in the universe?"

UFOs can be seen as a poignant symptom of frightening political times, meshing nicely with the Red scare, McCarthyism, polio, the H-bomb and other dark cultural markers of the 1950s. "The next war will be an interplanetary war," said General Douglas MacArthur in 1955, a statement which at the time was an expression of optimism. Mac noted that, after the arrival of doom from the skies, "nations of the world will be forced to unite."

More than anything else, belief in UFOs is both a tiny rebellion against a menacing system and a terrified bleat of hope that some responsible party will show up quick and fix everything before it's too late. UFOs are the equivalent of the naval officer in white who appears at the end of *Lord of the Flies*—civilization and authority arriving at the last moment.

"Now that science has run amok and is threatening us with atomic annihilation it does seem reasonable to expect that if ever another intervention was needed, the time would be now," writes Desmond Leslie, betraying the wish fulfillment common to UFO believers. The Venetian who George Adamski said contacted him in 1952 was there out of benevolent concern over radiation which, coincidentally, was worrying people on earth too.

"On his face there was no trace of resentment or judgment," Adamski writes. "His expression was one of understanding, and great compassion; as one would have toward a much beloved child who had erred through ignorance and lack of understanding."

How nice—here to help, and not a touch of blame.

Adamski, a California handyman, was the first person to report contact with an extraterrestrial, and he set the stage for the thousands of claims that would follow and—incredibly—be given serious consideration in our day by those who should know better.

Adamski unknowingly reveals the giddy mindset in which people start seeing saucers:

> Winter and summer, day and night, through heat and cold, winds, rains, and fog, I have spent every moment possible outdoors watching the skies for space craft and hoping without end that for some reason, some time, one of them would come in close, and even land.

And then they came! How coincidentally cool! Adamski later claimed to have traveled with the UFOs to the moon, Venus and Mars (those who believe most fervently in UFOs have the convenient ability to summon them like faithful dogs).

While believed at the time, Adamski is dismissed by current UFOlogists as being overly fantastic for modern tastes. Looking back on visitation reports of past decades, the accounts of alien contact do seem strangely culturally specific. Aliens never land and warn us that we must save string. Rather, their concerns always resonate with earth troubles. By the 1970s, the aliens were worried more about pollution than radiation, and their homilies were about saving the environment. In the 1990s they are hot to conduct sex experiments, as if advanced cultures would cross intergalactic space to cop a feel. Soon the aliens will be reported delivering messages about the unstable dollar, and that, for a while, will convince certain people.

The idea that UFOs represent some sort of mass psychosis was suggested fairly early on by Carl Jung, the psychoanalytic pioneer, who was so taken by the UFO question that he wrote a charming little book about it, published in English in 1958 as *Flying Saucers: A Modern Myth of Things Seen in the Skies.*

Jung called UFOs a "visionary rumor" and compared the sightings to crowds witnessing the Virgin Mary at Fátima. He is an example of how the sharpened mind and the slack-jawed believer can view the same evidence and draw completely different conclusions. UFO proponents comb history for anything they can use to prop up their sagging premise, dragooning vague Aztec paintings and superheated Vishnic mythology to prove that UFOs have hung around in the shadows throughout all history.

Jung takes the same material—the tales of floating eyes, burning orbs, hovering bloody crosses—and sees, not documentary snapshots of unfiltered extraterrestrial reality misread by the yokels of the day, but evidence of a deep human yearning for signs and reassurance from the skies, a need now dressed in modern clothing.

"It is characteristic of our time that the archetype . . . should now take the form of an object, a technological construction, in order to avoid the odiousness of mythological personification," he writes. "Anything that looks technological goes down without difficulty with modern man."

In other words, while a lonely sheepherder in the twelfth century might interpret the visions he's been having as "angels," nowadays those circles of light and voices from trees are apt to be mentally repackaged into glowing mother ships and chatty alien homunculi with big heads.

Tying UFOs into the rich tradition of human self-delusion also explains how the phenomenon has outlived Cold War paranoia. By constantly upping the ante—first sightings, then discovery of crash sites, then face-to-face encounters, then trips to outer space, and finally the present carnival atmosphere of sex probes and Nazi saucers—the UFO cult moves forward by sheer momentum, building on the popularity of former claims, a formula eerily reminiscent of previous spasms of unfounded belief.

Consider the evolution of UFO culture in the light of philosopher Loyal Rue's description, in his book *By the Grace of Guile,* of how public desire for Christian relics exploded midway through the first millennium:

> By the early fifth century, however, the demand for relics had gone upmarket as reports circulated about remains from more distinguished saints, such as the head of John the Baptist and the body of St. Stephen. Response to the "discovery" of these relics was so intense that even more spectacular finds followed: the staff of Moses, manna from the wilderness . . . Jesus' milk teeth, his umbilical cord, the foreskin from his circumcision, and so on. The only limitation on discoveries appears to have been the imagination of the discoverer. Inevitably, of course, problems of duplication arose. At least three churches claimed to have the head of John the Baptist, and eventually there were enough fragments of the cross about to build a battleship, and enough of the virgin's milk to sink it.

As with UFOs, there was a fierce debate about the authenticity of these relics, with pesky questions popping up, such as how Mary Magdalene came to be buried in France.

One asset unavailable to the fifth-century Catholic Church but enjoyed now by UFO faithful are the media, which do much to keep the myth of UFOs alive.

Jung has a valuable insight about the press. Noting how a distorted news account claiming that he believed in the extraterrestrial reality of UFOs "spread like wildfire from the far West round the earth to the far East," Jung expresses quaint nineteenth-century amazement that his measured denial of the story garnered almost no notice.

"As the behavior of the press is a sort of Gallup test with reference to world opinion, one must draw the conclusion that news affirming the existence of UFOs is welcome, but that skepticism seems to be undesirable," he writes. "To believe that UFOs are real suits the general opinion, whereas disbelief is to be discouraged."

Bingo. We hear so much about UFOs—from patently false *Weekly World News* photos of the President shaking hands with little green men to unsubstantiated claims by the unlettered—because UFOs are news.

"Where UFOs are concerned, it is almost impossible to distinguish the editorial policies and ethics of the *New York Times* or the *Washington Post* from those of the *National Enquirer* or the *Midnight Star,*" writes Hines, citing embarrassing examples of gullible press sensation. "The most absurd UFO reports are accepted at face value and published as news stories. Attempts are seldom made to verify the truth of the report or to seek comment from skeptical investigators."

This is terrible for several reasons. First, most people,

in their secret hearts, wish that these stories were true—that we were indeed being visited by our benign brethren from other worlds. I certainly do. If nothing else, it would cut the ennui layering our lives. To spark even a brief, irrational hope, based on the warblings of fakes and psychotics, is cruel.

Second, these reports tend to reinforce belief in UFOs among the unscientific and the impressionable. This can't help them, and makes the world seem even more dismal than it already is for the rest of us. One likes to take pride in one's fellow citizens, and not be reminded that they are, in the main, dupes and boobs capable of believing anything. It bodes ill. If a significant portion of the population is willing to discard the known scheme of the universe based on some odd lights somebody else saw at night, what hope do we have that the population will—oh, for instance—cling to its civil rights in the face of the coming storm of conservative reaction? Not a lot, I'm afraid.

And finally, UFOlogists are insulting. Nonbelievers are accused of being a dull herd grazing contentedly on the status quo, unwilling to look up from our feedage to acknowledge the wonders streaking by in the sky, despite the frantic pleadings and pointings of our intellectual betters. The scientific community, which at the advent of UFOs was burying its head in the sand of nuclear physics, electronics, computer science, genetics and space travel, is constantly tarred by the UFOlogists, smug and secure in their private phantasm, as reactionaries, in league with those who doubted the reality of meteorites, bacteria and heavier-than-air flight. UFOs give open-mindedness a bad name.

Like many annoyances, the UFO funhouse is an endless maze that one could become lost in, if it weren't ultimately so tedious. This observation, the most elegant and compelling refutation of UFOs that I know of, comes from Dr. Frank Drake, an astrophysicist who spent thirty years straining to hear an intelligent peep out of the infinite cosmos through increasingly massive international radio-telescope efforts. To his credit, Drake's lack of catching so much as a "Hi!" from outer space has neither dimmed his belief that one day the greeting will come, nor inspired him to start manufacturing faux greetings, as so many others seem so eager to do.

In his book on the patient search for extraterrestrial life, *Is Anyone Out There?* it takes Drake less than a paragraph to neatly demolish the entire mass of UFO literature over the past half century:

> When I talk to contactees who claim they've been given information by occupants of UFOs, the material turns out to be totally uninteresting. It is never anything that we didn't already know, and usually consists of blandishments of friendship and goodwill. This is what makes every story ultimately unbelievable, because if a civilization could master interstellar travel—something that is beyond even my wildest dreams right now—wouldn't they have the most striking news to report?

Should the day come when an alien spacecraft lands on earth and its occupants emerge to tell us things, the things they tell us, whatever they are, won't be *boring*. What they have to say will come as a *surprise,* and a bigger one than can be cooked up by the arid imaginations of housewives in Nebraska. The aliens will not have crossed the vastness of interstellar space to shake hands and wish us a good day.

If not—if the arrival of alien life will offer nothing new, but only serve to reflect back at us our own neuroses, social fears and sexual anxieties—then what's the big fuss about? If space aliens are going to turn out to be the same ooo-scary monsters we've been watching in the movies all these years, they might as well stay home.

V Is for Victim

 Once people wanted to come from good places. They put on airs. If your father was the Pope, if your forebears came over on the *Mayflower,* then you crowed about it, and decorated your home with family crests and genealogies and framed oil portraits of Great-Grandpap fondling his hunting rifles. Those without illustrious pasts either lied and invented them, or took pride in what they could. If you were Irish, you fancied yourself the descendant of poets and kings, not part of the wretched refuse the English viewed as dogs and treated as subhumans.

Now it's the other way around. People like to identify themselves as the downtrodden. Rhodes scholar Bill Clinton likes to talk about his alcoholic father. Louis Farrakhan, who lives in a mansion and drives Rolls-Royces bought with money extracted from the poorest elements in America, complains about rich Jews. We haven't seen Queen Elizabeth, sitting in front of Balmoral Castle with her corgis on her lap, sobbing to David Frost about how traumatic it is to think of the flight of Charles II from the Roundheads, and how she needs therapy because of it. But I suppose we will.

I'm always amazed how leaders of the highest accomplishment, those who have been to the poshest schools and benefited from both helping hands and the fruits of their own efforts, can, in some moment of extremity, suddenly start talking as if they were rag dolls.

Bob Packwood screeched hysterically and pointed at the bottle the second he was caught with his tongue in an array of unwilling mouths. Clarence Thomas, quavering at having allegations of his sexual peccadilloes trotted out in public, cried, "This is a high-tech lynching for uppity blacks." He's a Supreme Court justice now, so I guess he was overreacting.

That's what happens when victimhood gets trotted out—as it does so often nowadays: you quickly shed your individuality and find yourself clutching blindly at the historic wrongs committed against whatever people you happen to belong to.

The coercive power that victimhood offers in our civil society has been much commented on. Even though, like any currency, it has become devalued through overabundance, the temptation is to dig into your pocket and spend a little victimhood.

Identifying yourself with a certain group seems to mean you lose all sense of proportion. I am always utterly mystified at American Indians who protest over their image being used as athletic team mascots. Don't they have bigger problems? Isn't this something of a losing issue to pin your identity on?

One Indian advocate, in the constant hoopla over team mascots, raised the question of how Jews would feel if there was a team called "The Brooklyn Fighting Jews." My answer, honest, immediate, 100 percent sincere, is "Fantastic." I would buy a big Brooklyn Fighting Jews sweatshirt and wear it to the newspaper on the weekends. I'd buy a banner from the New York Sluggin' Hassids, complete with caricature of a hook-nosed rebbe blasting one out of the park. I'd put it over my kid's crib.

The native American response is that Jews are a secure, established, respected subgroup, and thus can afford to indulge in a little undignified humor. And I would respond that farmers in Iowa don't blame low crop prices on a conspiracy between the Sioux and the Pawnee. And they would say . . .

When you begin playing victimization, there is always, always, *always* a reaction. It's like a tennis game forever locked at love-love.

Even if, for some reason, the sports teams capitulated and scrapped their symbols, this does not mean that the grim activists who showed up on network TV the week of the Indians-Braves World Series would then heave a satisfied sigh and get back to whatever real lives they might enjoy. No, they would seize on those red plastic Indian figures sold at Woolworth's, or reruns of "The Lone Ranger," or something else to bitch about. Because once you taste the fruit of victimhood, you can't just give it up. The tonic is too heady, too addictive. The March of Dimes used to fight polio; once polio was cured, it switched to birth defects. The victims don't want to fold their tents and go away. What fun is that?

There's an editorial assistant at my office who sometimes wears a big sweatshirt with the image of that famous woodcut of slaves packed together in the hold of a ship on the front as well as the phrase: IMPORTED FROM AFRICA . . . On the back: AND I DIDN'T ASK TO COME.

Whenever I see it, I have the overwhelming urge to make up my own shirt, with that Margaret Bourke-White photo of concentration camp survivors peering weakly through a barbed-wire fence on the front. And on the back, in huge letters: MY FAMILY DIED IN THE HOLOCAUST AND ALL I GOT WAS THIS LOUSY T-SHIRT.

But I figure the subtlety would be lost on people, and other Jews at the office would complain, the way they did when somebody in management put up a Christmas tree a couple years ago.

The cult of victimization widens the already yawning chasms between people. I dislike the editorial assistant, based entirely on her wardrobe, which I consider a not-so-subtle way of flipping everybody the bird, all day long. Maybe she already doesn't like me, based on the color of my skin, and just wants to make the feeling mutual. The point is that we'll never get to know each other now, because great historical wrongs are being casually used for cheap effect.

You don't even have to be a victim to feel victimized. In 1995 at Northwestern University, a smug enclave of money and comfort if ever there was one, the Asian-American students, who comprise more than 20 percent of the student population, demanded an Asian-American studies program be installed.

The university, which already has an Asian studies department, agreed in principle but didn't move quickly enough. A dozen students staged a hunger strike—the classic protest of the powerless—demanding the university implement the program *now.* "We've been waiting three years," explained one of the hungry students, as if that were an unbearably long time for a new academic department to be crafted.

The student protest is just another symptom of viewing your ethnicity as a charge card to buy status with. It wasn't about education. Any of the students could get their masters degrees studying how the Chinese built the railroads, or the Japanese were interred in camps during World War II, or whatever. But individual study doesn't have the political clout and social cachet of a *department,* and the students figured, heck, if we comprise nearly a quarter of the school, we should get our own building. After all, the blacks have a department. The Slavs have a department. Even the Germans have a department. It's only fair. Waaaaaa.

How long will it be before Northwestern institutes a Department of Horny Teen Studies? Or offers a major in Indolent Sorority Girlhood, once the great number of students who fall into that category realize their power? ("We are not merely a sorority, we are a *people,*" declares Missy Taylor, leading the sit-down protest at the Tri Delt house. "And our stories must be told!")

The assault on Western Culture spearheaded by this type of thinking has been discussed, ad nauseam, and I don't intend to further the debate here, except to add that there is something terribly immature and sad about only being able to relate to your own victim group and demanding that the main culture bow to it. When I was twelve, I segregated my baseball cards of Jewish players into an all-Jew team—Sandy Koufax on the mound, Ken

Holtzman in the bullpen, Al Rosen on third base, etc.— and took a certain pride and satisfaction out of reading the lives of the great Jewish ballplayers, such as Hank Greenberg.

But I grew up. And realized that to view the world purely from the perspective of your own culture is to build a wall around yourself, constructing a private ghetto of the mind. My favorite writer is James Thurber, who suffered from the same genteel anti-Semitism that afflicted just about every single American born in the nineteenth century. Now, I suppose I could refuse to read him, based on his feelings about Jews, and maybe lobby to get his books pulled out of North Shore schools.

But I wouldn't be harming Thurber, who is safely in the grave—all I would be doing is denying great writing to myself and others based on a complete non sequitur, the way that many Jews reject Wagner's operas because he was an anti-Semite and the Nazis liked him—as if Wagner had some sort of retroactive complicity in World War II. Such thinking is so selective—Hitler liked Mickey Mouse, too, remember, but you never hear about people turning up their noses at *Fantasia* because of the aid and comfort that Mickey gave the Führer.

This subject is perhaps one that would have prudently been left out of a book aspiring to humor. But for anyone working in a big office in downtown Chicago, victimhood and class, race and ethnicity are such a swirling undercurrent, causing so many annoying and uncomfortable, if not downright awful, incidents and situations, that I felt dishonest and cowardly not to address it, if only in a half-ass way. The solemn donning of the mantle of victimhood has become a particularly acute modern annoyance.

I used to sit directly across from a large, effervescent black reporter. We were friends, I thought. I invited her to my wedding and she came. She invited me to her wedding and I went. One night we stayed out late and drank together.

Then one day I wrote a story on Boy Scouts from a troop at the Cabrini Green housing project attending a Scout camp in Michigan. It was a fun story. I got to go to camp in Michigan. The kids were cool, the setting great. Since the tiny town around the camp was dry, and none of the restaurants served booze, in the evening the Boy Scout publicist and I stopped by a supermarket and bought a frozen pizza and a bottle of Jack Daniel's and consumed them back at a cabin. For years, I cherished the remnant of the bottle as the whiskey that had been purchased for me by the Boy Scouts of America.

I wrote a story about these city teens who found themselves, suddenly, in the Michigan woods. I always like to start an article with a sharp image, and the sharpest image that caught my eye was a Scout who was sweeping out a fire ring, wearing a pair of new patent leather oxford shoes. The contrast between the shiny dancing shoes and the crumbly brown leaves told it all. "I ain't got no camp shoes," he explained, and I quoted him in the front-page article.

This, my reporter friend decided, was racism, and she went directly to the editor and complained about it. Had the Scout been white, she said, I'd have cleaned up the quote to "I do not possess any camping-type footwear" or something.

She was wrong. If the Scout had been some Irish punk from Bridgeport I would have done the same thing, be-

cause the slangy comment increased the sense of citifica-
tion and emphasized the contrast I was trying to point out.
But that wasn't what bothered me. I could comprehend
her feeling the way she did—it wasn't utterly insane. What
mystified me was her feeling that way and going straight to
my boss's boss's boss's boss. She sat across from me. Directly. When I looked up from my desk, I looked right into
her eyes, eight hours a day. She knew me. She was, I
thought, *my friend.* If she felt that I had done this terrible
thing, why not just talk to me?

This all came out during the screaming argument we
had right smack in the center of the newsroom foyer. She
said something akin to "Why do *they* always . . ." and I
said "There is no *they;* it was *me.* Me! I did it! . . ." and the
issue lingered for a few hours until I had the presence of
mind to do a computer check on her byline and the phrase
"ain't got no." Taking a red china marker, I circled each
time she quoted black people, including Jesse Jackson, using that phrase. I gave a copy to her and left a copy in the
editor's mailbox. End of tempest.

We didn't speak again for a year, not even to say hello,
and we barely speak now. To tell you the truth, I felt
wronged. I felt sort of like a victim. Perhaps I am due
something. . . .

W Is for Workplace

Like the innocent little ants and grasshoppers grown to enormous size by exposure to radiation in those cheap 1950s horror movies, the cozy corner groceries and local hardware stores of the hazy past have become monstrous by exposure to corruptive market forces.

Joining the giant supermarkets and colossal lumber palaces are mammoth electronics outlets, gigantic bookstores and geomorphic discount warehouses, each new site larger than the one before, swelling, pulsating, threatening to devour the landscape. The megastores are so immense that birds sometimes fly through their yawning entranceways and take up residence in the rafters, set so dizzyingly high that nobody dares attempt to rescue the terrified creatures from their perches.

Such voluminous space is necessary because these establishments try to crush their competition, not through improved service, but by offering every item imaginable within their chosen product range at prices impossible to match. At Office Depot stores, for instance, you can purchase anything from desks to pencils to computers to Waterman pens to bulk coffee and Italian cookies to go with the coffee.

Nothing is left to chance in chains like these. No elderly clerk named Paul will wander over, inquire about the kids and the sciatica, then mention that you should think about getting one of those new ergonomic chairs—better for the back. You will never see a homemade sign pushing a special on paper clips.

Rather, everything at Office Depot is sharp and bright and anonymous. The employees, most under the age of twenty-one, learning the ropes of their first jobs. The signs, professionally typeset, printed up at a central location and distributed along the chain.

The only impulses for human contact are those decreed by corporate headquarters. I walked into an Office Depot once and the manager of the hour, reacting to the arrival of a customer unit, barked to no one in particular: "Where is our greeter? Who is our greeter?" Nothing happened and, as I hurried past, embarrassed, she assumed the odious duty herself, grinning and exuding false bonhomie like gas. "Hello, welcome to Office Depot," she yelled after me as I fled into the boundless expanse of the store.

With no discretion left to individual stores, and all personal contact carefully scripted, if not executed, it is curious in the extreme that customers entering any Office Depot are confronted, first thing, immediately after the big pneumatic doors whoosh open, with a glaring sign: WE TEST ALL JOB APPLICANTS FOR ILLEGAL DRUG USE! The letters are three and a half inches high, red on a vivid orange background.

The signs are intended, no doubt, to comfort customers, who might otherwise worry that the gangly clerk tracking down their Pink Pearl eraser has taken a little something to allay the tedium of working in such a place. The signs let customers know that they may purchase freely, without fear of any nasty surprises later on because their selections had been rung up by a cashier with a head full of psilocybin. ("Hey, *wait a minute!* They charged me forty-five bucks for that box of chalk!")

That is the idea, though to me the signs are not soothing but rather mystifying, hateful and offensive. I see them as a political statement, no less than if they read KEEP FOREIGNERS OUT! or AN ARMED SOCIETY IS A FREE SOCIETY.

True, it makes sense that school bus drivers should control their intake of heroin during business hours. And it is wrong that every Amtrak accident is followed by revelation that the employees responsible for the train's safety had spent the last moments before the crash lounging in their private opium den car, holding smoldering bamboo shoots to the tarry black chunks of pen yan in the bowls of their long pipes.

But Office Depot? What's the worry? It's not as if customers running in for some No. 2 pencils are concerned that the clerk assisting them is benefiting from a fog of psychedelics. ("Look, Mr. Henderson! The colored pencils . . . are *beautiful!*") Maybe wacked-out clerks were shedding their red vests and scampering into the overhead storage racks, à la Quasimodo on the ramparts of Notre Dame

Cathedral, hurling crates of ring binders down on the terrified customers below.

But I doubt it.

My guess is that the purpose of crowing about drug testing is just that, to crow about drug testing—another way of bragging OUR EMPLOYEES ARE UNDER A TIGHT LEASH. Companies have a historic horror of employees somehow retaining individual characteristics after hiring. Today the main concern is employing pharmacopoeians. In the 1960s it was good employee grooming. In the fifties, Communism. Twenty years earlier, trade unionism.

It's always something. Ever since efficiency expert Frederick Winslow Taylor first espoused his "scientific management" theories ninety years ago, big business has been enamored of the idea that workers are uniformly lazy, morally corrupt, would-be felons, snoozing on the job and stealing the rubber bands. That is, unless keenly watched by ever growing layers of managers and foremen and observers and spies. Taylorism has at times threatened to go out of style, particularly when America noticed that Japanese companies were somehow squeaking by with a system of respect for rather than distrust of employees. But that moment quickly passed, into the neo-Taylorism of today, as evidenced by the belief that drug addicts are bungling stationery sales. Office Depot obviously thinks the situation is so bad that it can derive competitive advantage by proudly announcing it has managed to recruit the handful of clerks who aren't junkies, at least when hired. (If anything could drive a person to the needle, working at a giant discount store could. Perhaps the sign should read: WE MONITOR OUR EMPLOYEES FOR SIGNS OF INCIPIENT ILLEGAL DRUG USE!)

The drug test is just another of the ritual humiliations involved with becoming employed. A rite of passage, from proud if penurious freedom to indentured sufficiency. Businesses love to extend the ring then, as the prospective employee goes to kiss it, slowly lower the hand to hip level. Kneel.

When they hired me at the *Chicago Sun-Times,* years ago, they never said what the blood test I had to take was testing for, and I never asked. I didn't have to. I knew, or thought I did. Looking back at it now, even if the blood wasn't tested at all—for dope or AIDS or whatever—it was a neat little bit of symbolic theater. *"Ahh, welcome to what we like to think of as 'our little family.' Now, if you'll just roll up your sleeve, we'd like to have some of your lifeblood, just for safekeeping. . . ."* I guess I should be grateful they used a needle and not a vise.

Of course, Taylor didn't invent workplace degradation—ever since work began bosses have been grinding their underlings in whatever way they saw fit, with unsafe conditions, irrational demands and crushing workloads. "A job," Brendan Behan once wrote, "is death without the dignity."

In fact, it is the idea that work should be anything but torture that is relatively new.

New, though not by any means universally accepted. In many instances, taking a job is a trip back in time to some Dickensian workhouse where conditions are so horrid they would be funny if they weren't also real.

The tales are legion. The *Wall Street Journal* reported in 1995 that women working on a Nabisco chili-canning production line in Oxnard, California, had taken to wearing adult diapers, because the company wouldn't give them sufficient bathroom breaks.

Also in 1995, the government accused a Chicago manufacturer, the Chicago Faucet Company, of skirting safety regulations by monitoring the lead levels in employees' blood and firing workers who had too much lead in their systems.

And not so terribly long ago McDonald's was famous for forcing its employees to take lie-detector tests, at peril of losing their degrading minimum-wage jobs, to determine whether they harbored pro-union sympathies or, worse, had ever given away a free hamburger.

The list could go on forever. Starry-eyed futurists like to talk about the End of Work in the Information Age (I am actually showing my age: nowadays they talk about the End of Physical Reality itself) and we like to pretend that technology has eliminated unpleasant work conditions. But that just isn't so. Some jobs resist automation. Those frozen egg rolls you buy at the supermarket? Wrapped by hand, usually. Egg-roll-wrapping machines are still an evolving technology. I was amazed to discover, touring a seafood wholesaler called the Chicago Fish House, that there is a group of men whose job it is to debone whitefish fillets. They stand eight hours a day, in a 45-degree room, running their bare hands over the cold, wet fish fillets, feeling for the delicate, translucent bones and then pulling them out with needle-nosed pliers. No piece of equipment could do the same without reducing the fillets to mush. The deboners can't wear gloves; they would miss the bones.

The men seem to like their work and have been doing it for years, which brings to mind a recent BBC special called "The Worst Job in the World." It began, I'm told, with a bathroom attendant, who of course didn't think his job was so bad, but said that prostitutes have a worse job. Then the show talked to a prostitute, who thought she had it better off than morticians. A mortician was glad he wasn't a slaughterhouse worker, who felt he had it better than maggot farmers, and so on, until the program ended up with the Prime Minister, who didn't comment. He probably would have agreed that he had the worst job in the world—bosses are always the ones to feel sorriest for themselves—"lonely at the top" and all that crap.

Those at the top have the luxury of being able to complain without fear. Employees have a reluctance to bitch in public, because you never know who's listening. The most you can usually get out of a beleaguered employee is a grudging admission of the obvious. I remember visiting a mid-sized public relations firm in Chicago, run by an outsized, flashy woman. Over the secretary's head was a giant sign, spelling out the woman's name—Margie—in pink neon. Like all neon signs, it had a transformer—a big one, since the sign was so big—and it put out a hum. A loud hum, buzzing right next to the secretary's head. "Doesn't that hum drive you crazy?" I asked the secretary, while waiting for the great woman to present herself. She looked up with an expression of infinite weariness. "On some days more than others," she said.

That actually sums up the dilemma of the workplace in one elegant sentence. "On some days more than others." I'm sure that even the best job in the world—the guy who runs up with a little sable brush to fleck the sand off the hind ends of swimsuit models posing on tropical beaches for *Sports Illustrated* fashion shoots—must have its dreary days, when the models are grumpy ("Get that brush away from my butt, you foul little man!"), or the weather is chill, or the hangover lingers, or the langouste is chewy.

Which is why workplaces are so bothersome—generally good or generally bad, whether a giant, clangorous factory or a suite of sedate offices, you are always required to show up. If work is, by definition, something you don't want to do but have to, then the workplace is anywhere you don't want to be but, tragically, unavoidably, *are.*

Not only do you have to actually physically appear at your workplace, but often you have to wear some sort of special outfit. These uniforms range from the uncomfortable to the ugly to the merely mindless. While the chicken hats and hot dog suits of food workers are the subject of much ridicule, even more laughable are the unspoken, unwritten, yet nevertheless equally rigid strictures put on lawyers and managers and the like, who don't usually even recognize that their dress is as tightly controlled as a counterman's at Burger World. I once interviewed at IBM for a writer's job. As they led me to the communications office, I noticed that everybody wore a blue tie. Sitting down for the interview, the first words out of my mouth were, "Do you all gotta wear those blue ties?" I was not hired.

This may be changing. A decade after young guys in scraggly beards and T-shirts at companies such as Microsoft and Apple nearly mooted IBM into obscurity, Big Blue announced that the employees it hadn't laid off could now dress more casually. Many staid law firms and advertising agencies followed suit, some issuing press releases, as if they had discovered the special secret of the energetic companies running rings around them: khakis. There is something ineffably sad about a billion-dollar corporation crowing about letting its managers wear golf shirts on Fridays akin to a faded tearoom in the basement of a moribund hotel grandly announcing that ladies will no longer be required to wear gloves at the second seating.

Loss of control over how you dress is just one way that the workplace saps the self-determination adults imagine is their right. Having to labor within the usually ghastly setting of the workplace is another. I work at a typical place of employment, the Chicago Sun-Times Building, a squat, gray, trapezoidal monstrosity built in 1958—once called "the ugliest building in Chicago" by *Time* magazine, quite a statement in a city with so many hideous structures that a local paper once polled architects about which buildings they would most like to dynamite.

The Sun-Times Building made the list; a person can hardly approach the building without reflecting on the utter aesthetic bankruptcy of whoever constructed it, especially since it is next door to the spun-sugar fantasy of the Wrigley Building, with its rococo clock tower and its quaint little sky bridge. Taken together, the pair of buildings looks like a fancy Victorian wedding cake set next to an overturned galvanized metal bucket. (Though, give the *Sun-Times* credit; its location has one of the most beautiful urban vistas in the world, provided you are inside the building, looking out.)

Turning from the windows, however, is another matter. Most reporters don't have offices, and the attendant office walls, so all you can do is pretty up your desk space with snow domes and bobbing-head dolls and ironic little signs and pointed cartoons, anything to rest your eyes on during the interminable span while waiting to see if the Grieving Mother will take your call.

Comforting as they may be to the owner, these little stabs at whimsy, the satirical cartoons often plastered on the chest-level office dividers, are ultimately in vain. Instead of actually rebelling against the soul-sucking demands of the workplace, the posted "Blondie" with Mr. Dithers kicking Dagwood in the pants, or whatever, is really a surrender to the status quo. Life sucks—chuckle and keep working. More than summoning up even a shred of the comfort of the beach at Waikiki, the postcard of Hawaii serves more to underscore the reality that one is laboring under fluorescent lights in a little soundproofed cubicle.

Another downside to the tradition of spicing up your work area with a splash of decoration and personality is that everybody else does so too. Thus while your own particular brand of taste and humor invariably strikes you as true and ennobling, other people's effluvia typically range from dull to ugly to offensive.

Photographs of people's kids are common decorations in offices. They can be extra annoying. It's troubling to be reminded that office mates have children, because coworkers are generally such putzes, and it is painful to think that impressionable children are looking up to these idiots as godlike parents, learning from them, idolizing them. Such an evil fate—these poor innocent tots will go through their entire sad lives, tortured that Mommy didn't love them, endlessly analyzing Daddy's pat sayings and banal aphorisms, never knowing that in the real world Mom was the office moron and people could hardly wait until Dad got out of earshot so they could begin singing their rondos of ridicule, the avowed enemies beginning the tune, then the false friends chiming in and the bemused bystanders finishing out the round.

Whenever colleagues bring their children to the office, so as to enjoy a proud moment of cynosure, it takes restraint not to draw the tykes aside, get down on one knee, make intense eye contact and repeat several times, slowly: "It isn't your fault. Your father is just an idiot. Please remember that. Not your fault; father an idiot; please remember."

I should also add—just in case any of my confreres break down and buy my book this time ("We're all waiting for you to show up with a big box and hand them out," a fellow reporter once said by way of explanation)—that, all told, being a newspaper reporter is probably one of the better occupations a person can have, particularly at a union newspaper like the *Sun-Times,* where the normal cringing subservience of those on the lower rungs is mitigated by a sense of mutual security. Basically unfirable unless they copy directly from the *Tribune* and steal office equipment, both within the same thirty-day period, while drunk, my fellow reporters therefore display, shall we say, a certain *je ne sais quoi* not found at your average insurance office.

Add to this freedom the enormous benefit that, as a reporter, you are constantly being sent away, out of the office, someplace else. True, that place is frequently on fire. Or an apartment on the upper floors of a dismal and dangerous housing project. But you are just as likely to be sent to a cocktail party. Once, after some pathetic schlepp embezzled $250,000 from his company and spent it, the police said, at a strip club, I was dispatched to the club in question. There I spent a couple of days, sitting at a table up front, sipping Heineken and trying to strike up conversations with nearly naked women. Believe me, you haven't lived until you've turned in an expense account form with "Tips to strippers," and "Table dances" itemized on it. My only disappointment was that accounting paid it, no questions asked. The bastards.

X Is for Xerox®

 For years now, villains in movies have not waved around big bundles of obviously fake currency, the kind with the pair of oval portraits that look like reprints of Confederate money.

And one rarely sees the backdrop ripple in a major studio production anymore. They've got that problem licked, with computer imaging and glass matte painting and blue screens and the million other magical tricks that have created a population of ten-year-olds who can yawn into their fists and wonder about dinner while heads explode on matinee screens and asteroids sprout arms and legs and start tap dancing as they twirl through outer space.

So why do we have the "555" phone number prefix? I can't be the only person who hates it, who finds the most thrilling adventure plot, with Bruce Willis and ka-powing weaponry and careening cars, stop dead in its tracks as the hero, rubbing the side of a pencil over the pad found in the villain's hotel room, finds a clue: the phone number 555-1234.

It's worse than the boom mike dunking briefly but noticeably into a scene. Worse than a Roman senator checking his watch to see if it's time to assassinate Caesar. Worse, even, than Horatio, kneeling next to Hamlet's body, looking straight into the camera, winking largely and whispering from behind the back of his hand: "Don't worry—it's okay. He's not really dead. We're just acting."

Sure, I know why they do it. Some segment of the population is brain dead enough that if they see a phone number on the screen they'll call it, the way certain idiots stick their fingers into running machinery to see what happens. The person getting the calls—invariably an old lady in Sandusky—then screams bloody murder and sues the film company.

So AT&T rolled out the 555 prefix. It had been reserved for long-distance directory assistance numbers, and thus no real phone numbers began with it. Now 555 would serve as a code for phony phone numbers.

And it did fool people, for about a week. But now, after years of seeing it in every movie, television show, print ad and even a few books that need to mention a phone number, 555 has become as irksome as if, for legal reasons, novelists started calling their characters Adam Alpha, Bill Beta, George Gamma and such, so as not to provoke lawsuits from living people who might actually share a character's name.

The thoroughly obvious 555 isn't the only solution, you know. With every plot line more complex than the story of a man tossing playing cards into a hat costing $100 million to film, how much more would it cost to rent a phone line for three years to handle the calls of the bored and the inquisitive? Two hundred bucks? That's a wax job on the Batmobile. Half a wax job. Maybe.

One film actually did do that. The generally forgettable *Sneakers* with Robert Redford. Call the number seen in the movie, and you got a recorded message touting the film. But nobody else, to my knowledge, made use of such a fine idea. It is as puzzling as if nobody thought to follow up *The Great Train Robbery* with more Westerns.

The 555 flaw is just another blindness of movie makers, who are able to insert the weirdest annoying bits into their movies without care for the effect on the audience. I know that by the third time a character fondles a Diet Coke can, or drives by yet another Taco Bell delivery truck, the screen might as well go blank as far as my involvement in the movie is concerned. You might as well have Humphrey Bogart throw his arm over Claude Raines's shoulders at the end of *Casablanca* and say, "You know, Louie, I think this is the start of big savings week at Venture . . ." With digital sampling, someday he probably will.

I'm not a director. But I imagine it is a long road to become one, a struggle, an uphill apprenticeship, fetching bags of doughnuts and coffee for Oliver Stone while he screams at you, spittle flying off his lips. "Not *these* doughnuts! Not *this* coffee!" You'd think after scrabbling to a position where you're telling Arnold Schwarzenegger to try raising an eyebrow when he pulls the trigger, that you sure wouldn't start littering the scene with pizza boxes just so Pizza Hut will add a couple hundred G to the bottom line. Maybe that part of the process is outside your control. The producers do it, or some third party—the famous "they"—whom nobody has any control over does it, just another tick toward mediocrity of the vast corporate effort that films have been for a long, long time.

Movies of course are not the only place where commerce sticks its big unwanted bazoo into artistic effort. We've already talked about advertisements jangling everywhere we look. As if metastasizing ads weren't bad enough, corporations also want to control how you speak, write and think, especially when it comes to their multitudinous brand names. For instance, if I wrote the sentence, "Whenever I get hopping mad I calm myself by sticking a fistful of Oreos into my big gaping maw," the Nabisco Company, rather than being happy to see its product plugged in such a high-quality Doubleday book, would instead zip off a terse legalistic letter informing me that they prefer the sentence to read, "Whenever I get hopping mad I calm myself by sticking a fistful of Oreo® brand sandwich cookies into my big gaping maw," thank you, and would I please be so good as to conform my writing to suit their pleasure in the future.

Perhaps I'm only sensitive to this because I'm a journalist. The *Columbia Journalism Review* seems to be underwritten, at times, by companies sternly admonishing the press exactly how to use one of their 700,000 and counting registered trademarks. "The word Jeep can indicate only our brand," warns Chrysler. "Sometimes people say they want a 'weedeater' when they really want a Weed Eater® brand trimmer," instructs an ad from the Weed Eater people. "When it's just bleach, it's just bleach . . . it's not CLOROX!" commands Clorox.

As with the 555 prefix, there is a common-sense reason for this. I understand they are just trying to protect their trademarks. That if they don't, they run the risk of losing their rights to the brand name they so carefully built up over the years, the way Bayer lost "aspirin," the way Kimberly-Clark lost "Kleenex." (Ah, ha-ha-hah, just kidding. Of course Kimberly-Clark still owns the name "Kleenex"—*so far!*)

Okay, to a point. But here's my question: where's my cut? If I want to start my new novel, *Windsurfing in a Winnebago,* with "Karen sneezed into a Kleenex," what do I care if that puts Kimberly-Clark one microstep toward insolvency? "Karen sneezed into a tissue" might not carry the sort of cultural Zeitgeist I want to convey. There isn't that doubling of the K's that so titillates us alliteration fans, or the soft echo of "sneeze" in "Kleenex," so important to those of us sensitive to these things.

You perhaps remember that, in J is for Journalism, I mention a barfly keeping his wallet in a "Baggie." That should of course have been a "Baggies® brand plastic sandwich bag." But so what? The second way sounds stupid. As does "Big Mac hamburger sandwich" and "Kool-Aid soft drink mix" and most of the other preferred trademark usages.

If I'm policing my writing, if I'm an editor scrutinizing copy, what do I care if some multinational corporation loses control of the product name it has already made uncounted millions from? Let them lose it. If I am talking about the sculpted young people rolling up and down the lakefront, the best way to express that is: "Fabulous babes were rollerblading under the cloudless blue sky." Now I know Rollerblade Inc. would prefer "Fabulous babes were in-line skating under the cloudless blue sky," or, ideally, "Fabulous babes were enjoying Rollerblade® brand skates under the cloudless blue sky."

Tough. Come and get me, coppers. Take me to Trademark Jail. I think the corporations' stand is as morally indefensible as if Ted Turner started taking out ads urging people to view only the colorized version of *Casablanca,* which he has copyright to, and not the superior black and white original, now in the public domain.

Companies should be thankful if their brand is so popular that people want to misuse the name. If they're not careful, they won't have trademark problems because nobody will be familiar with their products. Among the dozen hectoring trademark ads in a single issue of the *Columbia Journalism Review,* one was from Frigidaire, claiming, "It's a name that's so popular some people call every refrigerator a Frigidaire®." People in nursing homes, maybe.

That's the only reason I stopped saying I was "Xeroxing" something. Not because Xerox has lawyers stomping around, waggling their fingers at usage criminals. (During the Watergate hearings, Xerox dispatched a letter to Sam Erwin nearly every day, asking him to request that documents be "photocopied." He ignored them, and wisely so.)

What got me to stop using "Xerox" as a verb was the realization that I never saw actual Xerox photocopying machines anymore. They were always Canons or Toshibas or some such thing. Calling every photocopier a "Xerox machine" is like calling every CD player a "Victrola." Soon their trademark will be as secure as Hupmobile's.

At least companies are overt about protecting their trademarks. Particularly scary is the way commerce can warp public discourse without anyone knowing. Newspapers kowtow to advertisers in a reflexive, automatic way. The advertisers don't even have to complain anymore—editors censor themselves. When an enterprising Chicago photographer shot pictures of vice cops arresting perverts in the restroom of Marshall Field's, there was never a question of any local newspaper running the dramatic shots, or reporting on the story, even though the cops said that trysting in the restrooms of downtown department stores is a common problem, and you'd think Mr. and Mrs. Charge Card would want to know about it before they packed Timmy off to the john.

Marshall Field's, I'm sure, would argue that it pays good money to run advertisements, and thus it is only fair that the newspapers show a little gratitude.

But that's not how it works, at least in my mind. You pay a fee to your doctor, but that doesn't mean he should smile and whack you on the back and tell you how hale and hearty you are, when he knows there's a tumor on your X ray the size of a catawba melon. You pay a doctor to be a professional and tell you the truth. Nobody ever shrieks, *"Cancer?!* Look, bub, I'm shelling out $95 for this visit, so just go on back and see if you can't come up with something a little better than that!"

The problem isn't limited to news. A writer can't care about corporate niceties and still be funny. Let's say that I was one day struck by how much the symbol on the new Toyotas—an oval with an upward arc cutting through it—resembles a horned head. A devil's head, really, with two curving horns. It is not an immense leap of logic to deduce that Toyota Motors is somehow in league with Satan, the way that certain fundamentalists who happened to also be

Amway dealers caused a lot of concern for Procter & Gamble by accusing it of being a claque of devil-worshipers, based on the company's moon and stars logo.

Now, at least to me, accusing Toyota of being a satanic cult (they are based in Japan, aren't they?) is funny. I don't have any evidence that this is the case. (Isn't Japan where the Aum Shinrikyu cult was putting poison gas in the subways?) I haven't done any research. (How do we know that Toyota isn't in cahoots with remnants of the Aum cult?) But still, the mind does start to wander. (How do we know that Toyota automobiles don't all have secret cylinders of poison gas, which can be released on the same signal, perhaps sent via satellite by Toyota's Aum cult overlords?)

I would not in good conscience suggest such a thing. I myself have owned several Toyotas and find them wonderfully reliable cars. (Of course they're reliable. Were Satan to manufacture an automobile, it would be reliable, wouldn't it? How else to get millions of Americans behind the wheel of their Toyotas when the company's Aum cult masters unleash the poison gas?)

I'd hate to have such pleasant free associations reined in by concern over what threatening and litigious letters might be dispatched by the Toyota Corporation. (And the Devil would have good lawyers, wouldn't he? He'd probably be a lawyer himself, like in *The Devil and Daniel Webster. . . .*)

Attacking lawyers has become high fashion, but in truth lawyers are only the vehicle. It is the idea that the law is a cudgel with which to bash rivals that has so deteriorated modern life in every aspect. Anyone is free to pick up the club, but the more cash you have, the bigger wallop you can deliver, and that usually is enough to win the day. A delightful, elegant little eatery opened a few years ago on Adams Street, half a block from the Art Institute. It called itself the Russian Tea Café. Rich red booths, Russian music, and wonderful food as authentic as if my grandmother had clawed her way out of the grave and prepared it herself. The black bread, fresh. The vodka, ice cold, and in a variety of diverting flavors—tea, lemon, anise, you name it.

And best of all, the service is perfect. The owner's son, a modest, downy-faced young man of formal bearing, stands at the door and, as soon as you walk in, starts bowing and weeping and kissing your hand—well, close enough. He is really, really happy to see you, and makes you feel, if only for a moment, that you aren't just another anonymous cog taking your feed, marking time until you pitch forward with a coronary and the cold, indifferent city flows around you as if you had never been there. You are special.

Needless to say, the restaurant soon became enormously popular among Chicagoans, with crowds struggling to get in every night, and reservations needed weeks in advance. And then, in the middle of it, the place changed its name—to Russian Tea Time, a ridiculous moniker that sounds like a Slavic nursery school.

The explanation for the sudden change is that eventually word of the Russian Tea Café's success got to the people running the wheezy, inferior Russian Tea Room in New York City. They decided that the Russian Tea Café's name was too similar to its own august name, and the requisite legal letters of threat and demand were dispatched.

Now, the chances for confusion were nil. The restaurants are seven hundred miles apart. Few people would find themselves musing, "Mmmm, maybe I'll fly to New York and get a blini," then noticing the Russian Tea Café and thinking, "Oh, never mind, it's right here." But the fact was that the Russian Tea Room felt it had a case and got its way, simply because the tiny young restaurant it picked on wasn't about to pay the legal fees and go to court and challenge them.

The underlying thread running through these tales of legal bullying and commercial cravenness is a very fragile idea—words carry power, dignity and authority, or at least they can, and when words are twisted because of business considerations, they change in a way that is usually not an improvement.

A little-remembered episode that took place twenty years ago will serve as both a mark of hope and a note of caution. In February 1976, *Esquire* magazine published a 23-page article by Harrison Salisbury. The magazine didn't pay Salisbury to write the article—the Xerox Corporation did, a whopping $40,000 at that, for the privilege of "sponsoring" the article.

This was something new under the sun. Advertisers had, of course, bought ads in magazines. But this was the first time the author of an article had been the appointed squire of a particular advertiser. Most on the scene looked up from their wallow, grunted, then flopped over in the sun. But the article was a fire bell in the night to the late, great E. B. White, who reared out of his New England retirement to dispatch a letter to the *American,* a tiny newspaper in Ellsworth, Maine.

"It doesn't take a giant intellect to detect in all this the shadow of disaster," he wrote. "If magazines decide to farm out their writers to advertisers and accept the advertiser's payment to the writer and to the magazine, then the periodicals of this country will be far down the drain and will become so fuzzy as to be indistinguishable from the controlled press in other parts of the world."

Astonishingly, the letter caught the attention of sentient minds at Xerox, who invited White to elaborate on his concerns over their newly coined practice.

"Whenever money changes hands, something goes along with it—an intangible something that varies with the circumstances," White wrote. "It would be hard to resist the suspicion that *Esquire* feels indebted to Xerox, that Mr. Salisbury feels indebted to both, and that the ownership, or sovereignty, of *Esquire* has been nibbled all around the edges."

The sponsorship, White wrote, was "not in itself evil, but it is the beginning of evil and it is an invitation to evil."

Xerox stopped sponsoring articles, and direct corporate involvement with the content of major magazines never caught on. Today, of course, magazines—all media—are corrupted by commerce in a thousand ways, large and small. As this book goes to press, IBM and NBC have just announced that they will produce half-hour computer infomercials and fob them off as science programs. But the idea of an old man's letter in a tiny New England newspaper inhibiting a billion-dollar corporation, at least for a while, is quite a comfort to us writers. Despite the money changing hands, despite all the loss of stature that comes from selling oneself, words still convey meaning. *Sometimes,* if luck holds, they can convey meaning.

Y Is for Yugoslavia

 In college I actually took a class in Eastern European politics. I was studying Russian and fancied that I might go into the foreign service. The class was taught by a crusty old professor named R. Barry Farrell. I used to be able to do a pretty good impression of R. Barry Farrell, contorting my tongue and talking through my nose so I could reproduce his gruff squawk. "So . . . Yorgi Yorgidezhe goes to *Mas*cow and . . . *maybe* he was *pushed* and *maybe* he *jahmped* . . . but either way he ended up at Lubyanka Prison on a *slaaaaab.*"

The amazing thing is, I actually used a bit of the knowledge gained in that class. Just once, years later. I started getting my hair cut at a place up the street. The lady cutting my hair had an accent, and during our idle, haircut conversation I asked where she was from. "Albania," she said. "Albania," I replied. "Is Enver Hoxha still running the place?" He wasn't, but I could tell the stylist was really impressed. Not many people can dredge up any information at all about Albania. I don't know how I retained Hoxha's name—I guess it's just the sort of odd name that lodges in your mind.

If American readers pick up the *Economist,* they may notice how extensively the politics of other lands are reported on and analyzed in the British periodical. Not only does the *Economist* give a frank, hard look at this country, free from the How-Can-We-Lose-When-We're-So-Sincere gauze of good will that we use when viewing ourselves, but it also analyzes the rest of the world, from discussing what the opposition party in the Sudan is planning to do about the government's water purification project to how grass-roots banking in Kashmir is affecting women's issues there.

Europeans really care about other countries—maybe because there are so many of them, packed together in such a tight space. Europe is the size of Texas, practically, and has about ninety countries in it now, with new countries being added every day. They get in the habit of keeping an eye on one another, just to make sure they aren't about to be invaded, again. And with so many former European colonies and protectorates scattered about the globe, they keep tabs on everyone else as well.

Not us. American news magazines concentrate on presenting in-depth reports about fancy bras and unflinching examinations of this summer's crop of Hollywood thrillers. Most Americans are only roughly aware of what state they live in, never mind who their governor is, or who their senators may be. We can barely pay attention to our own politics, and even when we do, politics tends to be presented as a kind of theatrical game—which new cynical pose is being adopted, which is being expeditiously cast off, which buzz lines are working this week, which are not.

Internationally, forget it. Surveys of American high school students are always showing that they think the earth is flat, or that Japan is a hundred miles off the coast of California. Huge occurrences sweep right by, unnoticed. There was more press about the plight of Dian Fossey's gorillas in Rwanda than there was about the prelude to one of the most atrocious slaughters of human history in Rwanda. Oh, the nightmare may have made the cover of *Newsweek* once, but it was replaced the next week by Hootie and the Blowfish and quickly fell from public scrutiny.

The bottom line is: we don't care. That may sound harsh, but it's the truth. Why would we? We're having fun, here on the deck of the SS *United States,* big stupid drinks in hand, all of the women in pretty summer dresses, the men wearing those blue blazers with the gold buttons and those idiotic captain's hats with the patent leather brims. The vibraphone is burbling away, the conversation light and pleasant. Who would be so *callous* as to bring some distant, *negative* thing to our attention? Only people who have an ax to grind, who have a stake in the matter, who are somehow directly involved, like immigrants. Or malcontents, like the Barbra Streisand character in *The Way We Were,* always spoiling those nice parties with her leftist babble. The wonder isn't that Robert Redford left her but that he ever gave her the time of day to begin with. Only in the movies.

If we cared about anything overseas, the fact that our Nikes are made by slaves in Thailand, that our Gap pocket

T-shirts are assembled by eleven-year-olds in sweatshops in Indonesia, would bother us. We would pay an extra dollar and buy jeans made by impoverished people right here in our own country.

But we don't care. Suffering in some distant tropical port doesn't mean as much as getting a few bucks off the price of a pair of linen pants.

I'm not running our country down—we aren't any worse than anybody else in the world. We have problems here, too, you know, and you never see bighearted people in Japan filling shipping containers with warm clothing and sending them to New York to help the homeless. They aren't beating themselves up in Germany, wondering how crime has gotten so bad in the United States and what they, as Germans, should be doing about it. They laugh at us.

Each human heart only has so much sympathy in it— a small amount, at that—and it gets used up pretty fast right around town. Heck, your family usually uses up most of it, and anything left is spent trying to keep your own neighborhood from devolving into a Hobbesian state of nature. It is the rare heart that has enough concern in it to start exporting.

About fifteen years ago a prosaic encounter lodged in my mind as representing an important dilemma.

I was meeting a girl for a date. She was a little late getting ready, and I waited in the living room with her roommate, watching television. The latest horror was on—the famine was in Ethiopia that year, I believe, and the pictures were as bad as ever.

My date, finally ready, came into the room and the three of us watched for a moment. Then the roommate stood up and announced, "I can't stand to watch this." She walked out of the room.

At dinner, a good part of the conversation was spent discussing the roommate's action. Was it callousness, as my date insisted? Or was her leaving, as I suggested, the more human response? Were we two, so eager to absorb this nightmare, the ones who were unfeeling?

Years have passed since then, and I really haven't answered the question. A lot of people automatically ignore such things, just let it flow over their consciousness long enough to glom out the basic details, then tune the rest out. Others plunge into the latest reports from overseas as if fully exposing themselves to the horror is a way of doing penance for being in a good place. Are the viewers kind-hearted people who can't allow crimes to be committed in darkness? Or just voyeurs titillating themselves with the latest atrocity?

I never saw *Schindler's List*. I just couldn't bring myself to do it. Another friend did, however, and urged me to go. "It has a lot of cute women," he said.

It is a luxury, of course, to be only annoyed by the woes of the world. Usually, troubles from other places arrive in a much more concrete form. Bombs, for instance. Or the horrors of the world get into trucks and rumble into your small village. Ignoring the situation is not an option.

But the United States—nestled between our oceans, our pockets bulging with money, the best army ever training its night-vision goggles on the horizon—is fortunate enough to generally experience the world's sorrows vicariously, mostly on television. Even the poorest areas, the worst inner-city high-rise housing projects, are oases of calm and comfort compared to the stinking hellholes of real poverty in other countries.

Lately, the central international horror in the American public's consciousness has been the disintegration of Yugoslavia into its constituent parts, the way wine will turn into vinegar and sediment if left long enough in a hot cellar.

We relate to the former Yugoslavia better because it is located in Europe. The lovely medieval towns being pounded into rubble are our image of what towns should be. TV news crews can get in and out a lot easier than they can into Liberia.

The war in what was Yugoslavia has now gone on for longer than our own Civil War. I have been watching news reports about it for five years, about Muslims being slaughtered. The haughty Serbs slaughtering them wipe off their bayonets then turn to the world with a "Who me?" shrug. There are also Bosnians and Croats and Hercegovinians involved somehow, and they all overlap as well, into Bosnian Serbs and Croatian Muslims and the like. The whole thing seems to be over now, but since it has gone on so long, I imagine the peace is just a temporary interregnum to give the principals time to reload before it starts all over again.

The above represents my entire knowledge of the matter. I can list a few towns—Sarajevo is one; Bihac another, places I've memorized from hearing them on the evening news every damned night.

I have little sympathy for the Slavs, or Yugoslavs, or

whatever they are called, as a class. They did it to themselves. You'd think they'd have been happy to finally get Marshal Tito off their asses, after all those years. You'd think fifty years of Communism dissolving as easily as snow on a spring day would have kept people waving to their neighbors for just a few years before they set about vivisecting their country.

But no. Everybody has to start trying to boot everybody out, in a lingering, pointless war of snipers and ragamuffin militia that is hardly worthy of the name "war." And I'm supposed to keep track of it all? No way. Not anymore.

One Sunday, years ago, over at the State of Illinois Center, they held a big celebration of "Latvian Independence Day"—a rather optimistically titled holiday, since at the time the Berlin Wall had not yet fallen and Latvia had, for nearly half a century, been locked firmly in the iron grasp of the Soviet Union.

I watched this band of pretty Latvian school kids, dressed in embroidered outfits and Alpine dirndls, going through the steps of their elaborate Latvian folk dances. Their elders carried signs saying LATVIA SHALL BE FREE and SOVIETS OUT OF LATVIA. When they got together to sing the Latvian national anthem at the end, it was an emotional moment for many people. Tears filled dozens of eyes.

Not mine. Me, I had to suppress a sneer. "Cripe," I thought to myself. "Poor deluded boobs. Latvia's never, ever gonna be free. Never. Forget it."

Within the year Latvia was free, free of the Soviet

Union, anyway. Shows you what I know. And give them credit. They didn't immediately invade Estonia, or try to annex Lapland, or any of the thousand other suicidal courses of delusional self-destruction they might have taken. Happy to be rid of the Reds, they are living their lives in what we might assume is mundane Latvian normality. You never hear about Latvia. And a good thing, too.

Z Is for Zealot

On January 10, 1457, before the judge Nicolas Quarroillon in the French province of Savigny, a sow and her six piglets were put on trial for the murder of a five-year-old boy who had strayed too close to their pen and been killed.

The guilt of the mother pig was well established, and she was sentenced to hang, but the attorney for the six piglets managed to convince the court that, though bloodied, their role in the death of the boy was uncertain. A new trial for the piglets was ordered, and the next month they were exonerated. The orphan pigs were released to the custody of the Countess de Savigny, since their owner could not vouch for their future good behavior. Their ultimate fate is unknown.

Criminal prosecution of animals had gone on in Europe for about two hundred years at the time of the trial of the sow and her piglets, and had another two hundred years to go before the phenomenon would wilt in the glare of the Enlightenment. For more than four centuries, however, cats, dogs, mules, bulls, horses and particularly pigs were tried for a variety of crimes and often punished—imprisoned in the same jails with human prisoners, executed upon the same scaffolds as human felons, often dressed in clothing to enhance the effect. A French archive records a pig, clad in breeches and a waistcoat, being led to the gallows in a tumbrel.

Such somber judicial treatment of animals brings a smile today, a self-satisfied smirk at the expense of medieval justice for being so zealous in its approach to law that it held unreasoning beasts morally responsible for the results of their actions.

But before we get too smug we should realize that our own society is at this very moment at the zenith of a mirror phenomenon. Wide popular acceptance has been given to the notion that, instead of responsibilities, animals hold a wide spectrum of inalienable rights, privileges that are equal to and, in some cases, surpassing those of humans.

That attitude, promulgated by People for the Ethical Treatment of Animals and other quasi-terrorist groups, leads to misreadings of reality which, to future generations, will be just as ridiculous as a medieval French judge ordering hungry mice to vacate a farmer's field. Dog owners insist their carnivore pets share in their vegetarian lifestyle. High school biology classes are told they cannot dissect frogs. Silk products are denounced for the wrongs inflicted upon silkworms. Protesters assault fly fishermen in midstream. Women wearing fur are attacked in the name of the rights of dead animals.

As social discourse breaks down, as respect for other

people's attitudes and opinions dissolves like a Fudgsicle left out in the sun, zealotry threatens to completely engulf the country. People cleave tighter and tighter to their own beliefs even as those beliefs float away into the highest stratosphere of extremism.

Most of the attention goes to fanatics in a narrow band of causes—gimlet-eyed ministers from Kansas waving bloody fetuses in the faces of terrified teenagers, or delusional unemployed truckers from Michigan tilting at a comic book cabal of evil intrigue that exists only in their fevered imaginations.

But concoct any sort of stance and you can find people devoting their lives to supporting it. Should horses wear diapers? One Chicago alderman made an impassioned speech on the floor of the council chambers, urging there be a law. Should circumcision be banned? A California group believes that circumcision of males is the greatest atrocity in the world today, and actively campaigns for it to be stopped. The moon landing a hoax? People believe it. The dissolution of the Soviet Union merely an ingenuous ploy by the Red Menace to lull us into complacency before the takeover? A guy walks up and down Michigan Avenue with a sandwich sign to that effect.

Like any bores, zealots don't know when to quit. They grab you by the elbow, hard, and start talking, and don't notice you shrinking away, trying to free yourself, rolling your eyes. Zealots want to affect the outcome of discourse without actually entering into it.

They can't. The idea of discussion, of moderation, of a gray zone in between their single favored extreme and something else, is anathema to a zealot. If PETA were merely battling against leopard hats, I'd be a member. Just trying to stop cosmetic companies from torturing bunnies? Here's $20.

But they also think that your keeping a goldfish is an act of tyranny.

"A rat is a pig is a dog is a boy," said PETA director Ingrid Newkirk, summing up PETA's philosophy more succinctly, and more damningly, than her opponents ever could.

There are three important aspects to zealotry. The first is the one that gets all the attention—burning absolutism. Zealots *know*. They never reevaluate. They never begin a sentence, "Now, I may be wrong about this . . ."

Which leads to the second important factor. Zealots are wrong. They have taken whatever little shred of truth they may have had when they started out and stretched it so much it is in tatters and no longer true.

Look at Louis Farrakhan. The real tragedy is not that Farrakhan is a hatemonger and an anti-Semite. He's small change when it comes to hatemongers and anti-Semites. I could walk to any street corner in Cicero and spit and hit a more rabid anti-Semite than Louis Farrakhan.

No, the sad thing about Louis Farrakhan is he's *wrong*. There are a lot of problems facing black people in America, the Jews aren't one of them, and every minute Farrakhan spends haranguing his audiences about the pan-global Jewish conspiracy is an opportunity for progress squandered. Go to a Farrakhan rally. He's got 5,000 people in a room, hopping up and down, fired up by the power of his charisma, hanging on his every word. And what is he talking about? *The Protocols of the Elders of Zion*. The sense of opportunity lost is almost maddening. What could Louis Farrakhan have accomplished had he not side-tracked himself with visiting spaceships and ice people and computing how many Southern Jews owned slaves in the eighteenth century? We'll never know.

The irony is, of course, if there *was* a Jewish conspiracy, trying to thwart black ambitions and render Farrakhan ineffectual, they couldn't do more damage than to direct him to carry on exactly the way he does. No evil puppeteer could have constructed a more egregious misstep than Farrakhan's pilgrimage to kiss the feet of Saddam Hussein and Muammar Qaddafi. (And there had better not be a Jewish conspiracy—I haven't been receiving my checks.)

The third aspect of zealotry is that zealots must try to win you over to their cause. This is crucial, and the truly annoying thing about zealotry. A wild-eyed fanatic burning with absolute belief in some idiotic misconception isn't much harm to anyone if he stays at home, clonically rocking and emitting a loud humming sound. He has to go out and win people over, or at least try.

In one sense, this can be funny. Zealots never realize how much joy they unintentionally bring to thinking people in their efforts to recruit new faithful to the flock. I have a big file of urgent updates from Tony Alamo, World Pastor of the Holy Alamo Christian Church. They're a hoot. DID YOU KNOW THAT THE *POPE* AND *RONALD REAGAN* ARE A COUPLE OF *ANTICHRIST DEVILS* AND THAT THEY ARE SELLING US ALL DOWN THE DRAIN? READ ABOUT IT!!! screams one headline. Finding a new Alamo update shoved under my windshield wiper just about makes my day.

The most amazing dribble gets passed off as knowledge. Go to any of the animal rights texts that clog any library and ask the simple question: What is the natural state of humanity? Where did we come from?

"The First People were wise, taking no more from life than what would satisfy their most basic, simple needs," marvels Michael W. Fox, in his book, *The New Eden,* a typical specimen. Fox not only romanticizes hunter/gathering into an ethos of childish gentility but forms nature to fit his vision. "There were probably no crazed grasshoppers turned into locusts then," he fantabulizes. "They came as changed, frenzied, and ravenous beings soon after man began to change the land."

That's right, we did it. We *made* locusts, by daring to plow the fields. I bet he thinks rats are our fault too. Rats are just cute mice grown huge on the leftovers from meatpacking plants. And if we give dogs enough soy bean Alpo, then those nasty curving canine incisors developed over ten million years of gutting hedgehogs will melt away too. Here, Fido, *celery.*

Of course, anyone with a sense of history can't help but feel a twinge while laughing off zealots. You have to, what with the occasional Oklahoma City bombing or the periodic Patrick Buchanan candidacy, to deliver a sobering slap and remind us that the funny little monkey dancing in a cage can suddenly change into the big scary gorilla running the show.

The issue of school prayer illustrates how easily an extreme form of intimidation can be presented as desirable public policy.

Any kid can pray in school, virtually any time. Glance down, commune with God, and who's to say you weren't just thinking about lunch or hoping you didn't get called on? This is an unarguable fact. Kids can pray all day, to themselves, if they want. Their grades may suffer, but nobody is going to stop them.

But silent prayer doesn't feed the unspoken, "Well-of-*course*-it's-our-country-isn't-it?" superiority that is barely contained by the religious and political zealots on the national scene. Certainly not the way that an authorized, public period of open school prayer would. So right wingers who, perhaps in their secret hearts, would like to solve the problem by lining up the nonbelievers and malcontents in front of a slit trench and blazing away, instead stand before the cameras and offer up the laughable notion that the problem with America is that grade schoolers don't all bow their heads together each morning and give thanks.

Remember the part about zealots being wrong? When considering school prayer, the central error its advocates make is assuming that, should they manage to take this baby step back toward the White Protestant Anglo-Saxon aristocracy that has been fading for the entire twentieth century, everyone else would meekly follow along.

I myself hope that a constitutional amendment permitting school prayer is passed, since I know the assumptions behind it—that praying means pressing your palms together and thanking Jesus for the milk, while the one or two oddballs who don't feel like joining in go stand back in the lockers with their noses against the wall—won't be written into law as well. That means my son will be free to use the devotional minute to slaughter a chicken in the name of Erzulie Dantor, the Haitian Goddess of Love and Luxury. If you've never seen it, it's a wild ceremony, involving the consumption of rum and possession by spirits. Not quite public school stuff. The desks would have to be moved aside to permit twirling. But heck, once the door is legally propped open, who among the public school officials will dare challenge the sincerity of my child's religious beliefs? At least it will start class off each day with a bang.

Acknowledgments

This book is dedicated to my wife Edie for the simple reason that without her there would be no book, no author, nothing. She is as necessary as the air, and a lot prettier. Thanks for the time, the love, and for little Ross.

As with my previous book, this book's topic and title came from Bill Thomas, my skillful and enthusiastic editor at Doubleday. Thanks as well to his assistant, Jacky LaPierre, whose good humor and willingness to listen kept me from going mad.

I tell prospective writers that a good agent is everything. By "a good agent" I mean David Black, who is actually a great agent, but I don't like to brag. I'm also indebted to his able associate, Susan Raihofer, a tireless advocate who held my hand endlessly and without complaint during the writing of this book.

I can't thank my superiors at the *Chicago Sun-Times* enough for their indulgence, affection and support. My boss, Steve Huntley, is the finest gentleman I have ever had the pleasure of working with. He was shockingly kind to me when I told him I was taking a year off, and I will always appreciate it. I am also in debt to Nigel Wade, the editor of the *Sun-Times,* who literally changed my life, giving me a column and inviting me into the warmth of acceptance when I had just about resigned myself to always dwelling on the frozen periphery.

Also thanks to Robert A. Davis, Mark Jacob, Bill Zwecker and everyone else at the paper, particularly Rich Roeper, my constant friend, and to the *Tribune*'s Eric Zorn, who graciously permitted me to steal his Rob Sherman vignette. Eric V. Copage, of *The New York Times*, was patience itself in adapting a chapter of this book to appear in his newspaper's outstanding Sunday magazine. A big hello to Alison True and everybody at the *Reader.* And a nod to Robert Pinsky, whose fine translation of Dante's *Inferno* inspired "G Is for Gimmick."

I require a lot of support from my good friends. Thanks to Jim and Laura Sayler, Cate Plys and Ron Garzotto, Kier Strejcek and Cathleen Cregier, Larry and Ilene Lubell, Carol Weston and Robert Ackerman, Robert Leighton and Val Green, Bob and Caroline Shrago, Elisa and Don Staniszewski, Sharon Hunt, and Coleen Hall.

And Didier Thys—wherever you are. Don't drink the water, keep in touch with the embassy, and watch out for mines.

The staff of the Northwestern University library was helpful in my research. Robert Seyfried at Northwestern's Traffic Institute gave me a glimpse into the world of traffic engineering. Thanks as well to Joe Pratt and his superiors over at the city of Chicago's Department of the Environment. All government should work so well.

My wife's family in Chicago—Irv and Dorothy Goldberg, Alan Goldberg and Cookie Gluck, Jay and Janice Sackett, and all the wonderful children—have given me great joy, peace and security.

And finally, to my own family—mother June, father Robert, brother Sam and sister Debbie—wonderful people to whom I owe everything. Thank you for your love and steady support, and for taking my occasional jabs with your characteristic good humor.